Mrs. Henry Wood

Mrs. Henry Wood

Mariaconcetta Costantini

Professor of English Literature, G. d'Annunzio University of Chieti-Pescara, Italy

EER
Edward Everett Root, Publishers, Brighton, 2020.

EER
Edward Everett Root, Publishers, Co. Ltd.,
30 New Road, Brighton, Sussex, BN1 1BN, England.
Full details of our overseas agents are given on our website.
www.eerpublishing.com

edwardeverettroot@yahoo.co.uk

Mariaconcetta Costantini, *Mrs. Henry Wood*

Key Popular Women Writers series, Volume 4.

First published in Great Britain in 2020.

© Mariaconcetta Costantini 2020.

This edition © Edward Everett Root 2020.

ISBN: 978-1-912224-93-7 Paperback
ISBN: 978-1-912224-94-4 Hardback
ISBN: 978-1-912224-95-1 eBook

Mariaconcetta Costantini has asserted her right to be identified as the author of this Work in accordance with the Copyright, Designs and Patents Act 1988 as the owner of this Work.

All rights reserved. No part of this publication may be reproduced, stored in a retrieval system or transmitted in any form or by any means, electronic, mechanical, photocopying, recording or otherwise, without the prior permission of the copyright owner.

Cover designed by Pageset Limited, High Wycombe, Buckinghamshire.

Series editors:
Janine Hatter and Helena Ifill.

This innovative new series delivers original and transformative, peer reviewed, feminist research into the work of leading women writers who were widely read in their time, but who have been under-represented in the canon.

The series offers critical, historical and aesthetic contributions to current literary and theoretical work. Each volume concentrates on one writer.

The first five titles are available:

- *Geraldine Jewsbury*   by Abigail Burnham Bloom.
- *Florence Marryat*   by Catherine Pope.
- *Margaret Oliphant*   by Valerie Sanders.
- *Mrs. Henry Wood*   by Mariaconcetta Costantini.
- *Frances Trollope*   by Carolyn Lambert.

These will be followed by volumes on:

- *Mary Braddon*
- *Rhoda Broughton*
- *Daphne Du Maurier*
- *Ouida*
- *Mary Shelley*
- *Marie Corelli*
- *Charlotte Riddell*
- *Edith Wharton*

We welcome suggestions for other titles.

The series volumes interrogate the ways in which women writers, their creative processes and published material can be considered feminist, and explore how recent developments in feminist theory can enrich our understanding of popular women writer's lives and literature.

The authors rethink established popular writers and their works, and rediscover and re-evaluate authors who have been largely neglected – often since their initial burst of success in their own historical period. This neglect is often due to the exclusivity and insular nature of the canon which has its roots in the Victorian critical drive to perpetuate a division between high and low culture.

In response, our definition of the "popular" is broadly interpreted to encompass women writers who were read by large sections of the public, and who wrote for the mass publishing market. The series therefore challenges this arbitrary divide, creating a new and dynamic dialogue regarding the canon's expansion by introducing readers to previously under-researched women writers who were nevertheless prolific, known and influential.

Studying the work of these authors can tell us much about women's writing, creativity and publishing practice, and about how popular fiction intervened in pressing political, social and cultural issues surrounding gender, history and women's roles in society.

This is an important and timely series that is inspired by, interrogates, and speaks to a new wave of feminism, new definitions of sex and gender, and new considerations of inter-sectionality. It also reflects growing interest in popular fiction, as well as a feminist desire to broaden and diversify the literary canon.

Ultimately the series sheds light on women writers whose work deserves greater recognition, facilitates and inspires further research, and paves the way for introducing these key women writers into the canon and modern-day studies.

The editors

DR. JANINE HATTER is an Early Career Researcher based at the University of Hull. With Nickianne Moody she has edited the volume *Fashion and Material Culture in Victorian Fiction and Periodicals,* already published by *EER.* Her research interests centre on nineteenth-century literature, art and culture, with particular emphasis on popular fiction. She has published on Mary Braddon, Bram Stoker, the theatre and identity, and Victorian women's life writing, as well as on her wider research interests of nineteenth to twenty-first century Science Fiction and the Gothic. She has also co-edited special issues for *Revenant, Supernatural Studies, Nineteenth-Century Gender Studies, Femspec* and the *Wilkie Collins Journal.* Janine is conference co-organiser for the Victorian Popular Fiction Association, and co-founded the Mary Elizabeth Braddon Association.

DR. HELENA IFILL is a Lecturer in English Studies at the University of Aberdeen where she is the Director of the Centre for the Novel. Her research focuses on the interactions between Victorian popular fiction, (pseudo)science and medicine. She is the Secretary of the Victorian Popular Fiction Association and a co-organiser of the Association's annual conference. As well as her monograph, *Creating Character: Theories of Nature and Nurture in Victorian Sensation Fiction* (2018), she has published work on Charlotte Riddell, Florence Marryat, Wilkie Collins, Bram Stoker, and Victorian mesmerism. She has also co-edited special issues for *Nineteenth-Century Gender Studies* and the *Wilkie Collins Journal.*

The author

MARIACONCETTA COSTANTINI is full professor of English Literature at G. d'Annunzio University of Chieti-Pescara, Italy. Her research mainly focuses on Victorian literature and culture, with a special interest in sensation fiction and the Gothic. She is the author of five books and has edited volumes on Victorian literature and culture, in addition to publishing numerous articles and book chapters both in Italy and abroad. Her publications on sensation novelists include the monographs *Venturing into Unknown Waters: Wilkie Collins and the Challenge of Modernity* (2008) and *Sensation and Professionalism in the Victorian Novel* (2015), as well as the collection of essays *Armadale: Wilkie Collins and the Dark Threads of Life*, ed. M. Costantini (2009).

Contents

Acknowledgements xi

A Note on the Text xiii

Introduction 1

Chapter 1. The necessity and traps of Victorian marriage 33

Chapter 2. Variations of the Griselda theme 67

Chapter 3. Desiring subjects and the effects of immoderacy . . 97

Chapter 4. The transgressive lady and the failings of
 patriarchy 129

Chapter 5. Unconventional low-class women 157

Conclusion 191

Notes 195

Works Cited 207

Index. 217

Acknowledgements

Thanks firstly to the series editors, Janine Hatter and Helena Ifill, for their constructive feedback and the much-needed corrections to draft chapters, and to John Spiers for his professional support and patience. At various stages of this project, I have benefited from the insights of Francesco Marroni, who generously read some parts of the manuscript and offered precious suggestions. I am indebted to various colleagues and friends for advice and assistance with bibliographical resources. Among them, I wish to express my special gratitude to Raffaella Antinucci, Andrew King, Andrew Mangham, Mara Mattoscio, Jude V. Nixon, and Saverio Tomaiuolo. Thanks to Tanya Izzard for indexing the volume. Staff at the British Library, the Senate House Library, the Staatsbibliothek of Berlin and the Salem State University Library has always been efficient in fulfilling my requests. Finally, thanks to Arndt Wilke for understanding my dark moods and providing warm encouragement at crucial moments.

A Note on the Text

"Mrs. Henry Wood" was the trademark name chosen by Ellen Wood, née Price, when she started to write professionally. It became a successful commercial logo in her age and is still used to identify her in most literary studies. For these reasons, she is referred to as "Mrs. Henry Wood" in the title of this book, even though she is called Ellen Wood throughout. In quoting from Wood's and other works, including secondary sources, I have added no emphasis; all italics are in the originals. Similarly, foreign expressions that are not italicized in the originals have been reproduced without emphasis.

Introduction

In her contribution to *Women Novelists of Queen Victoria's Reign* (1897), Adeline Sergeant described some changes in literary tastes that were likely to affect the fame of Mrs. Henry [Ellen] Wood at the *fin de siècle*. Highly successful since the 1860s and still widely read at the turn of the century, Wood was destined to dwindle to a minor literary figure soon afterwards and to be rediscovered almost one century later. Sergeant offers some food for thought in her appreciation. Besides attributing the waning fame of "the Scheherazade of our quiet evenings and holiday afternoons" to the *fin-de-siècle* undervaluing of "the art of the *raconteur*", she hypothesizes that Wood "would possibly have taken a higher place amongst English novelists if she had avoided mere sensation, and confined herself to what she could do well – namely, the faithful and realistic rendering of English middle class life" (Sergeant, 1897: 174, 191).

The missed opportunity suggested here is somehow at odds with the complexity of Wood's professional image. In recent decades, scholars like Lyn Pykett (1992), Andrew Maunder (2000) and Jennifer Phegley (2005) have acknowledged that Ellen Wood was no amateur writer. She made a remarkable career as novelist and editor, acquired a deep knowledge of the Victorian print industry and devised her own ways to participate in the literary debates of her age. Why would such a clever professional of the pen deliberately practise a genre that would prevent her from gaining "a higher place amongst English novelists"? Her entrepreneurial flair might partly account for her use of sensational strategies that targeted a large cross-class readership. But her narrative experiments have further reaching implications. As this work will show, Wood was not simply a market-oriented novelist who authored Victorian bestsellers. An active participant in the transformation of nineteenth-century literature, she contributed to developing alternative forms of the novel that defied her readers' expectations and, in so doing, exposed some inconsistencies of the society she lived in. The Woman Question, in particular, plays an important role in her "domesticated sensationalism" (Wynne, 2001a: 90) which, by grafting subversive elements onto commonplace domestic realism, both enforces and questions orthodox femininity. Unlike Wood's contemporaries, who were puzzled by a fiction they were unable to contain into a single category, we should consider the extent to which the jarring formal aspects of her prose were the results of a conscious experimentation through which she produced effects of epistemic stridency.

The elusiveness of Wood's figure and writing is most evident in the critical debate on the contribution she gave to the sensational school of fiction, which became an object of controversy immediately after the publication of *East Lynne* (1861). Insistently paired with Wilkie Collins and Mary Elizabeth Braddon in mid-century discussions on the scandalous sensation genre, Wood was attacked by such orthodox reviewers as Margaret Oliphant who made disparaging comments on the popularity, the inherent dangers, the vulgarity and the lack of realism of novels like *East Lynne* ([Oliphant], 1862: 567). Other Victorians were less critical of Wood's particular use of sensationalism which, in their view, was tempered by the pathos and moral messages permeating her fiction. In the following centuries, scholars continued to classify her as a practitioner of the sensation genre. Despite her distinctive conservatism, she has been labelled as an imitator of Collins (Baker, 1950: 214; Rance, 1991: 5), or compared to female sensationalists like Braddon and Rhoda Broughton who, as Oliphant herself claimed, were most likely inspired by the transgressive works of the Brontë sisters (Radford, 2009: 13).

Another widely debated issue is the role Wood played within a tradition of women's popular writing long excluded from the canon. Initially triggered by Antonio Gramsci's views of popular culture in the 1940s-50s (Longhurst, 1989: 3), the twentieth-century rethinking of the canon was further developed in the 1970s, when feminists started to object to a gendered and class-biased process of standardization of literary worth. Elaine Showalter's theorization of "a literature of their own" famously expressed the need to unearth and reinterpret the lost works of women novelists who, in different ways during the previous century, had started to articulate the experiences of their gender group. Wood's positioning within this newly canonized genealogy has proved difficult. Classified by Showalter as an early "feminine novelist" whose literary talents never took precedence over domestic duties (1977: 61), Wood has been differently interpreted by later critics who have explored some novelties of the career she pursued in a predominantly male field (Palmer, 2011). Similarly open to question is the part her novels might play in a revisionist project aiming to discover "feminist forbears in unexpected places" (Maunder, 2000: 25). Unmentioned in the female literary tradition reconstructed by Sandra Gilbert and Susan Gubar (1979 [2000]), Wood's writing is partly in line, partly at odds, with this tradition, as shown by its puzzling combination of anti-feminist rhetoric with a covert critique of domestic ideologies.

These apparent contradictions pose the problem of reconsidering Wood's life and fiction from new perspectives. Drawing on different feminist theories, this study aims to shed light on the complexities of her professional experiences and her writing practices which, as hinted above, cannot be encompassed within single critical categories. The approach adopted here derives from a variety of theories selected on the basis of their efficacy and arranged into a multi-layered framework that is used to unravel controversial aspects of Wood's context and texts. A bulwark against the shortcomings of "methodolatry",[1] this framework is also a protection from the dangers of essentialism inherent in gynocriticism that generally emerge in critical projects that seek to develop female-specific models of experience and production. By combining multiple theories together, I instead propose to explore Wood's negotiations between conflicting groupings of ideas and to examine the effects of ideological stridency she produced by ambiguously juxtaposing these ideas within her fictional texts.

A main problem met by Wood scholars is that of solving the inconsistencies of her biographical profile, which is based on scarce, contradictory and sometimes unreliable documents. Besides a few extant letters written by Wood and short testimonies by her acquaintances, the main sources of information on her life and career are two biographies penned by her son Charles after her death: a series of three articles titled "Mrs. Henry Wood. In Memoriam" appeared in *The Argosy* in 1887 and *Memorials of Mrs. Henry Wood* published in volume form in 1894. A revised and expanded version of the previous series, the volume adds few relevant facts to our knowledge: most additions are in fact descriptive pieces of travel writing or imaginative reconstructions of Wood's emotional states. Both biographies are basically hagiographic works that turn Wood into a paragon of Victorian matronly virtues. This mythologizing quality accounts for many ellipses and contradictions found in the two texts, which fail to illuminate important facets of her personality. The limits of both memoirs are confirmed by some letters preserved in the archives of Richard Bentley that offer glimpses of a self-assured professional at variance with the saintly icon of domesticity portrayed by her son. Elliptical and inconsistent though they are, these scant sources should be nonetheless compared with each other to discover hidden aspects of Wood's personal history. If read through the lenses of feminist theories, moreover, their gaps give us interesting clues to Victorian gender practices, as they reveal important strategies of concealment and self-construction adopted by Wood and reinforced by her son.

Born in a Worcester manufacturing family in 1814, Ellen Wood (née Price) spent her childhood in the English province. The main events of her early life are the special relation she established with her father, Thomas, and the business troubles experienced by their family as an effect of England's new free trade policies. A gentleman of scholarly tastes who had inherited a glove manufactory from his father, Thomas Price awakened his daughter's literary genius by spending long hours reading and talking with her in his study (Charles Wood, 1887: 3–6). As Charles Wood claims in *Memorials*, moreover, the young Ellen was always present when her father taught Latin and Greek to her brothers and soon became proficient in classical knowledge (Charles Wood, 1894: 45–46). Thomas Price offered to his daughter a refined and gentle model of masculinity that counterbalanced the violence of her maternal grandfather – a tyrannical man who "was not beloved within [his own house], and was feared outside it" (Charles Wood, 1894: 24).

At the age of thirteen, Wood was affected by a serious curvature of the spine that forced her to spend the next four years on a reclining board or couch. The origins of her invalidism are unclear. Her son mentions a childhood accident as a possible cause but he also speculates that it might have been an inborn complaint triggered by her intellectual labours: "The strength and activity of the brain may have proved too much for the weaker physical powers" (Charles Wood, 1894: 24). The link between physical weakness and mental overwork established by Charles evidences the nineteenth-century tendency to associate illness with femininity. Largely explored by feminist theorists in recent decades, the gendering of sickness has led to three main views of Victorian invalidism: as a result of the oppressive use of male power, as a female resistance to that power, or as a means through which women exploited their vulnerable positions to achieve personal ends (Herndl, 1996). Taught to consider themselves frail beings unfit for intellectual exertion and in need of protection from their childhood, Victorian women experienced a strong cultural conditioning that made them prone to real and imaginary ailments. Wood was no exception. Besides her first-person experience as a young invalid, she continued to be affected by her spinal deformity for her whole life and suffered from various diseases, some of which were probably psychosomatic.[2] Suggested by Showalter (1977: 171), the idea that some of her ailments might have been self-induced is validated by the following anecdote, which is told in both biographies. During the serialization of *East Lynne*, Wood was struck by an undiagnosed illness that doctors proved unable to cure for eighteen months. In this painful period, she strove to find answers in medical books, became convinced that her affliction was incurable and was finally healed by a strange old woman with radical leanings (Charles Wood, 1887: 429–430; 1894: 184–196). The episode casts light on Wood's attitudes and ideas. Unable to understand the nature of her disease, she first consulted some medical sources and was reproached by her doctor for indulging in unfeminine readings. Later on, she readily accepted the help of a female quack excluded from the medical profession. Besides suggesting Wood's limited trust in a male-exclusive professional group, these events confirm that she made significant personal experiences of illness during her life and, impelled to spend long periods of reclusion at home, she developed complex views of female invalidism that emerge in her thought-provoking fictional representations. As will be shown in the following chapters, her sick female characters substantiate the contradictions of a process of identity-making based on the assumption of women's frail corporeality. Their ailing bodies act out Victorian beliefs in women's physical inferiority, but they are also used to expose the flaws of gender stereotypes and to turn suffering into an instrument of feminine self-assertion.

In spite of her ailments, Wood did not conform to Victorian prejudices against the marriage of women invalids.[3] In 1836 she married Henry Wood, a good-looking man who was the head of a large banking and shipping firm. The newly-wed couple moved to the South of France where they lived for twenty years and where their five children were born. Imaginatively reconstructed in a number of colourful anecdotes added to the 1894 biography, the French period came to an abrupt end when some unspecified "trouble too deep for words" ensued, "setting its seal upon [Ellen Wood] for all time" while her husband "lost none of his gaiety or charm" (Charles Wood, 1894: 144). A significant omission in both biographies, the real nature of the "trouble" suffered by the Woods is still open to speculation. What scholars agree on is that Henry lost his job and the family was compelled to return to England where they faced financial difficulties. Another element that invites reflection is the contrast between Wood's and Henry's responses to the blow that struck their family. By highlighting the discordance between his mother's painful reticence and his father's light-heartedness, the biographer partly accounts for the economic autonomy Wood would gain in subsequent years. Without mentioning any conjugal crisis, he in fact hints at the more responsible attitude shown by his mother who would soon embark on a professional career and become the family's breadwinner.

Shortly after their homecoming, Wood decided to make a professional use of the literary talent she had until then cultivated amateurishly. She first took part in a literary competition organized by the Scottish Temperance League and won the prize with her first novel, *Danesbury House* (1860). The following year she rose to fame with the publication of *East Lynne*, which became a phenomenal bestseller and was followed by other successful works. In 1867, one year after her husband's death, she bought and relaunched the *Argosy* magazine, which she edited until her death. In addition to becoming a bestselling novelist, Wood proved to be a shrewd businesswoman, who learned to make profit in the expanding literary market without masculine guidance. Her entrepreneurial skills are not only evidenced by her successful management of *The Argosy*.[4] They also emerge in the tough negotiations she conducted with publishers and other leading figures of the Victorian print industry. The above-mentioned correspondence with Bentley bears witness to her proactive approach to the publishing process, her demands for profits, as well as her preoccupations with copyright issues and stage piracy (Newbolt 2001: 85; Phegley, 2005: 185–186; Sussex 2010: 108–119). Charles Wood himself offers clues to her entrepreneurial attitude by reconstructing her difficult relations with William Harrison Ainsworth, the editor of the two magazines in which she had published some early short stories in the 1850s: *Bentley's Miscellany* and *Colburn's New Monthly Magazine*. Mostly unpaid for her early contributions to these magazines, which tended to exploit women writers (Wynne, 2001b: 36), Wood began to make serious professional demands after her return to England. She first obtained small sums and then convinced Ainsworth to serialize *East Lynne* in the *New Monthly Magazine* (1860–61), thereby emancipating herself from an editorial bondage which, in her son's opinion, was meant to keep her in the position of cheap short-story contributor (Charles Wood, 1894: 206).

The successful negotiations with Ainsworth marked Ellen Wood's transition from amateur to professional writing. She rapidly learned to trust her literary talents and was not discouraged by two early rejections of *East Lynne*, which was finally published in volume form by Bentley. Her self-confidence emerges also in her sanguine defence of the originality of *East Lynne* against Caroline Norton's accusation of plagiarism, which appeared in the *Times* in 1871.[5] Further evidence of her painstaking commitment to her career is offered by her rigid work routine, which is minutely described by her son,[6] as well as by her unswerving dedication to writing *East Lynne* when she was affected by the mysterious illness mentioned above. These examples of professional rigour and self-assuredness are at variance with the icon of domesticity portrayed by her son, who strove to disguise the unfeminine aspects of her professionalism by claiming that she never "neglected or put aside" her home duties "for literary labours" (Charles Wood, 1894: 228). The difficulty of reconciling these two sides of her personality is increased by the fact that Wood herself cultivated her image of matronly respectability. An acute observer of the literary scene, she postured as a conservative novelist to avoid the virulent attacks launched by critics against the practitioners of the sensation genre. The comparison with Braddon is revealing. Both women novelists were industrious professionals who succeeded in a field dominated by male competitors.[7] Unlike Braddon, however, Wood lived no sensational life and was careful to tailor a respectable domestic role for herself.[8] This self-fashioning process was reinforced by her adoption of fine-tuning strategies of composition that enabled her to deal with inappropriate topics without offending the morality of her prevailingly middle-class readership.

Wood's use of camouflage strategies becomes more evident if we consider her pen names and authorial personae. The reasons why she decided to sign her major works as "Mrs. Henry Wood" are easy to surmise. In an age dominated by the law of coverture, the adoption of the husband's name could smooth the way for a woman's literary success as it counterbalanced her creative autonomy with ideas of guidance and propriety. As Maunder observes, Wood made "a spectacle of her absence" by using the name "Mrs. Henry Wood" which, together with her only portrait (an undated miniature by Reginald Easton), became an identifiable "commercial logo" that marketed her image of "impassive but respectable Victorian matron" (2000: 20).

Subtler mechanisms of self-concealment can be found in the male personae she assumed. In 1854, she contributed some letters to the male-orientated section of the *New Monthly Magazine* using the fake identity of Ensign Thomas Pepper, a young soldier at the Crimean front. Quite different in style from her later writings, these early pieces show her awareness of the demands of different audiences and her ability to imitate male discourse (Wynne, 2001a: 99–100). Wood used again a male voice in the Johnny Ludlow stories published anonymously in *The Argosy* in 1868, which were received as genuine narratives penned by a Worcester schoolboy. She kept the secret of the author's identity for a while and revealed it only when she published the second series of the Ludlow stories under her name. Both biographies mention the amusement she and her son Charles had in observing the public confusion of authorship; and both include funny anecdotes about people who pretended to have composed these successful stories. As Rolf Burgauer contends, the Ludlow case enabled Wood to invalidate some negative criticism she had previously received as she showed her ability to write in a style admired by her very detractors (1950: 19–20). But there is another aspect worth considering. The fun she had in assuming a male persona proves that Wood was conscious of the constructedness of discourses and was covertly challenging Victorian assumptions about the gendering of genres.

Further examples of this contrast between conservatism and heterodoxy can be found in Charles's narration of his mother's passing away. While lying on her deathbed in February 1887, Wood gave ample proof of "fortitude and patience" and, in conformity with Victorian myths of angelic womanhood, she accepted her fate with unwavering faith in God. Shortly before her death, however, she talked of a narrative project she had once devised: that of "writing the experiences of a governess in the same manner that I have written *Johnny Ludlow*". "I am quite sure they would have been very popular", she declared, before lamenting: "But it is all over – all over" (Charles Wood, 1894: 310–311). Although this expression of regret was followed by affectionate words and by a religious prayer, it is interesting to notice that her deathbed message included a reference to professional aspirations that had strongly animated her existence and were still cherished in her last living hours. As in other episodes of the biographies, the professional side of her personality comes to the fore unexpectedly in this dramatic scene in which her embodiment of female resignation is momentarily disturbed by her image of proactive career woman. The stridency thus produced confirms the idea that Charles deliberately downplayed his mother's public face to promote a domestic image of femininity – an image that she herself strove to fashion by concealing the most autonomous sides of her personality.

When she died aged seventy-three, Ellen Wood had produced over forty volumes of fiction including numerous short stories. Considered "the most intrinsically representative woman novelist of the mid-Victorian era", she was praised as "a remarkably competent story-teller" (Elwin, 1934: 232), even though she was not spared criticism. Blamed for her sensational themes, her unrealistic characterization and her careless prose by Victorian reviewers, she was posthumously disparaged for her "irritating tricks of style" and her melodramatic strategies (Elwin, 1934: 247–249), as well as for the "unexceptionably moral tone" of her works that were said to be "curiously commonplace and destitute of originality as of profundity" (Keddie, 1911: 319). A caustic remark on her combination of sensation and religious discourse was made by Charlotte Riddell who, probably animated by "splenetic envy", lamented Wood's "throw[ing] in bits of religion to slip her fodder down the public throat" (Elwin, 1934: 241). These comments stemmed from a variety of moral and aesthetic considerations that are too complex to analyse here. If examined all together, however, they suggest that, over the years, critics have shared the impression that something was amiss in Wood's characterization and syntax. While her skills for plot construction have been widely recognized, her depiction of credible characters and her stylistic peculiarities have been open to question if not overtly criticized.

These narrative aspects call for attention. How can we reconcile such apparent flaws with the interest in meta-literary issues that

Wood exhibited in her fiction and non-fiction? And why should a novelist concerned with the redefinition of the standards of literature fail to provide in some works the admirable realistic renderings she offered in other works? These questions are made more pressing by the active role Wood played within her cultural milieu. Phegley claims that she wrote at least half of the pieces published in *The Argosy*. These pieces included the "Log-Book", a book review section that raised such crucial issues as the need to blur the boundaries between elite and popular literature, the defence of women's ability to draw realistic characters, the attack on revered representatives of high realism and the revaluation of marginalized fictional forms (Phegley, 2005: 187–191). As editor and probable author of these anonymous reviews, Wood must have used the "Log-Book" to express her own ideas on fiction. The revision of literary standards, in particular, seems to have been a crucial objective of her editorial policy. This hypothesis is substantiated by numerous meta-literary comments found in her novels. Sometimes included in the form of narratorial intrusions, other times made through the characters' voices, these comments invite the reader to rethink the confines between realism and romance, moralism and sensationalism. Furthermore, Wood uses strategies of direct address to bring thorny problems to the reader's attention, especially when the narrative revolves around disquieting themes linked to the Woman Question.

A careful consideration of all these aspects raises doubts about the origins and the nature of Wood's supposed narrative flaws. Although some weaknesses of her fiction are undeniable, they should be viewed as the result of conscious experiments she conducted to develop new literary forms through which new experiences could be represented. These experiments are most visible in her combination of sensationalism and domestic realism. By grafting elements of the sensation novel – a centrifugal genre marked by the tendency to fragment the social order – onto the centripetal structure of the domestic novel, Wood inevitably produced the jarring effects detected, and often criticized, by her reviewers. Equally disturbing were the effects created by her integration of fairy-tale, gothic and supernatural elements into bildungsroman plots. The female novel of formation, in particular, was subject to revisions that curbed its norm-enforcing function. As shown in the following chapters, Wood created images of domestic suffering and violence that cast a shadow onto the desirability of the heroine's *Bildung*, and she exposed some traps of romantic love and marriage by making a demythologizing use of fairy-tale components. Her genre-breaking and genre-refashioning strategies also included the ironic fictionalization of conduct-book models of femininity (such as those enforcing idleness and home confinement), the development of crime narratives featuring women sleuths, and the sensational use of evangelical rhetoric to express a physicality of emotions purged of vulgarity.[9]

Most of these strategies were adopted in order to bring problematic issues into focus. By mixing conflicting literary genres together, Wood exposed some contradictions of feminine models validated by those genres, such as those of the modest maiden, the self-sacrificial wife, the loving mother, the unfeeling spinster and the demonic femme fatale. Her characterization of masculine figures was equally innovative: praised by an 1861 review for her remarkable delineation of male characters in *East Lynne*,[10] she represented some tensions inherent in the dominant category of Man and partly unmade this category to encourage a rethinking of masculine and gentlemanly ideals. She also explored class and professional matters imbricated with the gender problems of the age, and was particularly awake to the challenges faced by male and female members of the Victorian middle class, to which she herself belonged. The fact that she espoused bourgeois values did not prevent her from noticing the limits of her class's ideology, which she exposed in covert narrative critiques.

A main target of her irony was marriage, the institution upon which the Victorian middle class had founded its ideals of order and stability. Influenced like other contemporaries by the popularity of the Matrimonial Causes Act (1857), Wood depicted a number of ill-assorted matches, afflicted wives and discontented husbands in her novels, which seldom offer examples of happy companionate marriages. These conjugal pictures are made more disheartening by the frequent addresses to the reader with which her novels are punctuated. Often feminized, Wood's addressees are encouraged to sympathize with the novels' suffering heroines and to experience a process of identification that will bring their own dissatisfactions to the fore.

Even more complex was Wood's representation of separate-spheres ideology. When she started to write professionally around the middle of the century, the gap between masculine and feminine spaces was widening. In addition to working long hours outside the home, middle-class men tended to spend their leisure time in male-exclusive circles, while women were increasingly confined in domestic environments where they were allowed to perform few activities (Wolff, 1988). Additional problems were posed by the condition of redundant women who, as evidenced by the 1851 census, were forced to find a job outside their homes but, in so doing, risked losing the honourable status granted to non-working women. The negative effects of this situation are insistently dramatized in Wood's novels, in which female protagonists often complain about having to live a boring, uneventful and lonely existence.

Some of Wood's writings focus on the situation of redundant women and devise hopeful solutions by characterizing impoverished gentlewomen who manage to work without losing status. A paramount case is that of the eponymous protagonist of *Mrs. Halliburton's Troubles* (1862) examined in Chapter 1. Compelled to do various jobs to earn money for her family, Jane Halliburton performs a symbolic invasion of the public sphere but preserves her bourgeois respectability as she works within the safe walls of her home. This symbolic entry into the occupational world is an imaginative solution to a problem felt by the author herself who had an ambivalent social position. Although she cultivated an image of domestic respectability, Wood was no Victorian matron who idled her days away in her household. What she pursued at home was a full-time professional career that gained recognition outside the private sphere and enabled her to interact from a distance with the public sphere of the Victorian literary world. The complexity of her position was increased by her frail constitution. Forced to spend much time indoors by her lifelong invalidism, Wood transformed her space of domestic seclusion into a space of literary production within which she created works that influenced public taste and brought her public acclaim. By using illness as a means of professional self-empowerment, she changed some implications of the Victorian gendering of spheres from *within* the system, thereby substantiating recent feminist claims that Victorian women sometimes exploited their vulnerable condition to achieve unconventional aims (Herndl, 1996).

Such a view is validated by an interpretation of the separate-spheres dynamics offered in an article titled "Female Suffrage" which appeared in *The Argosy* in 1873. Written by Alice King, one of the evangelical contributors to Wood's magazine, the article objects to the prospect of female suffrage on the assumption that women could continue to assert a stronger spiritual influence upon men if they avoided turning into competitors for socio-political power. While championing the preservation of women's domestic roles, however, King makes the following thought-provoking remark on the influence that a woman writer could exert by simply holding the pen, a "peaceful weapon, which fits so well the female hand":

> English boys and girls, growing up in lands beyond the sea, learn to think with her thoughts. They who have never seen her face or heard her voice speak lovingly her name. She is ruler over hearts; perhaps can make us swell in anger or melt

in pity. The ideas she gives forth are discussed by the roadside and in the snug library. Her mind permeates other minds and tinges them with its colour. We fully believe that if a band of the literary sisterhood were to agree to try to abolish any one of the few real grievances of their sex, such as the right of a worthless husband to take his wife's earnings, they could make such a stir in public opinion that it would be abolished. (King, 1873: 194)

This statement, which cunningly teases out the potential for female empowerment within a conservative hegemony (Palmer, 2011: 113), offers a rationale for the complex role that the magazine's editor tailored for herself. In ways similar to the writer celebrated by King, Wood used her home-produced works to conquer the public sphere without violating social conventions. The underlying challenge she thus posed to separate-spheres ideology is confirmed by the worldwide diffusion of a novel like *East Lynne*,[11] which enabled her to "rule over the hearts" of readers in far-off lands and to "permeate other minds" from the safe distance of her domestic location.

While disclosing some camouflage strategies adopted by women writers, King's article deals with other pressing questions, such as female suffrage, which came to be widely debated at the time. Wood's ideological attitude to these questions still needs to be ascertained. How should we interpret her domesticated professionalism in light of the age's proto-feminist agendas? Was her conservatism in line with the varied, sometimes contradictory, convictions of anti-suffragist and anti-feminist Victorians? And if so, to what extent? The scarcity of biographical documentation prevents us from exploring these issues in depth. Both memoirs, for example, offer only vague references to her socio-political views. Besides observing that his mother "followed with keenest interest" "all social movements affecting the people or country", Charles Wood limits himself to declaring that she disliked argument, "took no part" in politics "beyond being a strong Conservative" and had "farreaching sympathies" for those affected by an inequality that "she recognised as a Divine law" (1894: 234).

Such vague comments must have contributed to the meagre interest Wood raised in 1970s feminists, whose sympathies lay with those Victorian authoresses who had openly rejected decorous models and expressed female anger and frustration. A sufficient example is the little relevance Showalter gives to a "sedate" sensationalist like Wood, who is accused of being too "reticent" in describing female passions (1977: 158, 172). In later decades, however, critics have recognized the existence of "a wide grey area" between Victorian feminism and anti-feminism, "where women who [were] indifferent to the whole controversy would place themselves ideologically" (Sanders, 1996: 5). As Valerie Sanders demonstrates in exploring this area, supposedly anti-feminist writers like Oliphant were full of inconsistencies in their life and writing. Despite their promotion of family values, these writers often undermined the ideologeme of the home with their personal ambition, their partial support of the feminist cause and their representation of ambiguous heroines divided between protest and submission. Successive studies have confirmed the inadequacy of the dichotomy of anti-feminism versus protofeminism, and the need for a more open-minded approach to nineteenth-century women writers, which should undercut "any easy identification of a specific genre with a specific ideology or doctrine" (Wagner, 2009: 7–8).

Although she is ignored or given little space in such studies as Sanders's *Eve's Renegades* (1996) or *Antifeminism and the Victorian Novel* edited by Tamara Wagner (2009), Wood can be profitably interpreted in light of this recuperative approach. By unravelling some contradictions apparent in her writing, including her puzzling representations of women, this book aims to overcome simplistic classifications,[12] which have deprived Wood's oeuvre of due critical attention, making it "largely untaught, unread, and out-of-print" (Maunder, 2000: 17).

Some complexities of Wood's conservative stance are clarified by comparison with contemporaries like Alice King, who uncomfortably negotiated between conflicting ideological views. An important issue at stake was undoubtedly the separate-spheres doctrine. Inextricably connected with the marriage question, this doctrine engendered heated debates among male commentators in the 1860s, as evidenced by the clashing positions of John Stuart Mill and John Ruskin. In *The Subjection of Women* (1869), most probably written with his wife Harriet, Mill famously opted for a realistic approach to Victorian sexual politics and condemned an enslaving system established through the marriage bond, urging for the complete emancipation of women. An opposite belief was expressed by Ruskin in "Of Queen's Gardens" (1865), where myth is used to romanticize the doctrine of separate spheres and to restrain the demands for autonomy made by insurgent women.[13] The attitudes of female intellectuals were similarly discordant. In 1857, for example, Barbara Leigh Smith Bodichon campaigned for the professionalization of women. In her essay "Women and Work", Bodichon convincingly used the bourgeois indictment of idleness as a source of vice and disease, declared that love (and marriage) was no profession, and strongly urged that women, "as children of God", should "be trained to do some work in the world" (1857: 7–9). One year later, Oliphant approached the question from an antithetical Ruskinian perspective:

> Equality is the mightiest of humbugs – these is no such thing in existence; and the idea of opening the professions and occupations and governments of men to women, seems to us the vainest as well as the vulgarest of chimeras. God has ordained visibly, by all the arrangements of nature and providence, one sphere and kind of work for a man and another for a woman. (1858: 145)

Clearly divergent in their attitudes, the two essays nonetheless share some strategies borrowed from religious discourse, which are used to validate the authors' claims. While Oliphant evokes God to naturalize the existence of separate spheres, Bodichon provides spiritual justifications for cultivating women's talents outside the home. Bodichon's rhetoric is not so distant from the religious discourse Wood employs in her novels to expose the dangers of forced idleness and to sanctify the work ethic of those women who were compelled to earn a living. Differently from Bodichon, however, Wood was concerned by the vulgarity of professionalism. The domestic role she tailored for herself and her working heroines was more in line with Oliphant's shunning of non-respectable occupations ("the vulgarest of chimeras"), even though the latter could not avoid self-contradictions in her stubborn pursuit of a literary career. Like Oliphant, moreover, Wood exhibited an ambivalent attitude to women's conjugal duties. Both novelists celebrated marriage as a founding social institution; but they also tended to represent the condition of married women in ironic or disheartening terms.[14]

Another influential writer of the time was Eliza Lynn Linton. An intellectual split between "self-effacement" and "a desire to destroy the status quo" (Sanders, 1996: 136), Linton has challenged scholars with the inconsistencies of her personality and her writings. In addition to living an unconventional life, she wavered between proto-feminism and anti-feminism, as evidenced by some irreconcilable ideas found in her oeuvre. Although she authored an early defence of Mary Wollstonecraft, for example, she opposed the prospect of higher education for women and was afraid of their entering into politics. She also urged a domestic life for her sex group but frequently represented conjugal life as oppressive "whereas her women who work are happy, vigorous and healthy" (Sanders, 1996: 131). In "The Girl of the Period" (1868), Linton confirmed her split view of femininity as she contrasted an old-fashioned ideal of womanhood (based on modesty and generosity) to the fast girl of the new times, who was depicted as too selfish and unfeeling, too interested in physical appearance and in making a mercenary marriage. A similar characterization is repeatedly found in Wood's fiction, which depicts fast girls in more complex and captivating terms. Differently from Linton, however, Wood recognized the value of female education that is visibly exalted in novels like *Mrs. Halliburton's Troubles*. The relevance given to her own learning in both biographies suggests that she cherished those childhood memories and was conscious of their importance for her future professional growth. Wood's promotion of a good education for women shows that she was less reticent than other conservative authoresses in dealing with such matters and that she did not dislike the "clever girls" celebrated in an essay by Joseph Johnson, who happily turned "self-culture" into "the means of self-maintenance" and proved to the world that they possessed "purpose, will, determination" (Johnson, 1862: iii-iv).

As shown by these comparisons, Ellen Wood developed her gender views in a highly contentious environment that was unsettled by women's demands for emancipation. Unlike the few Victorians who explicitly stood for or against these demands, she was one of the many intellectuals who positioned themselves in a grey area in which conservative and innovative forces ambiguously coexisted. Women of letters, in particular, tended to remain within this area as they demanded rights (especially in property matters) but were not yet convinced of the possibility of achieving equality between the sexes. Despite the lack of evidence, we can surmise that Wood had a good knowledge of this situation, read essays focusing on the Woman Question, and was influenced by the ideas that circulated widely within her milieu. Like most Victorians, she strove to combine proto-feminist agendas with conformist attitudes which, though perceived as harshly anti-feminist in later times, should rather be viewed as manifestations of the anxieties generated by the questioning of traditional models. The fact that

INTRODUCTION

Wood engaged with key social topics like the condition of married women proves that she was sensitive to contemporary issues but, still unready to espouse change uncompromisingly, she strove to express her concerns without violating established norms and tastes. This arduous negotiation did not escape notice. "Mrs. Wood is a writer who puzzles us", declared an anonymous contributor to the *London Quarterly Review* who made saucy comments on her alternation of pure stories with mischievous books that offended against "good morals and correct taste" ("Thackeray and Modern Fiction", 1864: 405–406).

The examples above show that the interrelations between nineteenth-century feminism and anti-feminism can be fruitfully explored to clarify various unresolved tensions of Wood's writings that have been overlooked or easily dismissed as flaws. In addition to ideas that were widely debated by the Victorians, this book draws upon a selection of post-Victorian theories that are used to unravel some discursive threads spun around the thorny question of women's roles and aspirations. The risk to avoid is, of course, that of anachronism. For this reason, I have based my selection of theoretical approaches on the methodological premise that theories developed after Wood's death cannot be interpreted as being anticipated in her oeuvre. They should rather be considered as the offspring of notions that began to surface in the nineteenth century but needed new epistemic contexts to be fully expanded and systematized. What these theories reveal, if carefully applied to Wood's texts and context, is her alertness to some cracks that were appearing in Victorian ideologies and her wish to explore the tensions produced by emerging forces that were challenging the world she lived in.

A female theorist that illuminates some important aspects of Wood's career and writings is Virginia Woolf, who developed ideas inherited from her Victorian predecessors. In conceptualizing the need of "a room of one's own", Woolf posed a problem strongly felt by nineteenth-century women, whose working spaces coincided with their family environment. "If a woman wrote, she would have to write in the common sitting-room", she declared in her famous 1929 essay, before lamenting the gender inequality of such a condition. Although a whole genealogy of authoresses had nurtured their sensitivity by observing "personal relations [that] were always before their eyes" in the sitting-room, the domestic reclusion and the forced inaction experienced by women over the centuries had caused acute suffering and deprived the history of literature of many undeveloped talents (Woolf, 1929 [2000]: 67–70). This reality could be changed, in Woolf's view, by granting women a space of their own in which they could use their pen to express their talents freely and to earn the money needed for their emancipation.

If applied to Ellen Wood, this spatial metaphor sheds light on the hardships she faced in developing her literary genius. Forced to carve her room of creativity within the home, Wood disguised her professional status by offering a model of female abnegation that concealed the reality of her economic and cultural capital. This model was an embodiment of a gendered domestic phantom facing all Victorian authoresses – a phantom that continued to hinder women's professional growth in the first half of the twentieth century. "Killing the Angel in the House was part of the occupation of a woman writer", Virginia Woolf provocatively admitted in the essay "Professions for Women",[15] before focussing on a second objective she strove to pursue in her literary career, albeit less successfully: that of "telling the truth about [her] own experiences as a body" (1931 [1981]: 151, 153). These Woolfian ideas can be used retrospectively to illuminate some challenges met by women novelists like Wood in an age dominated by the angel-in-the-house ideal. Instead of "killing" this ghostly presence, Wood adopted the cunning strategy of deflating its symbolism while wearing its garb. She cultivated a respectable image of womanhood to avoid social censorship and moral ostracism, but she simultaneously strove to find a new balance between professionalism and domesticity, as proved by her well-concealed pursuit of literary ambitions. In similar ways, Woolf's reflection on the difficulty of rendering the physicality of her experiences brings to light a problem faced by her Victorian predecessors: the public disapproval of extreme female emotions. In contrast with the age's tendency to conceive women in oppositional terms (as either disembodied angels or instinct-dominated Jezebels), Wood dared to represent the passions of respectable women in a strongly physical language which, as critics have lately observed, was obtained by blending evangelical emotionalism with sensational elements.[16] This generic combination is further proof of Wood's exploration of new ways of circumventing censorship while giving voice to those yearnings of womanhood that most Victorians were still unprepared to cope with.

The retrospective look Virginia Woolf cast upon Victorian paradigms of femininity enables us to decipher some intricacies of Ellen Wood's writing and to prove the complexity of her figure, which is not encompassed by the image of a domestic Scheherazade memorialized by Adeline Sergeant. One decade after Woolf, Simone de Beauvoir explored some aspects of womanhood that would significantly contribute to the development of later feminist theories. In *The Second Sex* (1949), Beauvoir drew on the distinction between Nature and Culture to expose the ideologies, discourses and practices through which the body is constructed as gendered. "One is not born, but rather becomes, a woman", she famously declared to explain that "woman" is not an essence but a construct within patriarchal culture (Beauvoir, 1949 [2011]: 283). What she thus suggested was that "women are not inferior by Nature but inferiorised by Culture: they are acculturated into inferiority" and men themselves are constructed through socializing processes that confer supremacy on them (Ruthven, 1984: 45). Beauvoir's articulation of the difference between biological sex and a culturally induced process of gendering is relevant to my reading of Wood. In addition to betraying some awareness of the fictitiousness of dominant masculine concepts, Wood characterized women as variable subjects that could not be encompassed within the unified, transhistorical category of the Eternal Feminine. Although they generally end up conforming to social rules, her female characters are heterogeneous in attitude, often yield to passions and pose subtle challenges to Victorian paradigms of femininity. To say this does not mean that Wood achieved a twentieth-century consciousness of the difference between sex and gender. Like most Victorians, she tended to found socio-sexual identity on biological distinctions; but she also started to perceive the constructedness of gender roles, as suggested by two aspects of her characterization examined in the following chapters: the parody of female ornamentation as an instrument of self-surveillance and the representation of some figures (both male and female) whose identity is not essentialized.

Beauvoir paved the way to a phenomenological approach to gendered subjectivity that was developed through several decades. Most relevant to our analysis is the evolution of her notion of "becoming woman" which, effectively combined with a variety of cultural and feminist theories during the twentieth century, led to late 1980s-early 1990s conceptualizations of the fluidity of gender. A significant example is Judith Butler's theorization of performativity. Drawing upon Beauvoir's reinterpretation of the phenomenological doctrine of constituting acts, Butler declared that "gender is in no way a stable identity"; "rather, it is an identity tenuously constituted in time – an identity instituted through a *stylized repetition of acts*" which are mostly performed through the body and "constitute the illusion of an abiding gendered self" (1988: 519). Similarly based on Beauvoir's thinking is the theory of the positionality of the subject developed by Linda Alcoff who, in exposing "the danger that essentialist conceptions of the subject pose specifically for women", asserted the desirability of construing gendered subjectivity "in relation to concrete habits, practices, and discourses while at the same time recognizing the fluidity of these" (1995: 450). Both theorists, moreover, appropriated and developed the Foucauldian notion that the body is not sexed prior to its acts and postures, but rather determined through discourses. Wood's fiction can be read in light of this phenomenological tradition which, though applied with caution, can help us ascertain the extent to which she showed a faint consciousness of ideas systematized by theorists one century later. Her representation of motherhood is a case in point. Without ever questioning the sacredness of women's procreation and nurturing, Wood cast doubt on the naturalness of these functions, as she portrayed excessive and recalcitrant mothers who learn to perform, and sometimes fail to embody, proper maternal roles.

Equally useful to our interpretation of Wood is Luce Irigaray's distinction between the "*two irreconcilable 'bodies*'" associated with a woman conceived as "*commodity*": "her 'natural' body and her socially valued, exchangeable body, which is a particularly mimetic expression of masculine values" (1977 [1985]: 180). An elaboration of the "becoming woman" concept, this distinction also draws upon anthropological notions developed by Claude Lévi-Strauss in *Les structures élémentaires de la parenté* (1949), where he theorizes on the commodification of women in patriarchal societies and explores the ways women are consumed and circulated among men like merchandise. In Irigaray's opinion, this process of commodification turns women into "*fetish-objects*" which are exchanged to strengthen homosocial bonds (1977 [1985]: 183). As a result, the female body becomes instrumental in reducing women to pure exchange value. Through a physical and symbolic manipulation of their bodies, women are forced to play the social roles of virgins, mothers and prostitutes. In so doing, they become part of an economy of desire managed by men, who assert their power also by imposing their proper names on their wives and daughters.

This male monopoly of power is extensively represented by Wood who, as we will see, focuses on different symbolic functions fulfilled by Victorian women within a strict patriarchal order. Her choice of pen names and authorial personae discussed above suggests her interest in these social dynamics. Her fictional texts, moreover, bear witness to her concerns over the gendered power relations of her world. Besides exposing the consequences of men's ownership of women through marriage, Wood characterized failing wives and mothers who disprove the naturalness of established roles, and rebellious heroines who defy their commodification by posturing as desiring subjects.

Another focus of attention in Wood's fiction is the female body – an object within which a variety of meanings are imbricated. Its complex signification is illuminated by twentieth-century feminist theories, and especially phenomenological approaches, which configure the body as the means through which the ego relates with the surrounding social space. As Elizabeth Grosz claims, our conception of reality and knowledge depends on sexually specific bodies implicated in power structures and subject to endless rewritings. A "corporeal feminism" should focus on specific ways in which women's bodies incarnate "the subject's access to spatiality" (Grosz, 1994: 85), render unique feminine experiences, give flesh to the sexualization of biological instincts and to the forms of protest women devise against their social construction. Such conceptualizations of the body are useful to decipher some perplexing images of corporeality found in Wood's fiction which, as demonstrated throughout this book, exposes the consequences of women's obsessive ornamentation of their bodies and describes thought-provoking cases of female anorexia and gluttony.

Directly connected with the social inscription of the female body is the problem of insanity, which is upsettingly represented in some works by Wood. Her ambivalent depictions of madwomen are clarified, for a twenty-first-century reader, by ideas developed by such feminist theorists as Elaine Showalter, Sandra Gilbert, Susan Gubar, and Luce Irigaray, who examine the mechanisms through which the Victorians designated women's bodies as sites of instability that favoured mental illness. Besides unveiling the oppressive mechanisms underlying such convictions, which were strongly validated by Victorian medical texts, these theorists explore the possibility of valorizing hysteria and madness as expressions of a proto-feminist discourse that was imbricated with dominant gender views in many novels of the age. As shown in Chapter 3, this discourse emerges in the writings of Wood herself whose characterization of mentally afflicted women poses thorny questions concerning their economic dependence and their emotional self-restraint.

Also worthy of notice is Wood's portrayal of physically and mentally weak men. Affected by a variety of disorders which endanger their households and are passed onto their children, these frail masculine figures are in line with the "flawed discourses of masculinity" woven in Victorian sensation fiction, which uses "repeated tropes of extreme affect, and domesticity under threat" to raise doubts about dominant constructions of manhood (Nemesvari, 2015: 88–89). Like other mid-century writers who started to interrogate standard masculinities (see MacDonald, 2015: 1–4), Wood drew on notions of male gentleness and psychophysical weakness to question the solidity (and the desirability) of established models, such as the domineering husband and the strict *pater familias*. This deconstructive tendency is further proof of Wood's interest in the permeability of those gender confines on which patriarchal heterosexuality was founded. What she and her fellow novelists began to explore in the mid-nineteenth century would be systematized into theory by twentieth-century feminists and appropriated by masculinity studies, which in recent times have emerged as "a significant outgrowth of feminist studies and an ally to its older sister in a complex and constantly shifting relationship" (Gardiner, 2002: ix).

By making a combined use of theories, this book intends to prove that Wood was "an important commentator on nineteenth-century gender politics, engaged in a project which is feminist in effect if not intent" despite her "seeming conventionality" (Maunder, 2000: 25). This project was in line with the attempts made by other mid-Victorian writers who, as Pykett suggests, strove to find forms that could articulate women's experiences and aspirations, even though no single ideological perspective or coherent range of perspectives was delineated (1992: 5). A main strategy Wood adopted to uncover some dark sides of women's lives was that of turning her implied addressee into an active interpreter of her texts. Frequently addressed by the narrator, Wood's readers (and especially female ones) no longer play the role of passive consumers influenced by conservative ideologies. They are rather encouraged to become what Judith Fetterley calls "resisting readers"[17] – textual interpreters who do not accept "as normal and legitimate a male system of values, one of whose central principles is misogyny" (1978: xx). Although Fetterley focuses on American literature, her definition of the "resisting reader" can be effectively applied to my analysis. As will be shown, a number of Wood's narratorial intrusions arouse sympathy for unorthodox female characters and, more generally, invite women readers to abandon essentializing viewpoints and to adopt a pluralism of perspectives which, by producing different interpretations, challenge the patriarchal notion of a single transcendent meaning.[18]

Together with the other theories mentioned above, this reader-response approach is functional to detecting significant aspects of Wood's oblique critique of established gender roles. Both her proto-feminist and her anti-feminist views are explored in the five following chapters, each of which pivots around a theme linked to the Woman Question or a relevant feminine model. Chapter 1 is devoted to Wood's representation of marriage, a recurrent motif in her fiction and the central institution on which Victorian bourgeois morality was founded. In line with her fellow novelists, Wood connoted marriage as the main instrument through which women achieved full social status. Still, she created very few images of conjugal bliss, and most of her married heroines are destined to experience domestic unhappiness and victimization. If read through the lenses of proto-feminist and feminist theories, the traps of wedded life she depicts reveal her subtle critique of the romantic-love ideal and the gendered roles constructed around this ideal. The chapter also investigates Wood's ambivalent depiction of the separate-spheres doctrine enforced by marriage, her polemical attitude to mercenary unions and her perplexing characterization of unhappy wives and mothers, who are both objects of pity and instruments to interrogate women's own responsibility in their sufferings.

Closely connected with marriage was the Victorian ideal of female forbearance, which contributed to keeping women under the strongholds of patriarchy. This ideal, deeply rooted in folklore, had been legitimized by a long literary tradition dating back to Boccaccio's characterization of the patient Griselda. Chapter 2 focuses on variations of the Griselda theme found in narratives by Wood who, while seeming to indict female rebellion, also encouraged her readers to sympathize with her humiliated heroines. Particularly interesting in her controversial depiction of women's patience, is her experimental combination of multiple genres, including the fairy-tale tradition from which she drew a variety of Griselda types that were grafted onto her domestic and bildungsroman plots. The results of such experiments are what Gilbert and Gubar would define as "palimpsestic texts", "whose surface designs conceal or obscure deeper, less accessible (and less socially acceptable) levels of meaning" (1979 [2000]: 73).

More sensational are the female models analysed in Chapter 3, which focuses on Wood's portrayal of women yielding to immoderacy. Although they are often condemned to expiate their sins, these characters fulfil a disruptive ideological function, as they are shown to be the victims of oppressive social mechanisms that force them to give vent to unfeminine cravings and sensations. In addition to inspecting Wood's complex (and often unorthodox) representations of female madness, the chapter draws on phenomenological feminist theories to detect the camouflage techniques that enabled the author to shun vulgarity while rendering female emotions in their strong physicality.

The last two chapters discuss the imbrication of gender and class roles in Wood's fiction. A champion of the Victorian bourgeoisie, to which she herself belonged, Wood adopted cunning strategies to expose some limits of the bourgeois ideology, especially with regards to its strict gendering of roles. The fact that most of her heroines belong to her own class confirms the primary interest she had in exploring bourgeois values and attitudes, which she partly endorsed, partly aimed to redefine in more libertarian terms. Less evident is her interest in women belonging to other classes, who nonetheless feature among her many female figures.

Chapter 4 is devoted to her characterization of upper-class ladies. A well-known example is that of Isabel Vane, the adulterous protagonist of *East Lynne*, who both fascinated and scandalized nineteenth-century reviewers. Like other gentlewomen portrayed by Wood, Isabel embodies bourgeois prejudices against the spoiled daughters of the degenerated upper echelons; but she also fulfils a thought-provoking function with her erring conduct, which raises thorny questions about the influence that class identity exerted on the moral responsibilities and the chances for autonomy offered to women.

An understudied aspect of Wood's fiction is at the core of Chapter 5, which focuses on her provocative portrayal of low-class women. After examining her representation of lower middle-class figures like governesses, who embody circulating anxieties about the permeability of class borders, the chapter analyses the challenging function fulfilled by women belonging to the lower social strata. Often portrayed as minor characters in Wood's fiction, these women are nonetheless important to understand the author's wavering between conservative and innovative views. If many bear evidence of circulating prejudices against the poor, others reveal Wood's interest in alternative feminine roles that might positively influence dominant bourgeois models. By creating an interesting gallery of resourceful maidservants and governesses, upright working-class women, weak but honest nurses, the author implicitly suggested that new spaces of action and autonomy could open for women if they could free themselves from such bourgeois strictures as the indictment of female labour. Most interesting, in this regard, is Wood's early experimentation with detection plots revolving around low-class women, who act as amateur sleuths and find essential clues to the discovery of middle-class perpetrators of ominous crimes.

By combining these neglected aspects of Wood's fiction with more studied ones, such as her depiction of marriage and female demureness, this book aims to explore her representation of the Victorian gendering of roles and other social practices of identity-making. The integrated theory used in the five chapters is meant to provide a critical alternative to simplistic readings of Wood's narratives which, too often interpreted in either/or terms, have contributed to her fading into obscurity in the post-Victorian age. In line with the recuperative approach inaugurated in recent years, the analyses offered in the next pages unravel many contradictions that have puzzled scholars for decades. Instead of being defined in sheer oppositional terms, such as conservative/unorthodox, domestic/sensational, anti-feminist/proto-feminist, Wood's works and professional role are read for their jarring aspects, which cast light on the complexity of her ideological position and narrative experimentation.

CHAPTER 1

The necessity and traps of Victorian marriage

Marriage was a central Victorian institution and the ideal around which the bourgeois concept of morality pivoted. From their early childhood, middle-class women were taught to aspire to a married status and encouraged to become respectful wives and devoted mothers. Advice books enforced this teaching by insisting on the "redemptive power of the home", the place where a gentle mistress was supposed to take care of her family and be "all attention" to her husband in order to "lighten his load and calm his spirit" (Tosh, 1999: 55, 54). Literature itself regularly represented marriage as the only ritual granting full status to women, whose expectations were those of making a good match that could provide them "with station, role, duties and economic security" (Mitchell, 1981: 10). In exchange for these advantages, women needed to be ready to perform the prescribed matrimonial duties. Even though girls tended to cherish the prospect of a romantic union, the marriage institution was mostly conceived as a social and financial transaction between two parties that gained unequal rights after entering into the contract.

Female dependence on men was validated by the supposed weakness of women, who were considered physically and mentally inferior to men and therefore in need of life-long protection and supervision. On a moral plane, contrastingly, women were thought to outstrip men, as the latter's sexual standards were less intransigent. Apparently at odds with each other, these views of women's simultaneous inferiority (psychophysical) and superiority (moral and sexual) were reconciled by the century's conceptualization of marriage as a bond based on the law of coverture and on uncompromising norms of female conduct. During the course of the century, however, the ideological framework of patriarchy was gradually shaken by demands for women's rights and autonomy that led to reforms such as the Matrimonial Causes Act (1857) and the Married Women's Property Acts (1870, 1882). All concerned with the legal position of women after signing the marriage contract, these Acts testify to the growing cultural awareness of the limits of an institution that forced wives to fully rely on their husbands' benevolence and granted insufficient shelter to the weaker party in case of troubles.

Another problem inherent in the traditional view of marriage was that of female seclusion and inactivity within the home. Increasingly discussed during the 1860s, the indictment of women's work inside and outside the household came to be perceived by many as a dangerous source of frustration and unhappiness. The result was an evolution of the notion of the conjugal bond and a slow revision of the couple's rights and duties. From the 1870s onwards, literature drew on the ideal of the companionate marriage[1] praised by proto-feminist thinkers like John Stuart Mill, who advocated the freeing of women from the straitjacket of a matrimonial contract entailing the unequal treatment of man and wife. Alternative views of this contract are offered in a number of writings which, increasingly in the late decades, responded to women's yearnings for less frustrating relations with their partners.

Despite her conservatism, Ellen Wood participated in this popular debate by offering very few images of conjugal bliss and by exposing some traps of marriage. Recurrent in her fiction is the indictment of mercenary marriage, represented as a consequence of a socioeconomic system founded on the notion of female dependence on male supply. Though morally biased,

Wood's mercenary wives are often shown to act under strong social pressures which, at the time, impelled women to marry for money. By focusing on this awkward situation, Wood offers glimpses into contradictions which, later in the century, would be polemically exposed by such feminists as the American writer Charlotte Perkins Gilman: "And yet why should we blame the woman for pursuing her vocation [the marriage of convenience]? Since marriage is her only way to get money, why should she not try to get money that way? [...] The mercenary marriage is a perfectly natural consequence of the economic dependence of women" (1898: 93).

Besides revealing the difficulty of escaping a contract enforced by women's socioeconomic dependence on men, Wood offers a disheartening picture of conjugal bonds after the wedding ceremony. What she represents in many novels are the hardships and discontent faced by a number of wives, including those who married for love. Worthy of notice, in her fiction, is also the infrequency of companionate marriages, which are achieved through much effort and rarely last in the face of adverse circumstances. By exposing different troubles experienced by Victorian wives without overtly criticizing the institution of marriage, Wood was caught in the same paradox faced by some anti-feminist novelists who, as hinted in the Introduction, made a destabilizing use of the traditional marriage plot. "If marriage is so important to them, and the only acceptable way out of the heroine's perplexities, why is it not made more attractive?" asks Sanders, thereby offering some important clues to this literary paradox (1996: 202). In ways similar to other women novelists, Wood officially sustained the ideology of the middle-class home, but she subtly challenged this ideology by drawing unhappy pictures of conjugal life that defied the age's assumptions about the real yearnings of womanhood.

The complexity of Ellen Wood's positioning is also evident in the matronly role she tailored for herself. As we have seen, her biographies lay stress on her embodiment of wifely and maternal values, but they fail to reconcile her iconic domesticity with the proactive professional role she came to play during her life. Although she spent a long time at home, Wood was no domestic recluse. A successful novelist and editor, she pursued professional activities that were patently at odds with the tasks performed by respectable matrons. When she started her literary career, moreover, she proved to be a shrewd businesswoman who surpassed Henry Wood in financial acumen and became the family's breadwinner.

The contradictions inherent in Wood's social status mirror the views about women and marriage intermingling in her works which, like most popular fiction of the age, both sustain and criticize the ideology of the middle-class home. What Vicky Simpson observes about *East Lynne* can be applied to most of Wood's narratives: they give voice to the characters' aspirations to the Victorian family ideal, but they also simultaneously destabilize the value of this ideal, thereby offering "a potent antidote to the 'familimania'" prevailing in the age's literature (2012: 586). Wood's critique of marriage is evident in her exploration of the financial relationships affecting gender and family roles. Her oeuvre bears witness to her indictment of mercenary unions and her exposure of the problems faced by women who lacked financial autonomy. In depicting the rights and duties of the marriage contract, moreover, she focuses on various social constraints that limited the freedom and self-development of Victorian wives. The cases of spousal neglect or abuse she represents, for instance, bring into sharp relief the fear of stigmatization that prevented many women from leaving their unfeeling or violent husbands.

Maternity is also connoted as a source of suffering and self-denial in some of Wood's works, such as *St. Martin's Eve* (1866) and *Court Netherleigh* (1881). Without ever questioning the sacredness of the mother's role, these works nonetheless reveal the undesirability of confining women into narrow domestic spaces where their minds and bodies are worn down by their frustrated aspirations to explore, and play some part in, the public sphere. Through a skilful combination of irony and camouflage techniques, Wood depicts the victimization of some women resulting from the social expectations placed on maternity. What she unveils are some negative aspects of female procreativity which, if viewed as the main defining function of womanhood, can engender rebellion or dangerous pathologies. Still, it is important to clarify that her portrayals of frustrated mothers bear no evidence of the abject conceptualization developed by twentieth-century feminists like Julia Kristeva (1980 [1982]) or Elizabeth Grosz (1994), who theorized about how patriarchal stereotypes of the maternal deprived women of independence and control over their lives.

With regard to space, it is revealing to see how often the household becomes a site of suffering, sometimes even terror, in Wood's fiction. Together with lonely wives oppressed by neglect and ennui, she portrays women haunted by external and internal ghosts within the domestic walls. By merging fairy-tale models with stereotypical elements of the Gothic tradition, Wood contributed to the nineteenth-century redefinition of the bourgeois home as a potential place of pain and fear. Uncaring husbands, dark family secrets and imaginative projections of conjugal unhappiness are some of the spectres that persecute her female figures, whose characterization bears traces of the age's taste for "homely Gothic".[2] In addition to setting some frightful stories in old upper-class mansions that incarnate the moral corruption of their owners, Wood's texts attach gothic connotations to some bourgeois homes, which become places of unhappiness and victimization of women disillusioned with marriage. The latter case is well exemplified by novels like *The Shadow of Ashlydyat* (1863) and *The House of Halliwell* (1890), in which bankers' and doctors' households are associated with suffering, humiliation and violence. As Chapter 2 demonstrates, a recurrent strategy used to render female persecution is the obsessive reference to figures like Bluebeard who, together with other fairy-tale characters embodying masculine oppression, are repeatedly evoked in her fiction. The gothicizing of domestic space is enhanced by the frequent addresses to readers who, as noted in the Introduction, are encouraged to identify and sympathize with the suffering heroines.

Alongside oppressed wives, Wood portrays two groups of characters that intriguingly challenge established gender roles. The first group consists of domestic men who, without being effeminate, set a new model of kindness and closeness to their wives. Probably inspired by Thomas Price, who successfully combined his business activities with the care of his children's education, these figures are a response to strict, muscular or overambitious models of masculinity that came to be viewed as inadequate after the mid-century, when some Victorians started to rethink domesticity as "a new arena for a different concept of [male] heroism" (Sanders, 1996: 98).

The second group that defies gender assumptions consists of single women who are either widows or spinsters. Like other women writers who explored the contradictions of widowhood, Wood drew on the complexity of this condition to expose some limits of the Victorian gender system. Her fictional widows are guaranteed respectability by their previous married condition. But they also reveal the strictures of the marriage system as they "capitalise on their freedom and reap the benefits of living without husbands" (Liggins, 2014: 36). This is the case of Jane Halliburton examined later in this chapter, whose self-help virtues are enhanced by the relative freedom she enjoys after losing her husband. Even more interesting is the function fulfilled by a group of women who never enter into a marriage contract. If some of them are hurt by the men they love and die prematurely, others set innovative models of conduct, as they achieve autonomy and wisdom. Wood generally avoids casting single women as pathetic figures or caricatures. The few eccentricities and comic aspects they exhibit tend to be counterbalanced by their business acumen, sagacity, generosity and by other qualities that turn them into points of reference for their family and their community.

A novel that betrays Wood's reservations about marriage is undoubtedly *East Lynne* (1861). As will be shown in Chapter 4, the disastrous union of Lady Isabel Vane with Archibald Carlyle is not only a warning against cross-class marriages that were thought to weaken the moral and social balance of the rising bourgeoisie. Their marriage also unveils some frustrating effects of the separate-spheres doctrine. Isabel's adultery is in fact presented as the result of her growing disappointment with married life – a feeling shared by many Victorian women. Compelled to find their satisfaction within the home, married women were often deprived of the companionship of their ambitious husbands who pursued their objectives in the public sphere. Unlike other female characters in *East Lynne* that exert power in the household by accepting conservative roles (Cornelia Carlyle and Barbara Hare), Isabel comes to see her husband's workplace as a rival and, driven by jealousy, she breaks a marriage contract that has betrayed her expectations. Even though she develops strong feelings for Carlyle after her marriage, Isabel initially agrees to marry him for social and economic reasons, as she is penniless and unable to sustain herself. Her conjugal tragedy confirms Wood's indictment of mercenary marriages, a practice stigmatized in most of her fiction, even in the few cases when these unions lead to mutual understanding and affection.

Another disastrous case is represented in *Anne Hereford* (1868), which depicts the materialistic union between Selina and Edwin Barley in all its dire consequences. After confessing that she used to hate her ugly husband, whom she still admits she does not love, the young and pretty wife declares "'I married for money'" and justifies her choice by mentioning the reverse case of Frances Carew, a relative who, despite her conjugal happiness, experiences social and financial troubles by marrying someone below her station "for love" (Wood, 1868a [1896]: 11). As the narrative unfolds, Selina is dreadfully punished for her materialistic attitude. Her flirting with an old suitor she had rejected leads to the accidental murder of another young man and, soon afterwards, to her own death that is caused by a cold caught during the tragic events. Vain and greedy, Selina is killed by the violent re-emergence of emotions and desires she had striven to cancel from her life after accepting a dispassionate union with a man she loathed. Her tragic destiny is contrasted with the situation of Frances Carew and Anne Hereford, both of whom get married for love and enjoy some conjugal happiness despite the obstacles posed by their strongly conservative society.[3]

The traps of marriage revealed in *Anne Hereford* become fully evident in *Court Netherleigh*. This late novel dramatizes the misadventures of two women who, after accepting a mercenary contract, fall prey to irrepressible desires and rebellious impulses. The indictment of money-oriented unions is achieved through an effective combination of fairy-tale elements with proto-feminist views that bring two thorny issues to the fore: the bartering of women in matrimonial transactions dominated by masculine power, and the extent to which consumerism contributed to the commodification of the female body. The two women who bring these issues to the fore are Selina Dalrymple and Adela Acorn, whose married parables offer disheartening pictures of gender and social discontent.

When an accident upsets her family peace and finances, Selina Dalrymple accepts the marriage proposal of Oscar Dalrymple, a sedate and calculating young relative who, after inheriting the property of her family, offers her protection and wealth. Defined as "one of the vainest girls living" who loves "pomp and show", she lures men with her natural charm and beauty (Wood, 1881 [1898]: 71, 106). This power of attraction increases when she settles in London and is, on her turn, captivated by the glamorous life of the capital: "Vain, giddy, and thoughtless, Selina's heart was revelling in the pleasures of this London life, her head turned with the admiration she received" (1881 [1898]: 109). Spoiled by her husband, who initially indulges all her desires, Selina falls prey to an irresistible compulsion to buy expensive clothes and accessories. Her purchase of luxury items gradually becomes a dangerous addiction, which makes her secretly incur huge debts. Described as "a skeleton in the closet" (1881 [1898]: 146), the debt resulting from her shopping mania brings ruin upon her family and contributes to souring a conjugal relationship she entered into for purely mercenary reasons.

What is noteworthy in Selina's story of addiction and downfall is the link it establishes between matrimonial compromise and the fashion market. First of all, the novel poses the dramatic problem of married women's lack of means, as Selina is economically dependent on Oscar. Her vulnerable position is confirmed by her willingness to be 'bought' in a socioeconomic bargain that excludes any affective involvement. Both aspects suggest that, like other Victorian novelists, Wood questioned the desirability of an institution that was inextricably conceived as a "financial transaction" (Calder, 1976: 31). These unappealing aspects are further emphasized by complex dynamics of oppression-rebellion associated with Selina's compulsive shopping. Instead of remaining a desired object, the woman gradually develops into a desiring subject who strives to escape her husband's control by purchasing ornaments without his permission. Her shopping "folly" – as mentioned in the title of Chapter 13 – is not only a form of pathology that draws attention to the age's mounting anxieties about consumerism; it is also a mechanism of self-assertion through which she rebels against the commodifying effects of gender relations founded on the law of coverture and male voyeurism.[4]

The pathological implications of Selina's impulses to buy are repeatedly equated to the self-destructive attitude of her brother Robert, who has disappeared and is believed to have taken his life. "'What if I put an end to it all, as Robert did?'" she muses in a fleeting suicidal thought, before comparing her weakness for shopping with Robert's addiction to gambling: "'It was always a fault of mine to be quick and fiery – like poor Robert'" (Wood, 1881 [1898]: 142, 158). Her particular compulsion is also connected with Victorian worries about the dangerous combination of market imperatives with the separate-spheres doctrine that threatened to transform shopping into "a fully articulated form of middle-class women's leisure" (Lysack, 2008: 2). Exactly because they could perform a limited range of activities, married women yielded to the lures of a trading system that embodied the commercial spirit of the rising bourgeoisie and was rarely perceived as dangerous in the early decades of the century. Despite the reservations manifested by orthodox thinkers like Ruskin, who detected a potential moral danger in women's appetite for wares, the Victorians were slow in developing an awareness of all the risks posed by compulsive buying. In an 1875 article entitled "The Philosophy of Shopping", for example, Eliza Lynn Linton still viewed the time spent in shops as a delightful activity through which women could escape "the monotony of more strictly domestic pursuits" and disprove assumptions about their "incapab[ility] of enjoying themselves apart from men" (488–489).

As mentioned above, a main target of criticism in *Court Netherleigh* is the threat of reification that consumerism posed to women, who increased their dependence on men's finances and controlling gazes by spending huge sums to embellish their bodies. Novelists became gradually aware of this threat during the century. An early literary exposure of its effects is the shopping expedition described in *Jane Eyre* (1847), in which the eponymous heroine struggles against Rochester's wish to turn her into an object of exchange by buying precious silks for her.[5] Charlotte Brontë's exposure of this sexual policy must have exerted some influence on later women novelists who, each in her own way, recast the idea of using men's money to purchase clothes and accessories that were meant to beautify (and commodify) women's bodies. Popular novelists, and particularly sensation authors, were sensitive to the increasing commercialization of Victorian society (Kimberly Harrison, 2011: 529–530) and curious to explore the different ways in which fashion turned women into merchandise. As Laurence Talairach-Vielmas observes, many representatives of the sensational school reworked fairy-tale elements in order to explore an "insolubly paradoxical terrain, where women oscillate[d] between subject and object": constructed "as desiring and consuming subjects" by advertisements, Victorian women were also objectified by a patriarchal system that encouraged them to dress beautifully in order to gratify men's voyeuristic pleasures (2007: 6).

These concepts apply to Wood herself, whose fiction reveals dangerous connections between men-owned money, consumerism and women's commodification through fashion. Well hidden under a conservative façade, such connections are nonetheless suggested by the author's skilful use of irony, which is most evident in the characterization of Selina Dalrymple. As we have seen, Selina is criticized for her vanity, but she is also connoted as a victim of socioeconomic transactions that objectify women. Though consciously accepted, the marriage contract she signs reduces her future autonomy. By spending her husband's money on glamorous clothing, moreover, she initially conforms to Victorian social rules that invited women to display their men's wealth through their attire. Shortly after her wedding, however, Selina turns shopping into a freely chosen "pleasurable course" that ruins her husband (Wood, 1881 [1898]: 134). What she performs, in so doing, is a symbolic act of disobedience that unveils pressing contradictions of the Victorian gendering of fashion. Besides 'punishing' her husband, she shows the possibility of acting as a desiring subject who purchases what she wants without her man's permission. At the same time, however, Selina's display of self-will is rife with ambiguities that confirm the limits of Victorian female autonomy. The self-liberating impulse she manifests, in spending her husband's money, is ironically neutralized by the commodifying effects of her compulsive shopping, as she purchases the very ornamentation that makes her an object of male desire.

Another thought-provoking figure in *Court Netherleigh* is Adela Acorn, whose stubborn rebellion against her husband unmasks worrying aspects of the alliance of patriarchy and capitalism. In a sub-plot strongly reminiscent of "Beauty and the Beast",[6] Adela is 'sold' by her father, Lord Acorn, to Francis Grubb, a "man in trade" who has offered to cancel the Lord's debts in exchange for his most beautiful daughter (1881 [1898]: 38). A vain, ambitious young woman who aspires to marry into the aristocracy, Adela initially rejects the proposal but is finally compelled to accept Grubb as her husband for the benefit of her family. Wood tempers the odious implications of this marriage transaction by narrowing the gap between the suitor's and the promised bride's personal endowments. While Adela's beauty is overshadowed by haughtiness, Grubb's "plebeian" status is counterbalanced by remarkable qualities: "a tall, noble-looking man, with intellect stamped on his ample forehead, and good feeling pervading his countenance" (1881 [1898]: 52, 35). What is promised by his physiognomy is confirmed by his gentlemanly conduct after their wedding: he treats his wife kindly and affectionately, and he patiently endures her whims and coldness until their union reaches a critical point.

Unlike her fond husband, Adela behaves like an unfeeling wife who despises his social status, squanders his money on fashionable objects, and neglects her household duties to pursue various leisure activities. In addition to enjoying parties, she ostentatiously flirts with men and, later in the narration, she falls prey to the vice of gambling, which makes her secretly incur large debts. Oppressed by financial troubles, Adela commits a criminal act that is the last straw in her marriage: she forges a cheque and lets a young wooer be jailed in her stead. The discovery of her crime is followed by the couple's separation – an act decided by Grubb who sends his guilty wife back to her parents. Upset by the loss of her social and financial privileges, Adela falls into a serious state of depression while her husband unexpectedly rises in rank through inheritance.[7] Physically and mentally wearied by her marginalization, Adela falls ill, repents her errors, develops a strong desire for her husband and even considers "going into a Sisterhood" or "a nursing institution" (1881 [1898]: 454) to escape her humiliating state. The latter course of action is providentially avoided by her reconciliation with her husband in the novel's conclusion. Before resuming her conjugal role, however, Adela is forced to enter into a new contract. She promises to become a "true and loving wife" and later proves to have espoused orthodox principles as she replaces "fashion and frivolity" with "higher aims and duties" which include giving birth to a son and heir (1881 [1898]: 469, 471–472).

The love Adela shows for her second son, in the novel's conclusion, counterbalances the irresponsibility of her previous conduct as mother. In a chapter titled "Perversity", Adela initially refuses to nurse her firstborn as she is impatient to resume her leisure activities. When the baby starts to fade away, she agrees to breastfeed him but the infant dies some weeks afterwards "long enough for her to get passionately attached to him, to use every means to make him strong" (1881 [1898]: 127). The affection described in this quotation is another camouflage strategy used by Wood who, while indicting Adela's initial lack of maternal care, simultaneously endows her with a disposition to nurture.

The taming of Adela Acorn is in line with the moral management devised for rebellious Victorian women who could escape stigmatization only by submitting to the gender norms they had violated. In addition to this social custom, the conclusion of *Court Netherleigh* seems to enforce views of marriage and household duties extolled in the domestic fiction of the age, which encouraged women to become dutiful wives and mothers. As Tamara Wagner observes, the "implausible" and "sudden" marital reconciliation with which the novel ends evidences Wood's conservative response to circulating anxieties produced by pressing debates on matrimonial reforms (2018: 126, 125). After laying out "negative guidelines on how to mismanage a marriage", Wood concocts a happy ending that exorcises the spectre of separation and, in so doing, upholds the bourgeois pragmatic view of a union based on financial security rather than romantic expectations (Wagner, 2018: 122). The orthodoxy of the novel's closure is undeniable. Yet, Wood also challenges her conservative message by using subtle narrative strategies that raise doubts about the very ideals that the text appears to champion.

First of all, Wood encourages her readers to sympathize with Adela who, unlike her husband, is repeatedly shown to suffer the dire consequences of their separation. Instead of highlighting the sinfulness of her previous conduct, the narrator lays stress on the woman's psychophysical afflictions and uses exclamations like "Poor Adela!" (Wood, 1881 [1898]: 388) to reinforce the effects produced by similar expressions employed by her family and friends. These narratorial intrusions are at odds with Victorian attitudes to fallen women who are rarely depicted as objects of compassion in the age's literature. One exception is the sensation novel's practice of drawing sympathetic portrayals of transgressive heroines – a practice largely attacked by reviewers in the 1860s-70s[8] – which Wood seems eager to continue in this late novel.

Also quite provocative is the symbolic function Adela fulfils in the economic transaction between her father and her suitor. Literally turned into currency by her spendthrift parent, who uses her market value to satisfy a demanding creditor, the young woman undergoes a process of commodification that increases her victim role. The gender implications of this symbolic exchange are enhanced by the novel's rewriting of "Beauty and the Beast". In anticipation of postmodern parodies, Wood makes an ironic use of figures and motifs drawn from this fairy tale, which are embedded into the realistic plot of her novel to unveil the objectification of women in a money-oriented patriarchal society. These effects are strengthened by the author's deletion and modification of sentimental and gender-enforcing elements of the fairy tale. An example is the absence of Beauty's request for a rose which, though made unknowingly, lays the premises for her father's debt with the Beast and her own victimization in the fairy-tale original.

By putting the most blame for the mismatch on the insolvent father and the desiring suitor, Wood not only reinforces her consistent critique of mercenary marriages, but she also alludes to the oppressive handling of women within a system that transforms their bodies into use values and exchange values.[9] Her description of the matrimonial transaction between Lord Acorn and Mr. Grubb offers some glimpses of a process of commodification that was only vaguely perceived by sensitive Victorians and would be theorized one century later: "Hence *women's role as fetish-objects*, inasmuch as, in exchanges, they are the manifestation and the circulation of a power of the Phallus, establishing relationships of men with each other" (Irigaray, 1977 [1985]: 183). A fetish-object exchanged between two men who little care for her feelings and desires, Adela is denied a part also in the second agreement Grubb makes with her father, when he resolves to send her back to her "maiden home": "The arrangements connected with this step had been settled between himself and Lord Acorn" (Wood, 1881 [1898]: 325). The marginal function she is forced to fulfil in both circumstances changes the meaning of the unfeeling attitude she initially adopts towards her husband. Although she is strongly blamed for her conjugal problems, Adela is not simply a capricious woman in need of moral management. What she embodies is primarily the role of a rebellious heroine who manifests her anger against her 'purchaser' by refusing to satisfy his love requests. Her disobedience is strengthened by her initial refusal to nurse their firstborn. Stigmatized as "perverse" and "unnatural" (1881 [1898]: 81–82), Adela's wish to escape the constraints of pregnancy and maternity is nonetheless partly justified by the reference to the "sacrifice" these functions entail[10] – an idea confirmed by the iterated adjective "rebellious" (1881 [1898]: 84, 86) suggesting her resolute rejection of conjugal duties imposed by an oppressive marriage contract.

Such a reading is validated by the different relationship Adela establishes with her husband in the novel's conclusion. Instead of being managed by her father, she personally negotiates her new wifely role with Grubb, whose newly acquired gentrified status contributes to purging their marriage contract of any commercial interests. Based on love rather than money, their second union suggests the possibility of overcoming patriarchal conceptions of marriage founded on the (literal and symbolic) bargaining of women. Although she renounces some pleasures and autonomy previously enjoyed as a rebellious wife, Adela freely chooses to espouse domestic principles in the novel's ending, thereby performing an act of volition that turns her from exchanged object into self-willed subject.

The conclusion of *Court Netherleigh* evidences the author's use of camouflage techniques in representing the problematic condition of Victorian married women. On the one hand, Wood seems to give official support to middle-class ideology as she concocts an orthodox solution to the problems caused by her rebellious heroine. On the other, she attaches innovative meanings to Adela's final domestication, which is interestingly connoted as a free choice made by a female individual after rebelling against a men-managed contract. Another aspect worth considering is the fact that the domestic happiness described in the final pages does not cancel the novel's consistent association of marriage with female reclusion and reification. Despite its late sentimental twist, the re-establishment of the conjugal relation Adela accepts in the end is not wholly in line with ideas of companionate union as it entails a wholesale 'reconversion' of the woman's "aims" and "tastes" (1881 [1898]: 471).

The effects of wifely rebellion described in *Court Netherleigh* are hardly surprising if we consider that this novel was composed in a decade marked by growing debates over women's rights and legal innovations, such as the Married Women's Property Act of 1882. What is noteworthy, however, is the fact that images of conjugal unhappiness are recurrent in Wood's earlier narratives, which employ similar motifs and strategies to cast doubt on the bliss of married life. Some disquieting links between mercenary unions and shopping mania are drawn, for instance, in *Verner's Pride* (1863), which unveils the dangerous effects these links have on personal relations and on women's psychophysical balance. In *Elster's Folly* (1866), the critique of venal marriages is combined with the idea of the husband's unreliability, as the blind trust Percival (Val) Elster asks of his wife Maude finally wreaks havoc in their household. Other novels, like *East Lynne, The Shadow of Ashlydyat* and *Bessy Rane* (1870), unveil many problems caused by Victorian models of female patience and endurance, which prevented wives from rebelling against oppressive conjugal bonds. Elsewhere, Wood denounces the psychological sufferings and the moral dilemmas generated by forms of gender inequality such as the sexual double standard, which are daringly explored in novels like *Lord Oakburn's Daughters* (1864) and *Within the Maze* (1872). These examples confirm Wood's persistent preoccupation with the risks Victorian women ran by accepting unions that turned them into homemakers dependent on the benevolence of their male partners.

The few depictions of successful marriages found in Wood's oeuvre are equally worthy of attention. In some cases, conjugal happiness is achieved after the two partners have experienced painful disagreements or misunderstandings that cast a shadow on their relationship. A good example is the troubled marriage between Karl Andinnian and Lucy Cleeve, whose conjugal distress is a central motif of *Within the Maze*. Initially separated by Lucy's parents, who firmly object to their wedding, the two young lovers manage to get married when the suitor rises in status and a mysterious illness threatens to kill the young woman.

Saddened by the coldness of her beloved when he accepts her father's prohibition, Lucy starts to refuse food and slowly develops a complaint that no doctor seems able to cure. Undoubtedly psychosomatic, her illness is a complex signifier of her vulnerable position in a society in which a woman's future was decided by her parents and prospective husband. The result of pathologized emotions that afflicted numerous women at the time (Vrettos, 1995), Lucy's ailment can be read in light of recent feminist theories which, as discussed in the Introduction, interpret disease both as a symptom of, and as resistance to, female powerlessness. This gendered reading is confirmed by textual elements that evoke mixed ideas of oppression and rebellion. A first element to consider is the fact that, before starting to decline, Lucy announces to her mother that she will never marry another suitor: "'I should resist to the end'" (Wood, 1872 [1891]: 27). By overtly expressing her dissent, she performs an act of rebellion that attaches provocative meanings to her self-induced disease. In successive episodes, however, the weakness of Lucy's position comes fully to the fore. It suffices to consider that the initiative to save her life is taken by Karl and her father in a conversation that turns the absent woman into an object of transaction between men. "'Therefore we have resolved to trust to this hope, and give you Lucy. It will be better than to let her die'", Colonel Cleeve declares to Karl, who later uses a similar reifying language to inform Lucy of their imminent wedding: "'It means, my darling, that you are to be mine for ever. My wife. They are going to give you to me'" (1872 [1891]: 79, 81).

The author's intention to explore the heroine's vulnerability is confirmed by the new abyss of despair into which Lucy falls after enjoying a short period of happiness and blooming. Soon after her honeymoon, her married life is spoiled by a family secret weighing on Karl's mind, which she fatally misinterprets. Influenced by a normative system that prescribes female shyness in sexual matters, Lucy refrains from asking for explanations and wrongly assumes that her husband keeps a beautiful lover in a nearby cottage he furtively visits at night.[11] Their misunderstanding leads to a long and painful breakup. Although she continues to live in their conjugal home, Lucy avoids any sentimental or sexual contact with Karl, and is consumed by passions that affect her psychophysical balance: "Lucy was fading. Her face, worn and thin, had that indescribable air of sadness in it that tells of some deep-seated, ever-present sorrow" (1872 [1891]: 408). It is only in the novel's ending that Karl clears away their disagreement by plainly mentioning his brother's presence in the cottage. His final decision to disclose his secret to his wife resolves their conflict. Lucy confesses that she is ashamed of her suspicions, while Karl praises her "gentle forbearance" and her embodiment of an admirable wifely model: "'Few young wives would have been as good and patient as you'" (1872 [1891]: 465).

As is often case with Wood, the novel closes with a conservative message that reinforces the values of domesticity. But the late reconciliation of the two partners does not dispel all the sensational and disquieting implications of their long matrimonial crisis. What the reader experiences is a gradual questioning of the institution of marriage as the couple betrays a persistent lack of trust and confidence. Another thorny issue unveiled by their disagreement is the sexual inequality sanctioned by Victorian norms. This issue, which would be a central theme in the sensation fiction of the 1860s, became more pressing after the 1857 Matrimonial Causes Act, which "served to consolidate the husband's position and, if anything, upheld the sexual double standard" (Jordan, 2011: 508). Even though it is finally disproved by fact, the 'potential' adultery committed by Karl is a serious problem for his suffering wife, whose overpowering emotions are minutely revealed and examined in the text. Torn by jealousy and rage, Lucy gives vent to an indignation felt by many Victorian women who had to tolerate their husbands' unfaithfulness: "Underlying all else in her mind was a keen sense of insult, of slight, of humiliation:

and she asked herself whether she ought to bear it" (Wood, 1872 [1891]: 201). By delving deep into Lucy's innermost thoughts and feelings, Wood encourages her readers to interrogate the gender policies of their age. What emerges in this and other passages is the unfairness of a society that, while sanctioning women's psychophysical inferiority, enforced female conformity to moral and sexual rules constantly violated by men. The sense of injustice and frustration is reinforced in some episodes in which Lucy is tempted to leave her husband. The prospect of separation is given up after a confidential talk with Margaret Sumnor, the disabled daughter of a churchman who convinces the outraged wife to patiently suffer her lot. The arguments used by Margaret, who narrates the sad anecdote of a wife "condemned to an unloved and solitary experience" after leaving her husband (1872 [1891]: 226), are practical rather than religious. "'Men and women are different'", she declares, before offering details about the freedom of movement and the pleasures enjoyed by any separated man. Quite different is the condition of a "right-minded" separated woman who, strongly limited by the doctrine of separate spheres, is condemned to "stay in her home-shell, and eat her heart away" (1872 [1891]: 226).

Humiliated by her husband's (assumed) misconduct, Lucy has to come to terms with the rigid prescriptions of her world, which denies legal rights and social support to women who threaten to dissolve the matrimonial bond. Another provocative element of her story is the reference to the strong passions by which she is gripped, including a sensual desire for her husband that surfaces in passages like the following: "Her whole heart yearned to him. He drew her face to his and kissed her lips with impassioned fervour" (1872 [1891]: 197). The sensuality of the scene lays stress on Victorian wives' expectations of "*mutual* conjugal passion as essential to a happy marriage" (Tosh, 1999: 158). These expectations, which would increase later in the century, are skilfully brought into focus in *Within the Maze* whose depiction of wifely unhappiness contributes to the representation of the sexual double standard of the age. Elsewhere in the novel, Lucy is assailed by morbid yearnings that contrast with the propriety and self-control prescribed to gentlewomen: "And it might be that, down deep in her woman's frail heart, there was a longing to see the inside of that place which contained her rival" (Wood, 1872 [1891]: 249). By characterizing a high-principled wife unable to stifle her emotions, Wood reveals the artificiality of the sexless model of angelic womanhood exalted by orthodox Victorians. This model is contrasted by the characterization of a woman of flesh and blood, subject to contradictory yearnings and passions, and frustrated by an institution that forced wives into a condition of "slavery" "not of the mildest form", in J. S. Mill's opinion (1869 [1870]: 59).

A similar picture is drawn in *Lord Oakburn's Daughters*. Published eight years before *Within the Maze*, this novel testifies to Wood's continued exploration of marital displeasure at a time when women were encouraged to find all their satisfactions within the marriage institution. In characterizing Laura Chesney, who unknowingly marries her sister's murderer, Wood reveals the frustrating effects that a husband's unfaithfulness can produce on a young wife. After eloping with Lewis Carlton in an act of filial disobedience, Laura experiences a growing sense of disappointment with her married life which reaches its climax when she is "rudely awakened" by the discovery of her husband's infidelity. "It is the *spécialité* of men to be fickle", the narrator notices ironically, before indulging in describing the rumours that had turned the wife's love into "something very like hatred":

> He had been lax in his notions of morality all his life; he was lax still. His love for his wife had been wild and passionate as a whirlwind; but these whirlwinds, you know, never last. Certain rumours reflecting on Mr. Carlton got whispered around; escapades now and again, in which there was, it

must be confessed, as much truth as scandal, and they unfortunately penetrated to the ear of his wife. [...] She contrived to acquire pretty good proof of their foundation, and they turned her love for her husband into something very like hatred. (Wood, 1864a [1872]: 334-335)

The narrator's remarks on men's inconstancy and the use of direct addresses like "you know" are subtle critiques of gender disparities through which Wood encourages her readership to disparage, rather than passively accept, Victorian sexual norms. The "resisting reader" (Fetterley, 1978; Culler, 1983)[12] that is thus created cannot but side with Laura who, despite some flaws of her characterization (i.e., her vanity and love of leisure), appears as a victim of her husband's deceitful disposition. Upset by Carlton's conduct in sexual matters, Laura unwillingly becomes instrumental to the discovery of his murderous actions. It is in fact blind jealousy that spurs her to spy on him like an amateur detective. Driven by her unbridled passion, she secretly opens his safe where she finds an incriminating letter that is later used by his enemies to prove his guilt. With much irony, Wood uses a wrongly assumed case of unfaithfulness to incense Laura's jealousy and make her avenge all the previous cases of (proven) marital infidelity. Although it is defined "insensate folly" (Wood, 1864a [1872]: 395) in this specific case, Laura's jealousy is shown to stem from her frustration at discovering the treachery of Carlton who, like most husbands charged with sexual laxity in this and others of Wood's novels, is held responsible for his wife's suffering.

It is no coincidence that the highly sensational depiction of Laura and Carlton's matrimonial wreck is offered in a novel that represents most conjugal bonds as sources of affliction. The author's pervasive irony about the traps of marriage is confirmed, in the conclusion, by a shadow cast onto the only potentially happy union in the novel: that between Frederick Grey and Lucy Chesney. In a humorous remark on his bride at the wedding party,

Frederick tells his young brother-in-law that Lucy is his now, because she has been 'bought' "with the gold ring that is upon her finger" and "can't ever be sold back again" (1864a [1872]: 517). The comment is significantly followed by a "lecture" Lucy receives from her elder sister Jane who, after recalling Laura's matrimonial disaster, entreats the young bride to "love, reverence, and obey [her] husband" (1864a [1872]: 520–521). If read in light of Jane's admonition and of the many unhappy unions in the novel, Frederick's comment loses part of its jocose undertones. It rather appears as a worrying remark on the condition of married women, as his reference to the "purchase" and "possession" of his bride suggests the dangerous dependence of wives on their husbands' fickle love and benevolence.

As shown so far, Wood tends to associate marriage with trouble and despondency in her fiction. One of the few pictures of conjugal happiness is found in *Mrs. Halliburton's Troubles* (1862), whose eponymous heroine is allowed to marry a man she loves and respects. In the first part of the novel, Jane and Edgar Halliburton set an imitable model of partnership-marriage, which is favoured by the husband's gentle and trusting disposition: "He had no secrets from his wife. He consulted her upon every point; she was his best friend, his confidant, his gentle counsellor" (Wood, 1862 [1897]: 31). After some years of good luck, however, the couple experiences a tragic reversal of fortune, as Edgar contracts a fatal disease that prevents him from keeping his job as professor at King's College. Deprived of his good income, husband and wife leave London with their four children and move to a countryside location, where they hope to find a healthier environment for Edgar's lungs and new job opportunities. But their hopes are soon crushed by the hostility of some dishonest relatives and by the sudden death of Edgar, who leaves his wife and children destitute.

Edgar's premature demise introduces an interesting twist in the plot. After telling a story of successful marriage in the opening chapters, the novel focuses on the "troubles" faced by the young widow, who returns to a single woman status and is impelled to earn a living for her children. Positioned outside middle-class normativity by the loss of her mate and forced to act autonomously, Jane poses a double threat to gender stereotypes. The courage and perseverance she displays in becoming her family's breadwinner question the stability of a system founded on men's protective and proactive roles. They also offer a potential solution to the problem of female redundancy raised by the 1851 census, which produced anxieties about the rising numbers of unmarried middle-class women forced to search for paid occupations outside the home. Jane's ability to work without losing her respectability during her widowhood suggests an idea that gradually became acceptable in the 1860s: the idea that single women in general "could avoid dependency on men by undertaking paid work in order to acquire incomes of their own" (Liggins, 2014: 33).

The daughter of a shabby-genteel family, Jane is trained in domestic duties in her girlhood. The household skills she learns not only enable her to become a good wife for Edgar, but they are also put to good use in her widowhood to save money, to attract tenants and to perform jobs requiring manual abilities, like that of glovemaker. Thanks to her good education, moreover, Jane becomes a private trainer of schoolchildren – an activity that significantly improves her income and social standing. Skilled, inflexible in her work ethic, and prudent in the management of their scanty means, she is finally rewarded with social and financial success. What she comes to embody is an outstanding model of self-help in line with the ideal celebrated in *Self-Help* (1859) by Samuel Smiles, who praised "the frugal use of money" and defined its "honest earning" as something "of the greatest importance" achieved through "patient industry and untiring effort" (1859 [2002]: 245). Besides her religious faith, it is moral strength that makes Jane capable of pursuing her objectives in the face of all the "troubles" anticipated in the novel's title, which include the loss of her only daughter. In the conclusion, the eponymous heroine is celebrated as a successful parent who has managed to raise three "high-minded, honourable, and educated [young] men" (Wood, 1862 [1897]: 459) by combing maternal care with the masculine role of breadwinner. Instead of being wearied by her sufferings, moreover, she is said to have a "lady-like" and "attractive" appearance, "not in the least like one who had had to toil hard for bread" (1862 [1897]: 459).

The anomaly of Jane Halliburton's characterization is undeniable. Although she incarnates domestic values, she is also endowed with self-help virtues typically associated with men, like courage, strong will and perseverance. Compelled to labour by adverse circumstances, Jane keeps her ladylike manners intact, thereby disproving Victorian assumptions about the debasing effects of paid work on gentlewomen ([Oliphant], 1858: 145). Her innovative portrayal is confirmed by the special training received from her parents. Besides learning her household skills from her mother, she is "so thoroughly educated in all essential branches" (Wood, 1862 [1897]: 202) by her father who also initiates her to unfeminine areas of study like Latin (1862 [1897]: 8–9). This early training, which enables the heroine to earn an income when she is in dire straits, is in line with Barbara Leigh Smith Bodichon's proto-feminist ideas on women's education and work. In an essay published in 1857, Bodichon urges parents to "give a girl a training for a trade" that can be put to good use in moments of trouble, especially when a woman "may be left to act as both father and mother to children dependent on her for daily bread". Furthermore, Bodichon enthusiastically defines work, "the great beautifier", as "[a]ctivity of brain, heart, and limb, gives health and beauty, and makes women fit to be the mothers of children" (1857: 10–11, 18).

All these ideas are validated in *Mrs. Halliburton's Troubles*. Besides showing how Jane becomes a "father and mother" who successfully employs her skills to feed her children, the novel suggests that the heroine is beautified by her professional activities that give her mental and physical health. Her model of cleverness also resembles the one set by Joseph Johnson's "clever girls" who, as noted in the Introduction, manage to turn "self-culture" into "the means of self-maintenance" (Johnson, 1862: iii-iv). What makes Jane's portrayal most challenging is the homage she is paid by a "learned professor" who exalts her erudition and teaching abilities by defining her as "a sister professor" (Wood, 1862 [1897]: 210). The epithet must have sounded provocative in an age when women were still denied possession of high professional talents. Although she tempers the subversive effects of this scene by confining Jane's activities within the home, Wood seems to espouse ideas of women's self-development championed by Bodichon and other proto-feminists, who rejected notions of biological determinism and lamented women's acculturation into inferiority.

The autobiographical elements of Jane's characterization[13] suggest the author's interest in alternative models of womanhood, which combine ideals of matronly gentility with new professional aspirations. This interest is confirmed by the "utopian" conclusion of *Mrs. Halliburton's Troubles* – a conclusion found in those popular novels that, as theorized by Sally Mitchell, depict a society changed by an individual (1977: 43–44). Although Mitchell never mentions Wood, her definition suits the compelling story of Jane Halliburton, whose unwonted transformation into a genteel, talented breadwinner is praised by all the novel's characters. Another element that deserves notice is the fact that the above-mentioned transformation takes place after Edgar's death, when misfortune impels Jane to develop. By connoting widowhood as a more empowering condition than marriage, Wood implicitly challenges the law of coverture, even though she tempers her subversive message by highlighting the short conjugal happiness and the virtuous domesticity of her protagonist.

The reduced autonomy of married women is also suggested in a minor episode of the novel that involves Jane's firstborn William. During his honeymoon on the Continent, William refuses to share the details of a scandalous story with his young wife Mary. The reason he offers for his silence – that of protecting the woman's peace of mind and morality – is reported by Mary in a letter to her mother in which she mistakenly signs herself with her maiden surname (Wood, 1862 [1897]: 436). Apparently irrelevant, the 'epistolary accident' gains meaning in light of its gendered implications as it conveys the vague sense of frustration felt by the young woman who complains about having "kept [her] letter open for nothing" because her husband considers the tale "more fit for papa's ears than for yours or mine" (1862 [1897]: 436). A symbolic rebellion against the law of coverture, Mary's adoption of her family name instead of her husband's is further proof of Wood's reservations about the possibilities for self-development that marriage offered to Victorian women.

These reservations are confirmed in the novel by an ironic reference to Mormon polygamy that is thus stigmatized by a minor character: "'One husband is enough to have at one's fireside, goodness knows, without being worried with an unlimited number'" (1862 [1897]: 338). Anti-Mormon arguments are also present in *Verner's Pride,* a novel pivoting around images of conjugal unhappiness and violence. Published one year after *Mrs. Hallilburton's Troubles, Verner's Pride* connotes Mormon matrimonial practices in oppressive terms and, despite some comic undertones, it uses polygamy to reinforce the dreariness of the experiences of many wives in the novel. Mormonism was one of the topics debated around the middle of the century when the legal handling of divorce raised much interest in irregular or alternative forms of marriage.[14] This interest is confirmed by the proliferation of the so-called "bigamy plots" in mid-Victorian literature. Wood herself evoked the spectre of bigamy in such novels as *East Lynne* and *Elster's Folly,* and she wrote *The Earl's Heirs* (1862), an early bigamous novel in which "'the same spot' contains three spouses" and the difference between "who is the predecessor and who is the criminal" remains provokingly unclear

(McAleavey, 2015: 61).

While exploring the pitfalls of marriage and the troubles faced by numerous wives, Wood also blames men for the limited autonomy and satisfaction of their female partners. In addition to violent, strict and overambitious husbands, she portrays potentially good men who care for their wives but nonetheless fail to set an admirable spousal model. In many cases, their failure is attributed to their fickleness in love, which makes them betray important promises made to their wives. Their inconstancy not only fuels destructive female passions, as in the case of Lewis Carlton discussed above, it also imperils the happiness and the well-being of their children, who are eclipsed by the arrival of a new wife demanding all the father's attentions. Novels like *Danesbury House* (1860), *East Lynne, St. Martin's Eve* and *The House of Halliwell* well render the dangers posed to the household by the sentimental weakness of the *pater familias* who, after experiencing a condition of real or assumed widowhood, entrusts his children to the care of an unsympathetic new wife. Generally connected with a broken promise and viewed in terms of 'betrayal', the choice of a younger, less caring second wife is imputed to the husband's inconstancy of feelings, which brings ruin on the family. A good example is the tragedy consequent on George Carleton St. John's second marriage narrated in *St. Martin's Eve*, in which the man's new wife murders his firstborn Benja. The brutal crime, which is induced by psychopathological and socioeconomic reasons, is also associated with St. John's inability to keep a promise made to his dying first wife: "'When […] you think of another wife, oh choose one that will be a *mother* to my child'" (Wood, 1866b [1893]: 3–4). In addition to this promise, the man breaks a second pledge he fretfully makes on her deathbed, that of never marrying again – a prospect ironically defined as impossible by the dying wife and the narrator, who share the conviction of men's innate weakness in sentimental and sexual matters: "'To remain faithful to the dead is not in man's nature'" (1866b [1893]: 4, 11).

As testified by the previous examples, most novels by Wood represent married men as flawed or weak figures that contribute to the troubles of their family. Yet, there are in her fiction some interesting portrayals of husbands that challenge dominant gender models. What marks their distinction is their close link with the domestic sphere which, no longer conceived in exclusively female terms, becomes "a new arena" for male heroism. Without renouncing their career or their social status, these gentle husbands tend to spend more time at home caring for their wives and children. Unconventionally domestic in their tastes, these figures dispel the gender anxieties conveyed by "mock-New Men stories" published around the mid-century.[15] While the latter parodied lonely husbands waiting at home for their partying wives, Wood's narratives connote such men in virtuous terms, as shown by the characterization of Francis Grubb who patiently puts up with Adela's pleasure-seeking conduct. The late composition of *Court Netherleigh*, written at a time of epistemic redefinition of manliness,[16] does not fully account for Wood's critique of restrictive marital models. A few portrayals of affectionate husbands and gentle fathers are also found in her early fiction. In *Verner's Pride*, for example, Lionel Verner convincingly plays the role of forbearing husband, while in *Danesbury House* Lord Temple's double conversion to the joys of temperance and domesticity is symbolically rendered by his fond nursing of his baby boy.[17] Probably influenced by her father's personality, Wood strove to develop alternative models of masculinity that could challenge "the three features most common to the early Victorian paterfamilias, namely remoteness, sovereignty, and benevolence" (Roberts, 1978: 59). But this aim was difficult to achieve. The few credible models of domestic gentlemen offered in her fiction are overshadowed by numerous figures embodying patriarchal values, whose inflexible conduct generates family tensions and despondency.

While representing the problems faced by wives within the marriage contract, Wood also warns her readers against the dangers of romantic love by characterizing some naïve women victimized by insensitive or distracted lovers. Frail and prone to dejection, these girls generally die of a broken heart after developing psychosomatic illnesses that are both a consequence of, and a protest against, their beloveds' careless conduct. The tragic story of Ellen Adair and Arthur Bohun told in *Bessy Rane* exemplifies such a relationship. Drawn to each other by "[t]rue love – idealistic, passionate, pure love" (Wood, 1870 [1872]: 19), the two young people are separated by Arthur's scheming mother who objects to their marriage. Arthur himself is held responsible for their separation, as he is driven by pride and social ambitions that make him doubt the desirability of their match. In the last part of the novel, the young suitor repents of his errors after discovering the high-rank status of Ellen's family and the secret reasons for his mother's hostility. But he finds his beloved on the verge of death. Affected by a consumptive disease, Ellen passes away in a melodramatic scene that underlines the "lingering pain and suffering" of "one of the sweetest girls this world has ever known" (1870 [1872]: 441). The novel closes with a picture of the inconsolable Arthur who pays solitary visits to Ellen's grave and expresses his hatred for "the rank and wealth to which he had, in a degree, sacrificed one who had been far dearer to him than life" (1870 [1872]: 448).

If Ellen's premature death epitomizes the senselessness of women's immolation on the altar of their lovers' ambitions, the tragic demise of Adeline de Castella narrated in *St. Martin's Eve* has gloomier implications, as it connects female sacrifice with other victimizing practices, including the voyeuristic consumption of women's bodies. Narrated in a long digression set in France,[18] the love story between Adeline and Frederick St. John is opposed by two stern representatives of patriarchal power: the girl's father, who has promised his daughter to the Baron de la Chasse, and a Roman Catholic priest, Father Marc, who tries to prevent Adeline's marriage with "an Englishman and a heretic" (Wood, 1866b [1893]: 289). By joining forces, the two men convince Adeline to accept the arranged marriage with the baron. Her surrender upsets Frederick who gives vent to all his rage. He not only disfigures the portrait of the young woman he has just painted, but also accuses her of being "[f]alse and fickle" (1866b [1893]: 301, 294). Overcome by negative emotions, Adeline experiences the breaking of a blood vessel, which paves the way to her premature death, "protracted across several, highly sentimentalized chapters" (Mangham, 2008: 294). The tragic climax is reached when Adeline's dead body is beautified and exhibited to the public gaze in a French ceremony called "the reception of the dead". The gothic exhibition of her corpse "arrayed in all the pomp and splendour of life" (Wood, 1866b [1893]: 356) is accepted by the dying girl who, initially revolted at the prospect, slowly comes to view it as a *post-mortem* occasion to be admired by Frederick.

If carefully read, however, the symbolism of the "reception" proves more complex than it might seem. A first thing to consider is the shocked response of Frederick who, unaware of his lover's death, staggers in a "fainting-fit" at the sight of her corpse (1866b [1893]: 364). In ways similar to her psychosomatic illness, the appalling exhibition is an instrument through which Adeline 'punishes' Frederick who, too absorbed by his own feelings, has abandoned her to a cruel destiny. By letting herself die, moreover, she frustrates the plans of her authoritative father, as she destroys the beautiful object of the marriage transaction he made with the baron. Even more disturbing are the necrophiliac implications of her displayed corpse which, strongly evocative of "Sleeping Beauty" and "Snow White", uncannily combines beauty with horror. Described as "inexpressibly beautiful" in its "festive attire", the body evidences some ghastly details that betray its cadaverous state and make it appear "fearfully strange" (1866b [1893]: 363). As Andrew Mangham observes, Wood's use of the cadaver as a weird object of admiration gives an early clue to the reifying effects of male voyeurism studied one century later by Elizabeth Bronfen, who draws on Freudian theories to demonstrate how "the female corpse has been fetishized by male-driven scopophiliac cultures" throughout the centuries (Mangham, 2008: 296; Bronfen 1992). The gothic paraphernalia of this episode confirm the victimized status of Adeline who, despite a few attempts to resist men's controlling power, embodies the "objectified figure of the incarcerated woman" before and after her death (Mangham, 2003: 92).

Unlike Ellen and Adeline, who are killed by the contradictions of a world that asks them to "fulfil woman's appointed destiny on earth" (Wood, 1866b [1893]: 290), other single women portrayed by Wood acquire autonomy and wisdom by escaping the marriage contract. Mostly characterized in positive terms, these women exhibit some eccentricities but are never derided by the author. Like Charlotte Brontë, Charlotte Yonge and other novelists writing around the mid-century, Wood starts to rethink earlier stereotypes of the old maid – a figure that, in the first half of the century, is generally cast as "pathetic", "a 'proper sport' for comedy and satire" (Liggins, 2014: 35). Even though they embody some anxieties of the age, the spinsters featured in Wood's oeuvre bear witness to the author's exploration of alternative models of femininity, as the qualities they display imply the possibility of living an acceptable life outside the boundaries of marriage.

A compelling portrayal of a single woman is that of Hester Halliwell who comes to play a central role in an early novel published posthumously: *The House of Halliwell*.[19] Abandoned by a fickle lover who is attracted by another woman, Hester is not killed by heartbreak and learns to keep her passions under control. Generous and wise, she helps her siblings on different occasions and performs different roles to assist her relatives, including that of amateur detective. Her ability in personal relations is coupled with professional skills that she reveals when she establishes "a ladies' boarding school" with good results (Wood, 1890 [1896]: 168). In the central part of the novel, moreover, she is assigned the function of narrator of interpolated passages, which report her experiences in the first person. If we consider the flimsiness of the other characters featured in the novel, we can interpret Hester as the heroine of *The House of Halliwell*. Sustained by moral strength and perseverance, she counterbalances the weakness and inability of the masculine figures and becomes the point of reference of a family struck by multiple misfortunes. In so doing, she fulfils an early prophecy uttered by Aunt Rebecca Copp, another strong woman who foresees that her niece will "never marry" and will always "be in the midst of business", living an existence "full of usefulness" (1890 [1896]: 8).

The model of spinsterhood set by Hester reverses Victorian convictions about the ways a woman could acquire status and fulfil her mission. Instead of serving a husband or a father, the heroine becomes an autonomous, strong individual that supports various family members and friends, including her former lover whom she meets "altered, worn, and wasted" (1890 [1896]: 210) and consoles before his untimely death. Less relevant but similarly endowed with common sense is the characterization of Bettina Davenal, who plays a minor role in *Oswald Cray* (1864). "A beautiful woman in her day" who has acquired "a cold hard look" after the tragic end of her "romance" (Wood, 1864b [1904]: 20, 41), Bettina becomes a point of reference for her orphaned niece, Sara. Impaired by deafness, she is occasionally the target of ironic comments on her disability (1864b [1904]: 20); but her rationality and wisdom are evidenced on many occasions. Despite her limited hearing, Bettina sees clearly beyond appearances. Careful in her investments (1864b [1904]: 285), she is quick in detecting the flaws of Markus Cray, whom she considers an unfit husband for young Caroline Davenal, and she openly rebukes the improvident couple for living as "rogues or idiots" (1864b [1904]: 41, 288–290). Her strict attitude does not, however, limit her generosity; in addition to Sara, she is ready to assist Caroline later in the novel, when the young woman returns to England sick and impoverished (1864b [1904]: 406–407).

Later in her career, Wood continued to portray autonomous

single women who fulfil a positive function within their community. A good example is Margery Upton characterized in *Court Netherleigh*. A "little woman" in her fifties, "very active and energetic, as little people often are" (Wood, 1881 [1898]: 2–3), Margery appears on the scene at critical moments when she helps others to handle disagreements and to make important decisions. Her judgment and mental balance are repeatedly highlighted in the text. An independent woman who skilfully manages the fortune she has inherited, she becomes a symbol of bourgeois virtues as opposed to aristocratic profligacy. This symbolic function is suggested by her strong dislike of the prodigal Lord Acorn and her preference for Francis Grubb to whom she leaves her patrimony and title. "'Would I allow Court Netherleigh to fall into the hands of a spendthrift?'" (1881 [1898]: 353), she exclaims after making her will, which allows Grubb to inherit the property he had lost owing to family conflicts. Even though she is killed by a fatal disease before the conclusion, Margery Upton is an important figure of the novel, as she fruitfully combines the role of ministering goddess with the image of an independent woman who generously helps others and restores justice in human affairs.

These unconventional spinster figures confirm Wood's provocative representation of romantic love and marriage as sources of trouble for women, who are more likely to thrive outside the matrimonial bond. In addition to denouncing mercenary unions that reify women within a marriage market dominated by men, Wood describes the afflictions of many wives who, for different reasons, are disillusioned by a contract entailing the unequal treatment of the two parties. Although she uses camouflage strategies to deflate some polemical effects of her discourse, she is decidedly unorthodox in exposing the pitfalls of married life. The well-know matrimonial crisis dramatized in *East Lynne* exemplifies her critique of an institution that often disappoints her heroines – a critique that, as shown above, marks the distinction of many narratives she wrote in the span of three decades.

CHAPTER 2

Variations of the Griselda theme

The Victorian conceptualization of marriage revolved around ideals of female patience and endurance, which contributed to keeping women under the strongholds of patriarchy. A basic tenet of bourgeois culture, these ideals had strong roots in folklore and myth that had enforced centuries-old representations of the "Eternal Feminine" in oppositional terms, as a contrast between "angelically selfless" women and "wickedly assertive" female monsters (Gilbert and Gubar, 1979 [2000]: 21, 28ff). Such representations were further elaborated by the fairy-tale tradition developed in Italian principalities and France during the sixteenth and seventeenth centuries. Drawing on folkloric sources, authors like Giambattista Basile and Charles Perrault cultivated a new literary genre "to ensure that young people would be properly groomed for their social functions" (Zipes, 1983 [2006]: 30). The following two centuries were marked by a proliferation of literary fairy tales in Europe and North America, a phenomenon favoured by the circulation of English translations and by middle-class attempts to preserve a rustic culture threatened by modernization.

The nineteenth century witnessed a climax of interest in fairy tales, whose leitmotifs and archetypes penetrated a variety of poetic and fictional works. Significant influence was exerted by the gendering of roles inherent in this genre, which perpetuated orthodox models of femininity to encode a patriarchal ideology. The demure beautiful heroine was an important model appropriated by Victorian writers, whose bourgeois values had much in common with the social and family values championed by fairy-tale authors. But the process of appropriation was far from uniform. Sensation novelists, for example, made particular use of fairy-tale motifs and figures to upset literary expectations. Whereas mainstream writers opted for "conventional happy endings" that "demanded that the heroines be married and securely locked up in their homes", practitioners of sensation fiction "seemed to debunk traditional tales and to rework narrative archetypes to launch their plots" (Talairach-Vielmas, 2007: 1).

Ellen Wood's oeuvre bears witness to this complex reworking. Her female figures are often modelled on recognizable fairy-tale heroines, who are evoked by intertextual references, plot patterns and psychophysical details. Unlike their prototypes, however, Wood's characters rarely experience a conventional happy ending. They either evolve in unforeseen ways or meet a tragic fate that unveils the gender disparities of their male-dominated system. Another specificity of Wood's fiction is the "non-disjunctive" quality of most of her characters (Kristeva, 1968), including male ones. The distinctive polarization of fairy tales, whose stock figures are "not ambivalent – not good and bad at the same time, as we are in reality" (Bettelheim, 1976 [1991]: 9), is seldom found in Wood's fiction. Her portrayals of half-flawed heroes, half-sympathetic villains, self-harming heroines and moderately evil stepmothers suggest her attempt to reshape traditional tales into realistic novels that had a different sociogenetic impact.

Without ever disputing the ideological foundations of the separate-spheres doctrine, Wood questioned the inflexibility of dominant gender discourses, which compelled men and women to play narrowly conceived roles. Her remissive heroines, in particular, are portrayed in highly ambiguous terms as they are often shown to contribute to their own victimization. Their unconventional depiction is reinforced by the revision of some morphological elements and syntactical relations typical of fairy tales (Propp, 1928 [1968]; Greimas, 1983). Two effective strategies are the denial of a happy ending and the male hero's limited reliability, which Wood adopted to challenge some conventions of a domestic culture that impelled women to be decorative, forbearing and submissive to male authority. By projecting naïve beauties and obedient wives into a nineteenth-century context obscured by the spectre of women's humiliation, Wood questioned the indoctrinating function of fairy tales that encouraged children, and especially girls, "to conform to dominant social standards that [were] not necessarily established in their behalf" (Zipes, 1983 [2006]: 34).

Wood made extensive use of fairy-tale motifs and figures, which she usually reworked to stigmatize women's passivity and victimhood. Lethal effects of female naivety and male voyeurism are for instance exposed in *St. Martin's Eve* (1866) which, as shown in Chapter 1, offers a disturbing necrophiliac version of the sleeping-beauty figure featured in Perrault's eponymous tale and in Grimm's "Snow White". Another revisionary strategy adopted by Wood is that of counterbalancing Adeline de Castella's tendency to self-destruction with the vitality of her friend and rival Rose Darling, who sets an unorthodox model of female self-assuredness. A "wild" girl who violates many gender prescriptions, Rose initially flirts with Frederick St. John and later marries the baron to whom Adeline had been promised (Wood, 1866b [1893]: 83, 383). In the conclusion, the nobleman becomes a good husband for Rose who, instead of being punished for her transgressions, is rewarded with an advantageous match and an enamoured mate (1866b [1893]: 458–459). Equally provocative is Wood's reinterpretation of "Beauty and the Beast" in *Court Netherleigh* (1881). Adela Acorn's story analysed in the previous chapter suggests the author's awareness of the commodification of women within a marriage market that transformed daughters and wives into fetish-objects exchanged between men. Other women-aimed tales reworked by Wood include "Cinderella", evoked for example by the eponymous heroine of *Bessy Rane* (1870) subjected to a manipulative stepmother; "Bluebeard", which is brought to mind by her narratives of wifely oppression; and "Little Red Riding Hood", strongly alluded to in *Anne Hereford* (1868), whose protagonist is threatened by sexual and social dangers represented by wolfish male figures.

All disquieting and unconventional, these pre-nuptial and bridal models of femininity testify to Wood's interest in the rites of passage women experienced during adolescence, when their social status came to be significantly defined by their romantic or filial relationships with men. It is, however, in representing victimized wifeliness that the author offers her most daring critique of gender constraints, as confirmed by the recurrent images of matrimonial unhappiness discussed in the previous chapter. What makes these images truly disheartening is Wood's refunctionalization of the Griselda theme, which offers a paradigmatic model of female suffering and patience. A folkloric figure turned into a literary character by Boccaccio (1353 [1973]), Petrarch and Chaucer during the fourteenth century, Griselda inspired a verse tale by Perrault in 1691 and influenced writers all over Europe, including British authors like Maria Edgeworth and Anthony Trollope, who respectively reworked the myth in *The Modern Griselda* (1804) and *Miss Mackenzie* (1865). The original story narrates the misadventures of a woman of humble origins who marries Gualtieri, the Marquis of Saluzzo, and is repeatedly put to the test by her authoritative husband. The man's reasons for humiliating his wife are vaguely offered in the early versions of the tale. Perrault himself attributes Gualtieri's actions to an impulse he is unable to suppress. Separated from her children and subject to various forms of mortification, including the request to serve Gualtieri's (presumed) new bride,[1] Griselda never fails to set a model of wifely obedience. Her constancy finally satisfies her husband who, after many years of testing, restores his exemplary wife to her social and family position.

The nineteenth-century popularity of this story is hardly surprising. If we consider the Victorian ideology of the home and the anxieties produced by women's growing discontent, it is easy to see why such models of female docility could attract mainstream novelists and conduct-book authors. Like the original Griselda, the many forbearing wives portrayed in the age's literature validated the gender rhetoric of the rising bourgeoisie, which founded its social and national power on women's willing acceptance of domestic roles. Wood herself praised the enduring force of a wife like Lucy Andinnian who, as shown in the previous chapter, manages to control her indignation aroused by her husband's (presumed) infidelity. In ways similar to the deeply humiliated Griselda, Lucy stays with Karl and is finally rewarded for her "gentle forbearance" (Wood, 1872 [1891]: 465). This conventional message is however obfuscated by the pitiful anatomy of Lucy's wounded feelings, which must have aroused the sympathy of many otherwise intransigent readers. The sense of injustice conveyed in the novel inscribes the author of *Within the Maze* (1872) into the "wide grey area" mentioned in the Introduction, an area inhabited by numerous writers who, while championing conservative values, could not refrain from depicting the pitfalls of women's married life.

Unlike Lucy Andinnian, who stays with her husband but gives voice to all her conjugal frustration, other female characters portrayed by Wood conform to gender prescriptions by silently accepting their lot. A telling case is that of Mrs. Hare in *East Lynne* (1861). The wife of an imperious and coarse magistrate, this minor figure exhibits the typical meekness of conventional heroines: "modest, [...] passive, unconscious of her sexuality", she has already experienced the transition from daughter to wife and mother, and has learned to embody the role of "proper Victorian heroine who neither acts nor plots" (Gruner, 1997: 303). The woman's passive demeanour is problematically linked with her psychophysical invalidity over the course of the narration. When she first appears on the scene, Mrs. Hare is described as "a pale, delicate woman, buried in shawls and cushions", a "poor invalid" who is constantly thirsty but unable even to order tea in her own household (Wood, 1861 [2000]: 60–61). Ironically underscored by the narrator, the woman's inability is attributed to habits of self-repression developed over the years as a result of her acquiescence to her husband's domineering attitude:

> Justice Hare was stern, imperative, obstinate, and self-conceited; she, timid, gentle, and submissive. She had loved him with all her heart, and her life had been one long yearning of her will to his: in fact, she had no will; his was all in all. (1861 [2000]: 61)

The reference to the timid wife's love for her husband strengthens the polemical undertones of the passage, which codes romantic love as a trap. An early study in female masochism, the characterization of Mrs. Hare is made more disquieting by the assertion that the woman did not feel her "servitude as a yoke" (1861 [2000]: 61). In later episodes, Mrs. Hare is obsessively portrayed as a demure suffering figure. Upset by the flight of her son Richard, who is wrongly accused of murder and abandoned by Mr. Hare, she develops anorexic habits that increase her invalidity. Her over-indulgence in tea – the only substance she likes to ingest – makes her "weak, shaky, and fit for nothing" while her frustrated maternal love produces dangerous grief and emotions (1861 [2000]: 280, 284). Nevertheless, Mrs. Hare continues to revere her husband and reproaches her rebellious daughter Barbara who, instead, deplores her father's arrogance and insensitivity.[2]

The negativity of Mrs. Hare's characterization is confirmed by narratorial observations, such as "[she] was always pleased when someone else decided for her" (1861 [2000]: 285). Like Griselda, Mrs. Hare is repeatedly put to the test by her domineering husband and plays her victim role with unwavering patience. What differs from the folktale, however, is the conclusion of her marriage story. Instead of passing her test and being celebrated as a model wife, she is unexpectedly freed from her conjugal yoke by two strokes suffered by Mr. Hare, who enters a "state of half imbecility" and becomes "[t]ractable almost as a little child" (1861 [2000]: 672). Coupled with the happy return of their son, which puts an end to Mrs. Hare's long-repressed maternal love (Gruner, 1997: 317), Mr. Hare's paralysis ironically produces liberating, joyful effects that show on his wife's countenance. "The change in her was wonderful: she was a young and happy woman again" (Wood, 1861 [2000]: 672), the narrator observes, thereby confirming that what had weighed on Mrs. Hare's mind and body was her distressed wifely role.

By revising some morphological and syntactical relations of the Griselda prototype, Wood altered the ideological implications of the original folktale. Her grotesque representation of the Hares' conjugal bond casts a shadow on the marriage institution, as it shows a victimized woman thriving when (accidentally) freed from her overbearing mate. A tyrannical husband and father who also adopts boorish conduct in the social arena, Mr. Hare incarnates an old-fashioned model of "masterful and repressive" masculinity (Tosh, 1999: 95) that slowly came to be questioned in the age of Victoria. As Talia Schaffer observes, moreover, Mr. Hare's embodiment of an "aggressive and indifferent patriarch" adds to the novel's problematic exploration of professionalism in relation to gender dynamics. On the one hand, the man's paralysis symbolizes the inadequacy of his archaic model of masculinity – a version of the "rural, crude", untrained "eighteenth-century squire" that contrasts with the new professional model set by Archibald Carlyle (Schaffer, 2016: 230). On the other hand, the Hares' troubled domesticity reveals disquieting parallels with the disastrous union of Carlyle and Isabel. Both "fallen men" (Schaffer, 2016: 227) who inadvertently destroy their households, Carlyle and Hare represent the threats posed by two different types of husbands who, independently from their manners and status, similarly poison the happiness of their families.

If manners and professional objectives are the main differences between the two husbands, the actions performed by their distressed wives are more at variance. Neglected by Carlyle, Isabel breaks their marriage bond as a form of revenge, even though she later repents her adultery and adopts an expiating conduct. For her part, Mrs. Hare commits no act of disobedience but is fortuitously liberated from her conjugal yoke. Their opposing conducts seem to validate orthodox views of wifeliness, as the text apparently condemns the rebellious woman to a tragic death while rewarding her forbearing counterpart. On reflection, however, this oppositional reading is challenged by the flawed characterization of Mrs. Hare. Freed by a chance event that might never have happened, the patient wife is slightly caricatured by the narrator, who tends to depict her passivity and inanity as defects rather than qualities. The fact that her figure is never conceived as an imitable model is validated by her persistent pathologization. Interpreted by Ann Kaplan as an expression of "maternal melodrama" so "sickly and confined as to be unable to help her [own] daughter" (1989: 39), Mrs. Hare is associated with female hysteria by Laurie Langbauer, who underlines how her figure resembles Isabel's in its liability to "nervous afflictions [that] appear to come from their motherhood" (1990: 171).

Another pathological element highlighted in the text is Mrs. Hare's eating disorder. Both a product and a critique of patriarchy, her anorexic leanings draw attention to the suffering corporeality of the frustrated wife and mother. By rejecting food, the woman not only deprives her body of strength; she also performs a symbolic action, as she establishes a relation of hate with the corporeal frame through which her ego is connected with the outside world. If "the ego is the meeting point, the point of conjunction, between the body and the social" (Grosz, 1994: 32), we can read Mrs. Hare's anorexia as a self-disabling process through which she silently protests against the Victorian social system. The rebellious implications of her self-starvation are confirmed by comparison with the Griselda tale, whose exemplary wife never impairs her own body. Unlike this folktale protagonist, Wood's anorexic characters such as Mrs. Hare reveal some psychosomatic effects of conjugal humiliation, thereby suggesting the author's awareness of contemporary debates on eating disorders that paved the way to the burgeoning disability studies of our times.

To say this does not mean that *East Lynne* conveys a strong critique of marriage relations. The provocative elements of the Hares' and the Carlyles' troubled unions are partly mollified by the paradigm of female orthodoxy offered by Barbara Hare, who becomes Carlyle's second wife. Respectively daughter and rival of the two unhappy women described above, Barbara turns into a patient Griselda later in the narration, when she learns to keep her passions under control and to play the role of compliant wife. As we will see in Chapter 4, Barbara is a character that raises multiple (sometimes contradictory) class and gender issues. A main function she fulfils is that of counterbalancing the negativity of her mother's and her rival's conjugal models, as she becomes a model-wife for Carlyle at the novel's ending. Undoubtedly reassuring for orthodox readers, her character conveys conservative views of femininity that are recurrent in Wood's novels. At the same time, however, her conservatism is instrumental to the author's subtle questioning of marriage and gender roles, as the growing self-restraint she adopts seems to confirm, rather than deny, the humiliation and oppression experienced by less fortunate spouses, such as Mrs. Hare and Isabel.

The conflation of anti-feminist and proto-feminist ideas becomes more jarring in two novels Wood published after *East Lynne*: *The Shadow of Ashlydyat* (1863) and *Lord Oakburn's Daughters* (1864), both of which provide thought-provoking variations on the Griselda theme. References to this theme are recurrent in *Lord Oakburn's Daughters*, which offers a perturbing rewriting of the story of a patient woman tyrannized by a patriarchal figure. The role of demure heroine is here played by the eldest daughter of the Chesney family, Jane. Different from her rebellious sisters Laura and Clarice, Jane is completely subject to the whims of their imperious father, whom she serves with exemplary patience: "if by walking through a sea of fire – and this is not speaking metaphorically – she could have eased him of a minute's pain, Jane Chesney would have stepped lovingly to the sacrifice" (Wood, 1864a [1872]: 98). Deliberately ironic, this hyperbolic image of self-sacrifice raises doubts about the soundness of Jane's filial devotion to a capricious man who fails to reciprocate her kindness and affection. The disparity of their relationship becomes evident when Captain Chesney (risen to the title of Lord Oakburn) marries his governess against Jane's will, thereby triggering his daughter's unquenchable jealousy.

The unnaturalness of their father-daughter relationship is confirmed by a conversation Jane has with Laura, to whom she confesses that her only aspiration is "to devote [her] life to warding off care from his" – an admission that almost shocks her interlocutor: "'Would you *wish* no better?'" (1864a [1872]: 112). Stubbornly compliant with Oakburn's wishes, Jane is painfully hurt by his clandestine marriage that makes her feel similar emotions as those assailing betrayed wives. "Utterly sick and faint" (1864a [1872]: 258) at hearing the news, she not only suffers the loss of her "post of authority" in the household; she is also distressed at the idea of being replaced in the affection of a man she has meekly served and adored:

> Oh, reader! surely you can feel for her! She was hurled without warning from the post of authority in her father's home, in which she had been mistress for years; *she was hurled from the chief place in her father's heart.* [...] but what she could not bear was that another should become more to her father than she was. He whom she had so revered and loved, he in whom her very life had been bound up, had now taken to himself an idol – and Jane henceforth was nothing. (1864a [1872]: 260)

The narrator's address to the reader, couched in the familiar Victorian and especially Brontëan conversation discourse,[3] not only raises sympathy for the suffering daughter. It also emphasizes some disquieting aspects of Jane's filial love, which is almost eroticized by her jealous rivalry with her father's newly-wed partner. The incestuous undertones of the quotation are increased by comparison with the Griselda tale, as Jane simultaneously plays the parts of the enduring wife and of the young daughter that Gualtieri pretends to wish to marry in order to further test his spouse's patience. Far from being praised by Wood, Jane's unnatural devotion to her parent is frequently ironized in the novel, which lays emphasis on the many sufferings resulting from her 'wifely' subjection to Oakburn.

These incestuous connotations are lacking in *The Shadow of Ashlydyat* whose elaboration of the Griselda myth is darkened by another perturbing element: the description of the lethal effects of forbearance on the wife's psychophysical balance. Instead of rewarding female patience in the end, the novel condemns the passive wife to a premature death, thereby highlighting the risks inherent in self-annihilating attitudes like those adopted by Mrs. Hare in *East Lynne*. The implications of this tragic twist appear more provocative if we read the novel in light of the bourgeois qualities celebrated by Samuel Smiles in *Self-Help* (1859). While Smiles praises (prevalently male) virtues of fortitude and perseverance, *The Shadow of Ashlydyat* configures female endurance as a frustrating habit that threatens to kill women. This gendered interpretation confirms that Wood wrote what Gilbert and Gubar would define a "palimpsestic text" (1979 [2000]: 73), which both conveys and camouflages messages that would sound unorthodox to most Victorian readers.

One of Wood's favourite novels, *The Shadow of Ashlydyat* is described as an exploration of "the workings of the human heart" by her son, who mentions the centrality of the "heart-history" of Maria Godolphin, a woman suffering for "the sins of others", depicted in all her "sorrow and anguish and endurance" (Charles Wood, 1894: 256). A "quiet, retiring, gentle" young woman endowed with sober tastes, Maria Hastings marries the handsome but "[g]raceless" George Godolphin, the spendthrift younger son of an affluent banker (Wood, 1863a [n.d.]: 11, 131). Despite his good intentions, George fails to make a good husband, as he is too insouciant in business, too incautious in managing finances and too fickle in love. Cheated by professional swindlers, he wrecks the family bank, ruins relatives and acquaintances, and brings shame on the Godolphin name. This chain of misfortunes comes to weigh on Maria, who becomes aware of George's faults only after the family's bankruptcy. Afflicted though she is by financial worries and shame, however, she refuses to blame her husband for his crimes, which include forgery and the wilful ruin of her father. Still in love with him, she feels it is her "duty to defend him against the world" (1863a [n.d.]: 366) and perseveres in her protective attitude in the face of people's criticism. Another source of trouble is the flirtatious conduct George adopts with the glamorous Charlotte Pain before and after his wedding. Consumed by jealousy, which adds to her many worries, Maria develops a psychosomatic illness that rapidly undermines her frail constitution. Her untimely death is followed by the repentance of her light-hearted husband, who decides to leave Britain and try his luck in the colonies.

At first glance, Maria seems to embody a wifely ideal perfectly in line with Victorian conduct books.[4] Serious-minded, ladylike in manners and submissive towards her husband, she also becomes a doting mother, as she gives birth to a beautiful girl, Meta, after losing three previous children. This exemplary picture poses the problem of interpreting her tragic death. Why is the novel 'cleansed' of such a paragon of virtue before its conclusion? And why is her characterization flawed by relational, intellectual, even moral imperfections that make her figure rather unappealing? These blemishes, which emerge in various passages, raise doubts about the imitability of her wifely model. In an early scene of the novel, for instance, Maria is compared with Charlotte Pain, her rival-in-love. Both beautiful, "but of a different type of beauty" (1863a [n.d.]: 50), the two women are the objects of a phrenological and behavioural analysis that brings meaningful differences to the fore. While Maria is "timid" but endowed with "integrity", "high principle" and "refinement", Charlotte is said to lack such qualities (1863a [n.d.]: 51). An anticipation of the binary "fair girl" *vs.* "fast girl" theorized by Eliza Lynn Linton in "The Girl of the Period",[5] this opposition is however challenged, in the same passage, by some comments made by the narrator who puzzlingly underlines Charlotte's endowments – "kind-hearted in the main, liberal natured, pleasant tempered, of a spirit firm and resolute"– while stigmatizing the other girl's idleness: "Maria – I grieve I have it to say of her in this very utilitarian age – was rather addicted to doing nothing" (1863a [n.d.]: 51–52).

The non-disjunctive effects of such remarks are reinforced in later episodes. Unlike Maria, who is prevented from acting by her shyness and self-restraint, Charlotte proves to be energetic, bold in speech and action, generous towards her rival and ready to assist her in distressing times. Despite some moral and aesthetic flaws – she is garish in dress, marries for money and exerts a masculine power over her husband – Charlotte exhibits an admirable vitality as the narrative unfolds, while Maria dwindles to a pale figure sadly afflicted by her lack of initiative. Disparaged by her own sister for her complacent passivity – "'You have been a blind simpleton, nothing else. George Godolphin has lavished his money and his attentions broadcast elsewhere, and you have looked complacently on'" (1863a [n.d.]: 366) –, Maria is even assailed by moral dilemmas in a passage resonant with Hawthornian echoes:

> Down deep in her heart she thrust that dreadful revelation of his falsity, and strove to bury it as an English wife and gentlewoman has no resource but to do. Ay! to bury it; and to

> keep it buried! though the concealment eat away her life – as that scarlet letter A you have read of, ate into the bosom of another woman renowned in story. It seemed to Maria that the time was come when she must inquire a little into the actual state of affairs, instead of hiding her head and spending her days in the indulgence of her fear and grief. (1863a [n.d.]: 382)

Besides commenting on the impotence of Victorian married women, who were impelled "to bury" their emotions to keep up appearances, the narrator traces a thought-provoking comparison between Maria's repressed feelings and the symbol of shame worn by Hester Prynne in Nathaniel Hawthorne's *The Scarlet Letter*, which had become an immediate success after its publication in 1850. Unlike Hawthorne's protagonist, who manages to reverse the meanings of the infamous letter from "Adultery" into "Able" while keeping quiet about the truth of the adultery, Maria is "eaten away" by her efforts to keep silent and to obey a man she no longer trusts. Her failure to develop into a self-assured woman is confirmed by her inability to violate the law of coverture and "inquire a little into the actual state of affairs". The sexual undertones of the quotation are also intriguing. Whereas Hester Prynne commits adultery, Maria is a victim of her husband's infidelity which, though never shown to be physical, gnaws at her constantly. With bitter irony, Wood suggests that, owing to her passivity, the betrayed wife is consumed by the sexual (and professional) misconduct of her husband, while the latter is protected by the age's tolerance of male infractions.

The irony of this situation is increased by the fact that, unlike the high-principled Maria, Charlotte Pain indulges her passions freely. Never overtly described as involved in adulterous affairs, Charlotte nonetheless flirts with George and other men throughout the novel and flourishes despite her unorthodox sexual mores. While the "fast girl" thrives, the patient wife is literally consumed by her efforts to be a paragon of virtue. When George brings ruin to their family, Maria withdraws from public life. The narrator remarks that she takes "an exaggerated view" of the disgrace, before adding that Charlotte would have reacted differently and "shown herself as usual" (1863a [n.d.]: 332). Owing to her self-indulged shame, moreover, Maria loses her appetite and develops dysphagia, a dysfunction generally associated with anorexia in medical literature.[6] Her symptoms get worse over the course of the narration, and are described as follows in the text: "But she found some difficulty in swallowing [food]. Throat and bread were alike dry" (1863a [n.d.]: 336). Most likely psychosomatic, her trouble evolves into a serious disease that doctors are unable to diagnose. Labelled "atrophy" by a medical professional, who describes it as a "curious complaint" and a "gradual wasting away of the system without apparent reason", it is also associated with psychological suffering by a household servant, who observes: "It is burying the grief within people's own breasts that kills them" (1863a [n.d.]: 499–500).

The self-induced disease kills Maria at the age of twenty-eight. Her premature death is narrated in a protracted melodramatic episode, which includes George's repentance for his errors and his promise that he will never marry Charlotte. Enveloped by narratorial irony, Maria's deathbed scene has Darwinian undertones, as her passing away is provocatively contrasted with her rival's ability to struggle and survive:

> You may remember it was observed at the beginning of her history that she was unfit to battle with the world's sharp storms – it had now proved so. Charlotte Pain would have braved them, whatever their nature, have weathered them jauntily on a prancing saddle-horse; Maria had shrunk down, crushed with their weight. Il y a – let me once more repeat it – il y a des femmes et des femmes. (1863a [n.d.]: 491)

While the angelic wife is "crushed with the weight" of life's storms and perishes, the unconventional Charlotte incarnates a new idea of femininity based on the "survival of the fittest" theorized by

Charles Darwin four years earlier. The use of a French sentence at the end of the quotation evidences Wood's use of camouflage techniques in portraying the two female protagonists. Without ever questioning Maria's moral superiority, the author raises doubts about the desirability of her sacrifice, which is unfavourably juxtaposed with her rival's exuberant vitality.

The contradictory meanings attached to Maria's passivity are evident in the wide-ranging interpretations offered by Wood scholars. As Anne-Marie Beller contends, "Maria's undoubted masochism is a key part of her status as a lady" and her death "serves as a vehicle for the punishment of George" (2008: 224–225). This conventional reading is validated by the central stage given to the husband's repentance in the long deathbed scene. As is often the case in Wood, however, the novel offers no single ideological perspective or coherent range of perspectives (Pykett, 1992). Drawing on this idea, Emma Liggins notices that, without precluding sympathy for the dying wife, *The Shadow of Ashlydyat* exposes Maria's behavioural and physical inadequacy "to activate a variety of interpretations of the domestic woman" and encourage readers to explore "alternative models of femininity" (2001: 64–65).

By reshaping the Griselda figure in half-ironic, half-melodramatic terms, Wood unveils some ambiguities of the Victorian conceptualization of the angelic wife, whose perfection is not granted by refinement and moral superiority. The evolution of Maria's apathetic attitude into deadly "atrophy" exemplifies the limits of her stereotyped figure, which lacks the vital elements of Charlotte's personality. While the frail wife is crushed by her efforts to conform, the ebullient Charlotte manages to survive and exposes, through her conduct, what twentieth-century feminists call "the danger that essentialist conceptions of the subject pose specifically for women" (Alcoff, 1995: 450). Her practice of masculine sports, her physical strength and her constant pursuit of freedom suggest the possibility of shunning the paralyzing models women were encouraged to incarnate at the time. Like the heroine of Braddon's *Aurora Floyd* serialized 1862–63, Charlotte displays an unfeminine love for dogs and horses. Her hobbies include the driving of horse carriages, which she performs with remarkable abilities despite people's reservations.[7] What is more, Charlotte praises the educational effects of being "reared among horses and dogs" and reproaches Maria for bringing up Meta to "the same deficiencies" that have marred her mother's personality (Wood, 1863a [n.d.]: 282). Some potentialities of the educational model proposed by Charlotte emerge in the novel's conclusion, which describes her last meeting with George who is embarking for Calcutta. The role she plays, in this final episode, is that of a strong, self-assured amazon, who boldly drives her horses, followed by her dogs and accompanied by her compliant husband. Treated coldly by her former lover, Charlotte nonetheless maintains a psychophysical dominance over the scene, which she leaves "dash[ing] away in style; her whip flourishing, the dogs barking, her red feather tossing and gleaming" (1863a [n.d.]: 519). The novel's closure lays further emphasis on the woman's vitality by describing her glamorous social activities: "And Mr. and Mrs. Pain's dinner-parties in Belgravia are a great success" (1863a [n.d.]: 519). The leisured life Charlotte continues to pursue in London is contrasted with the "weary sadness" exhibited by George in leaving England, a sadness that raises thorny problems of interpretations:

> Did he finally regret the inevitable PAST with all its mistakes and sins? – and think that if it could but come over again, he would act differently? Possibly so. (1863a [n.d.]: 519)

By implying that Maria's death might have failed to redeem her erring husband, the adverb "[p]ossibly" problematizes the woman's sacrifice. If it is true that the moral values to which Maria sticks are never questioned, it is also true that her wifely role is challenged by the emergence of alternative models of femininity that partly anticipate the late century. To say this does not mean that Wood configures Charlotte as an ideal homemaker. The humorous narratorial comments on her dress code and her ebullient personality, and George's observation that "'Men do not marry women such as Charlotte Pain'" (1863a [n.d.]: 491),[8] prevent us from reading her figure as an easy replacement of Maria.

What the novel poses, in the end, is the problem of redefining the condition of married women at a historical juncture marked by the clash between distressful emblems of the past and flamboyant harbingers of modernization. This idea is substantiated by the novel's characterization of another victimized wife: an ancestress of the Godolphins who was murdered by her husband and never interred, whose spectral projection (the "Shadow" mentioned in the title) haunts the family for generations (1863a [n.d.]: 238). The presence of this tormented revenant on the scene attaches gruesome connotations to the womanly model incarnated by Maria, which she uncannily mirrors; but it also highlights the difficulty in modernizing gender roles in an age haunted by the spectres of an oppressive past that keeps returning. As Andrew Mangham notices, the generic experimentation conducted in *The Shadow of Ashlydyat* confirms the author's "conflicting attitudes towards gender": by embedding "the Female Gothic's narrative of the incarcerated and excluded wife" into a realistic plot, Wood juxtaposes traditional and innovative models of femininity, none of which are unequivocally offered as exemplary to her readers (2003: 91, 88).[9]

Maria Godolphin's death is not the only tragic reworking of the Griselda story found in Wood's oeuvre, which offers multiple disturbing variations of the tale. In *The Red Court Farm* (1868), for example, the forbearing Clara Lake dies of an illness caused by her mental torments. The woman's parable of decline, analysed in the following chapter, is consequent on her husband's infidelity, which she suffers silently, consumed by a wild jealousy she avoids revealing to the world. Less dreary is the conclusion of a subplot of *Lady Adelaide's Oath* (1867), in which the young Edith Bordillion risks her life owing to her rebellious marriage with the son of a squire. Punished by her father-in-law who denies the couple any financial support, Edith experiences poverty and starvation. She starts to pine away as a consequence of her deprivation of proper food, but her condition worsens when she learns about her husband's involvement in criminal activities. The worries by which she is assailed make her develop anorexic leanings that threaten to kill her. Providentially saved by a benefactor, she nonetheless resembles Maria Godolphin in her performance of the role of victimized wife, as her eating disorder unveils the responsibilities of the two male figures that have wrecked her life: her husband and the heartless squire.

The sacrificial model that is physically embodied by Clara Lake and Edith Bordillion becomes symbolic in *Bessy Rane* (1870), whose eponymous protagonist agrees to fake her own death in a criminal plot hatched by her husband. A remissive girl initially tyrannized by her stepmother, Bessy turns into a forbearing wife after marrying Oliver Rane, who becomes the centre of all her attentions: "There was nothing she liked so much as to wait on her husband" (Wood, 1870 [1872]: 164). Her amorous care contrasts with the condescending attitude adopted by her husband. "'You young women can't be expected to understand business questions'" (1870 [1872]: 198), asserts the strong-willed Rane before convincing his wife to participate in the sensational staging of her own death. Although it has no legal consequences, the discovery of the fraud casts a dark shadow on Rane's professional image, as he uses his medical position to certify his wife's passing away. For her part, Bessy dwindles to a paler figure when she becomes an accomplice in the crime. Her passive submission to her husband makes her figuratively become the ghost that is seen by an inquisitive servant after the funeral: "If not Mrs. Rane – who? – or what?" (1870 [1872]: 259). A symbol of Bessy's psychophysical invisibility, the presumed manifestations of her spectre deprive the heroine of her fleshy presence on the scene and, in so doing, ironically invalidate the centrality she is given in the novel's title.

A different assemblage of folktale components is found in *Oswald Cray* (1864) which tells a typical story of female endurance. The Griselda role is here played by young Sara Davenal, who uncomplainingly bears with her father's and her beloved's irrational decisions. Put to a hard test before her wedding, Sara continues to cope with male whims after becoming a wife, thereby suggesting the inescapability of her condition. A meek and gentle girl used to caring for others, she patiently allows herself to be deprived of means by her father, Dr. Davenal, who refuses an inheritance to silence his guilty conscience.[10] Stigmatized by his lawyer – "but the time will come when your children will not thank you for this" (Wood, 1864b [1904]: 161) –, the doctor's selfish act is unquestioned by Sara who, though well aware of their financial problems, kindly complies with her father's wish: "Sara was silent. A shiver passed through her at the allusion. She did not dare reply to it. [...] 'I am sure you are right, papa', she murmured. 'Do not keep this money'" (1864b [1904]: 164). More trying is the responsibility for her brother that she is assigned on her father's deathbed. Prematurely killed by pneumonia, Davenal is unable to resolve an incident involving his son and entrusts Sara with the difficult task. In addition to selling their properties to pay off her brother's debts, the orphaned and destitute girl is compelled to deal with an unscrupulous blackmailer whom she manages to silence later in the narration. While receiving this grievous burden, she is however denied knowledge of the real nature of the crime committed by her brother, which is later revealed to be forging bills. The irrationality of Davenal's refusal to share the full story with his daughter is hinted in a conversation that brings their unbalance of power into focus:

> "I don't know one thing", she whispered. "Papa, I don't know what – the crime – was".
> "And better that you should not know", he answered with a vehemence surprising in his weak state. (1864b [1904]: 227)

With subtle irony, Wood juxtaposes the "surprising vehemence" of the dying man with the elliptical speech of the timid woman to prove that the gender roles performed by father and daughter do not match the situation. Exactly because she is entrusted with unfeminine responsibilities, Sara should receive all the information she needs instead of being censored by an authoritative man who is about to leave her unprotected.

Dr. Davenal's death is followed by other misadventures, which contribute to troping his daughter as a Victorian child visited by her father's sins. Abandoned by her fiancé, Oswald Cray, Sara faces various financial problems and is tyrannized by Neal, a cruel servant who symbolically joins the ranks of her male 'torturers'. In the novel's conclusion, Sara receives a marriage proposal from Oswald who silences his pride and asks for her forgiveness. What is lacking in his speech, however, are full explanations for their long separation.[11] "'Don't ask me, Sara! In mercy to myself'", asks the proud man who obstinately rejects all her requests to know: "'Ah, don't press me further, Sara, for I cannot tell you. [...] *Will* you – will you generously let my confession rest here?'" (1864b [1904]: 441–442).

In ways similar to Dr. Davenal, Oswald refuses to share the complete truth with the young woman and appeals to her generosity to silence her requests. The scene is repeated in the novel's closure with an interesting variation. Now a married couple, Oswald and Sara are recollecting their difficult past when the wife suddenly asks to learn the untold secret:

> "Oswald", she resume in low tones, "won't you tell me what your suspicion was?"
>
> "I will tell you some time, Sara; not now. Oh, my darling wife, how much is there in the past for many of us to repent of!" he continued in what seemed an uncontrollable impulse. "And it is only through God's mercy that we do repent".
>
> She laid her head upon his shoulder and let it rest there.

Its safe abiding-place, so long as the world, for them, should last.

Only through God's mercy. My friends, may it be shed on us all throughout our pilgrimage in this chequered life, and abide with us unto the end! Fare you well. (1864b [1904]: 455–456)

The religious tone of the last sentence, a recurrent motif in Wood's novel closures, does not dispel the worrying implications of the husband's obstinate silence. By postponing to an undefined future ("some time") the revelation of the truth, Oswald validates biblical and folkloric models that indicted female curiosity and justified the male testing of female patience. For her part, Sara seems to accept the prospect of not getting to know. The loving gesture she performs, in laying her head upon Oswald's shoulder, is undoubtedly a validation of the conjugal roles enforced by her husband. Yet, his request to be trusted blindly contrasts with her multiple attempts to learn the truth. Her repeated entreaties to know, in this and earlier scenes, produce a sense of frustration in the reader who, prevented from witnessing the effects that a disclosure might produce, is encouraged to reflect on the gender disparities of a society that extolled women's bearing with male whims.

The frustrated curiosity epitomized by Sara Davenal is a motif variously reworked in Wood's fiction, which often associates women's psychophysical sufferings with the prohibition of female knowledge. An interesting combination of these themes is found in *Elster's Folly* (1866), whose eponymous hero is examined in Chapter 4. Fascinating but fatally irresolute, Val Elster is trapped into a mercenary marriage by Maude Kirton who, driven by her mother's unlimited ambition, prevents Val from marrying his first love, Anne Ashton. Upset by her lover's infidelity, Anne develops anorexic tendencies and shows symptoms of a dysphagia that is often connected with female nervous disorders in Wood's oeuvre: "Try as she would, she could not eat: all she confessed to, when questioned by Mrs. Ashton, was 'a pain in her throat'" (Wood, 1866a [1903]: 292–293). Her affliction is attributed to her sentimental constancy and her timidity, two personality traits exalted in mainstream literature, but here connoted in negative terms, as elements of a "romance" that kills "quiet, sensitive, refined" natures "in silence" (1866a [1903]: 292). Although it is said to affect both genders, the tendency to fall ill after experiencing love disillusionment evokes female paradigms of patience rooted in folklore, which were developed to encourage women to silently withstand male fickleness. Yet, Anne is not killed by love labours. She becomes Val's second wife after Maude's untimely death. In ways similar to Griselda, she is thus rewarded with conjugal happiness for her long patience. Still, the narrator's description of her sorrows raises gender issues that are perturbingly left unanswered in the text. Why is a sweet and refined young woman condemned to stifle her feelings when disappointed by an inconstant lover? If morally superior to male light-heartedness, why is female self-restraint pathologized?

These questions are made more disquieting by Anne's submissiveness to Val's desires after their marriage. Forced to stand the aggressive presence of Maude's mother in their household, the patient wife asks Val to share the secret that prevents him from getting rid of their intrusive guest. Instead of information, she gets a typical request for forbearance by her husband who bids her to trust him blindly and indefinitely defers the moment of revelation: "'Not yet; in a little time, perhaps. Bear with me, still, my dear wife; bear with me'" (1866a [1903]: 434). Shortly afterwards, Anne gains access to the yearned-for knowledge; but it is Val's mother-in-law who impels him to the disclosure. Confronted by the elderly woman in hysterics, Val admits having been a bigamous husband who married Maude illegally and condemned their children to illegitimacy. Even though his wedding with Anne is validated by the fortuitous deaths of both his 'first wives',[12] he proves to be an untrustworthy partner who endangers the happiness and well-being of many people. By showing the legitimacy of Anne's bids to learn the secret, Wood obliquely questions the indictment of female curiosity by men who, in addition to curbing their women's aspirations, generate the troubles that afflict their beloved.

The polemical refunctionalization of the Griselda theme in *Elster's Folly* is reinforced by many intertextual references to "Bluebeard", another fairy tale that was extensively reworked by Victorian authors of "marital Gothic" fiction (Massé, 1992: 20–29; Talairach-Vielmas, 2007: 159). Whereas Anne is told the terrible secret that marred the life of her predecessor, Maude had spied on her husband and discovered his secret in an act of "[w]ilful, unpardonable disobedience" (Wood, 1866a [1903]: 347). The secret is that of Val's previous marriage with a girl named Alice Waterlow, which invalidates the latter union. Besides eavesdropping, Maude's investigation includes the use of a key to unlock "an ebony cabinet" where Val's private correspondence is kept (1866a [1903]: 331) – a hint at the trespass committed by Bluebeard's curious wife in Perrault's tale. Unlike the fairy tale, however, Wood's novel concocts a terrible punishment for "Maude's disobedience" (1866a [1903]: 344). Whereas Perrault warns all wives against prying into their husbands' secrets but lets his heroine be rescued by her brothers, *Elster's Folly* narrates how, shortly after discovering Val's bigamy, Maude develops the same congenital heart problem that killed her brother. Instead of being saved by her male sibling, the young woman is symbolically 'infected' by his disease that, coupled with Val's deceitful conduct, condemns her to die prematurely. Her victimization, which entices the reader's sympathy, is increased by her growing love for her husband. Initially characterized as a cold and ambitious girl, Maude gradually evolves into a conforming wife deceived by a fickle man who wrecks her and their children's lives. The dangerous model she embodies is what Anne must avoid duplicating after her wedding. By learning Val's secret, his third wife is symbolically protected from the risks run by her predecessor who, in imitation of Griselda and the various Bluebeard's spouses, becomes a victim of her husband's injunctions and unruly sexuality.

Indirectly evoked by Val's conjugal relations, Bluebeard was "the prototype" of many Victorian bigamy novels that associated domesticity "with dangerous marital multiplicity" (McAleavey, 2015: 50). In Wood's oeuvre, references to this grim Perrault tale are ubiquitous. Marital multiplicity is represented, among others, in *East Lynne* when the disguised Isabel is employed to work for Carlyle's new family. Other Wood fictions rework Perrault's eponymous protagonist into a demonic-lover figure. The lineage of these figures, which are both threatening and fascinating, includes nineteenth-century elaborations like those offered by the Brontë sisters. One sufficient example is the characterization of Edward Rochester who is framed "within a context of animalized and demonized masculine sexuality" in *Jane Eyre* (Hendershot, 1998: 168). Wood's indebtedness to this tradition is evident in *Anne Hereford*, whose portrayals of the heroine's lover and uncle draw on masculine figures featured in "Bluebeard" and "Little Red Riding Hood", as well as on Brontëan rewritings. As shown in Chapter 5, the dark attractive man with whom Anne falls in love and her tyrannical uncle are ambiguous projections of a threating conception of masculinity, as they both exert an oppressive power on the young woman while aiming to protect her.

The appeal "Bluebeard" had on Victorian writers, including Wood, is certainly due to its strong realism that well suited the novelistic form. Devoid as it is of any magical or supernatural element, the story of "the most monstrous and beastly of all fairy-tale husbands" (Zipes, 1983 [2006]: 299) enabled novelists to depict the dangers of an institution that subjected women to the social and sexual control of their male partners. By projecting Perrault's picture of aristocratic oppression onto their bourgeois milieu, moreover, many Victorian writers could explore the risks inherent in the gendering of roles enforced by their class, which conceived women's conjugal subjection as a prerequisite for social and national prosperity. It is no coincidence therefore that, in her most gothicized versions of the Bluebeard story, Wood represents the wives of rising professionals as victims of conjugal violence. Doctors, in particular, tend to play the role of domestic tyrants in her works which, besides exposing their deontological limits (Costantini, 2015: 325–329), often characterize them as tormentors or murderers of their spouses (Price 2016).

Symbolically embodied by Oliver Rane, who stages the fake death of his wife in *Bessy Rane*, the Bluebeard role is realistically played by other medical men featured in Wood's oeuvre. In *The House of Halliwell* (1890), for example, the flirtatious conduct of Dr. Matthew Goring leads to the murder of his wife, poisoned by strychnia in their household. Probably killed by their scheming governess who later marries Goring, the murdered wife is also a victim of her fickle husband whose complicity in the crime remains unascertained. Suspected by his sister-in-law who 'sees' him on the crime scene in a revelatory dream, the medical man plays an ambiguous role in the novel. His marital and ethical responsibilities cast a shadow on his professional group, thereby confirming the Victorian embourgeoisement of the upper-class prototype of villainous husband created by Perrault.

A more gothicized version of Bluebeard is found in *Lord Oakburn's Daughters*, in which the attractive Lewis Carlton uses his medical knowledge to kill his first wife (Price 2016). Driven by a strong passion for his sister-in-law, Carlton violates his deontological rules by becoming a heartless uxoricide, thus suggesting, with his slyness, that crime prospered among apparently respectable professionals. Clearly inspired by "Bluebeard" in the characterization of the fierce doctor, the novel also evidences other intertextual references to Perrault's tale, such as the dangerous curiosity of Carlton's wife Laura. As shown in Chapter 1, Laura is driven by jealousy to spy on her husband. She commits an act of marital disobedience by using a special "skeleton key" commissioned at a locksmith's to open the safe in which the doctor keeps his private documents (Wood, 1864a [1872]: 432). Better organized than Bluebeard's wife, she not only shows autonomy in getting the special key; she also wears dark clothes to disguise herself and, thanks to them, she escapes discovery in a thrilling scene: "But she cowered in the shade of the dark corner; moreover the clothes she wore were dark, and his eye passed her over" (1864a [1872]: 437). Although she cannot properly interpret the clues she has found, Laura becomes instrumental to the discovery of her husband's crime. Her violation of social rules, which prescribed loyalty and obedience to wives, is partly stigmatized, partly praised, in the text. If her spying on Carlton appears as conjugal betrayal, the role she plays in unmasking him acquires positive connotations as she performs a symbolic act of revenge against her sister's murderer and, more importantly, she unintentionally gives evidence to a group of lower-class women who, as shown in Chapter 5, join forces to unmask the criminal doctor.

A rebellious wife who contributes to punishing an awful crime committed by her husband, Laura is a figure of non-disjunction that exposes some inequalities of Victorian society. Even though she is indicted for violating the law of coverture in various passages, she performs actions that contribute to unveiling some gender disparities existing within the marriage contract. Carlton himself displays a patronizing attitude towards his disobedient spouse in a letter sent from his prison cell. After confessing that he committed the murder because of "How passionately [he] grew to love [her]", the man reproaches his nosy wife for her lack of trust ("Oh, why could you not have trusted me wholly?") and he closes the missive by granting her his "full and free forgiveness" (1864a [1872]: 503–504). Formulated in a language that confirms orthodox views of conjugal roles, the letter acquires a paradoxical meaning as it is written by an uxoricide. The forgiveness Carlton grants to Laura, moreover, recalls the benevolence displayed by Gualtieri towards his tyrannized wife. By incarnating two prototypes of oppressive masculinity, the criminal doctor demonstrates the extent to which the gruesome realism of "Bluebeard" and "Griselda" appealed to Victorian novelists, who reworked traditional tales to produce modernized stories of oppression.

To say this does not mean that all the defective husbands portrayed by Wood exhibit villainous features. If Carlton is unredeemed by his epistolary benevolence and his love for Laura, other domestic oppressors are shown to act under the pressure of external agents, as is the case of George Godolphin and Oliver Rane. Criminal in their actions but capable of repentance, such figures witness Wood's exploration of the challenges posed to Victorian men by gender prescriptions that encouraged them to behave like stern patriarchs.

In the same way as she avoided polarizing many male characters, Wood challenged dominant views of the Eternal Feminine by creating a wide range of heroines animated by unrestrained passions. She also drew interesting portrayals of women who commit wicked actions which are partly justified by circumstances. Particularly noteworthy is her reshaping of fairy-tale stepmothers that rarely appear as stock characters in her fiction. Often driven by passions they are unable to stifle, Wood's stepmothers differ from those featured in "Cinderella" or "Snow White", as they prove to be capable of good feelings or, at least, of repentance after oppressing their households. This is the case of Eliza St. John, who incautiously initiates her own children and stepchildren into dangerous drinking habits in *Danesbury House* (1860), or of Barbara Hare whose unsympathetic attitude is the result of her efforts to embody a proper wifely role. With a few exceptions, such as the governess portrayed in *The House of Halliwell*, Wood provides justifications for the violent actions committed by these women against their rivals or stepchildren. The case of Charlotte St. John examined in the next chapter is emblematic. A brutal murderer who upsets the life of her new home, Charlotte is also connoted as a victim of inherited madness and socioeconomic disparities that trigger her over-emotional conduct.

The characterization of Charlotte St. John suggests the extent to which Wood turned fairy-tale female 'monsters' into thought-provoking grey figures, whose disruptive agency is not always the result of the same evil disposition exhibited by their literary predecessors. Equally provocative is the function fulfilled by the remissive wives analysed above. All variations of the model of forbearance set by the patient Griselda and other archetypical figures, these characters show the innovative potential of Wood's reworking of the fairy-tale tradition, as they raise pressing doubts about the desirability of the Victorian gendering of roles especially within the marriage contract.

CHAPTER 3

Desiring subjects and the effects of immoderacy

The construction of women as feeling subjects was a basic tenet of Victorian culture. Discourses about affect dominated the age's conceptualization of gender, which was founded on the assumption of women's susceptibility to feelings. Middle-class Victorians in particular aligned femininity with a liability to emotional excess that provided ideological validations for various forms of parental and marital control, including the law of coverture. Owing to their alleged psychological weakness, women were thought to be potentially destabilizing for their family and society and consequently viewed as in need of strong male guidance. Most nineteenth-century medicine substantiated these presumptions. Besides offering pseudoscientific support to the control of female emotionality and to the moral management of transgressors, Victorian medical discourse contributed to creating the myth of a widespread "female malady" by configuring madness as "metaphorically and symbolically [...] feminine", "even when experienced by men" (Showalter, 1985: 4).

A product of "dualistic systems of language and representation" that situated women "on the side of irrationality, silence, nature, and body, while men [were] situated on the side of reason, discourse, culture, and mind" (Showalter, 1985: 3–4), this gender asymmetry became a literary *topos* during the nineteenth century, as evidenced by all the anxious, hysterical, depressed and deranged women featured in Victorian fiction. Sometimes dangerous for others, at other times these characters become victims of their own excess of affect that engenders a variety of psychophysical disorders. The manifestations of these disorders reflect the age's beliefs in the emotional and corporeal vulnerability of women, whose "heightened sensitivity" was assumed to "magnify the production of physical symptoms" (Vrettos, 1995: 23). Essentialized by doctors, the nineteenth-century conviction that "women's emotions were more somatic, and their diseases more complicated by emotions, than men's" (Vrettos, 1995: 23) not only accounts for the centrality of women's illness in the century's literature. It also explains the rationale behind the literary pathologization of women's deviance which, independently from its seriousness, tends to be associated with contemporary beliefs in the gender's psychophysical frailty.

Since the 1970s, feminist critics have offered a variety of readings of these cultural and literary reverberations. Special attention has been devoted to representations of female hysteria and madness, which bear witness to the oppressive effects produced by the Victorian alliance between patriarchy and medicine. These effects were strongly denounced by Elaine Showalter. Against sociomedical presumptions about the pathological interconnections between women's bodies and minds, Showalter imputes hysteria to the repressive actions of patriarchy, which frustrates female yearnings to obtain mobility and intellectual development (1985: 132). Other critics have explored the extent to which, during the nineteenth century, madness was used as an instrument of control and discipline against resisting women, who were labelled as insane in order to be contained, silenced and sometimes incarcerated into asylums.[1] Recuperative approaches to insanity are instead offered by feminists such as Hélène Cixous and Luce Irigaray, who conceive it as a liberating means through which women strive to escape normativity. If Cixous reappraises female madness as a form of anti-systemic behaviour,[2] Irigaray juxtaposes its conventional reading as "waste" (i.e., what is discarded because it "resists transparency") with its potential to be a *"resource* of reflection" (1977 [1985]: 77, 151). Specifically meta-literary is the recuperative version proposed by Sandra Gilbert and Susan Gubar in *The Madwoman in the Attic*, which invites a reconsideration of Victorian fiction by describing deranged female characters as projections of their angered authoresses.

These feminist efforts to rethink women's mental disorders outside the essentializing mechanisms of patriarchy have influenced later interpretations of Victorian literature. A compelling reading of "women's capacity for emotional expression" is provided by Ann Cvetkovich who contends that the discourses of affect found in the age's fiction both substantiate and threaten dominant gender views (1992: 6ff). The sensation novel in particular is, in her view, a literary space where conflicting models of femininity are provocatively envisaged and juxtaposed. Often associated with mental afflictions, the tormented heroines featured in this genre show that "the expression of affect is as much a way to dominate as it is a way to resist domination" (Cvetkovich, 1992: 10). Wood herself is described as an author who represents the contradictory condition of nineteenth-century women by making a spectacle of female suffering. In her analysis of *East Lynne* (1861), Cvetkovich highlights the ambivalent status of Isabel Vane who, "at once transgressive adulteress and suffering victim", suggests that Victorian melodrama "functioned both to install women in their place and to allow them to mourn that position" (1992: 97, 127).

Besides revealing Wood's interest in the Victorian gendering of affect, Isabel's development of a lethal affliction at the end of *East Lynne* is proof of the author's exploration of the bodily torments generated by women's over-emotionality. Similar links between self-repressed affect and pathology are established in other Wood narratives, as shown by the suffering Griseldas examined in Chapter 2. Probably a victim of psychosomatic problems herself, as hypothesized by Showalter (1977: 171), Wood fictionalized many cases in which affect comes to be somatically inscribed in the female body, thereby validating Victorian views of women as over-feeling creatures in need of control. Yet, she also challenged this deterministic approach by showing that female passions are ignited by frustrated desire. The anger felt by Lucy Andinnian when she suspects her husband of infidelity in *Within the Maze* (1872) is a case in point. Not only a manifestation of her wounded sentimentality, Lucy's anger is also an outraged response to a vexatious system that asks her to forbear in silence, thereby denying her status of desiring subject: "Underlying all else in her mind was a keen sense of insult, of slight, of humiliation: and she asked herself whether she ought to bear it" (Wood, 1872 [1891]: 201). The "sense of insult" expressed by the offended wife confirms the complexity of the anatomy of passions offered by Wood. The over-feeling women she portrays, which fall into two main groups, embody relevant aspects of the age's discourses on female affect; but they also question the essentializing approach of these discourses by giving clues to the social triggers of emotions that were instead assumed to be inborn in the female gender.

A first group of over-emotional heroines characterized by Wood consists of women like Lucy Andinnian and Anne Hereford (respectively analysed in Chapters 1 and 5), who manage to preserve a respectable status despite their affective excess. This type is partly reworked in *East Lynne*, where Isabel Vane keeps her refined manners after her fall and is redeemed by a reconversion of her sensual passions into strong maternal impulses. More distressful is another variation of the type exemplified by gentle female characters crushed by their efforts to silence their emotionality. Numerous in Wood's fiction, these women reveal with their sufferings the inflexibility of a normative system that forces them to stifle passions seldom connoted as improper in the texts. A telling example is Maria Godolphin featured in *The Shadow of Ashlydyat* (1863). Her painful efforts to repress spontaneous emotions like jealousy and rage are contrasted with the ebullient passions of Charlotte Pain who, though liable to social criticism, provides a thought-provoking model of emotional freedom.

The melodramatic devices used to characterize these feeling subjects are replaced by gothic paraphernalia in the characterization of a second group of women, who are driven to violence and crime by their impassionate personality. These characters, who are analysed later in this chapter, are further proof of the complexity of the author's representation of the Victorian female condition. On the one hand, their portrayals substantiate Victorian fears of unruliness that legitimized the social control of women's emotions. On the other hand, the violence they unleash upon their world unveils some socio-political and economic causes of hysteria which is not only configured as congenital, but is shown to be fuelled by a system that frustrates female desires. The ambiguous characterization of these fierce women sheds more light on Wood's subtle undermining of the ideologeme of female inborn emotionality. Besides disproving the idea of a "sedate" author too "reticent" about passions (Showalter, 1977: 158, 172), it suggests that Wood explored Victorian policies of containment of female affect and, by representing women's frustrated aspirations, unearthed some contradictions of a society that produced the negative passions it stigmatized.

Let us start our analysis with the first group of female figures which, though assailed by strong emotions, make efforts to keep them under control. At first glance, these figures reflect dominant assumptions. The mental and physical sufferings they experience owing to their affective excess validate Victorian beliefs in women's propensity to over-emotionality and the arguments in favour of parental surveillance and self-control offered in conduct books and advice manuals. What differs in Wood however is her rare demonization of female emotions, even when they lead to transgression. In contrast with didactic handbooks prescribing ladylike composure,[3] Wood seldom connotes her heroines' passions as irremediably sinful and, more importantly, she tends to arouse the readers' sympathy for impulsive erring women. With regard to class affiliation, it is noteworthy that the most distressful efforts to curb emotionality are made by characters belonging to the author's own class. With some exceptions, including the exemplary Charlotte East analysed in Chapter 5, Wood does not associate self-restraint with working-class women, most of whom are easy prey to instincts and desires. Immoderacy also prevails among her upper-class ladies, who tend to violate rules before learning to turn their overflowing emotions into self-redeeming impulses. It is instead among her bourgeois characters that self-restraining attitudes are shown to prevail, even though their consequences on the women's psyche and body are ominously depicted.

This bourgeois model of self-mastery owes much to the Ruskinian mythologizing of obedience as a social virtue entailing "the chastisement of the passions" which, though applicable to both sexes, is particularly recommended to women (Ruskin, 1849 [1903–12]: VIII.249). In Wood's narratives, obedience is eulogized by a number of upright middle-class heroines who struggle to suppress their overflowing emotions. The ordeal through which these women go is well rendered by the patient Griseldas analysed in the previous chapter. Another example is offered by the conduct of a minor character featured in *The Shadow of Ashlydyat*: Ethel Grame. In ways similar to Maria Godolphin, Ethel stifles her feelings to comply with other people's wishes. Patiently submitted to the capricious will of her selfish mother and sister, who treat her like a household servant, she sets their desires before her own and refuses to rush into marriage with the affluent Thomas Godolphin with whom she is engaged. Ethel's repression of her desires and emotions is an essential part of her notion of female obedience and submission to parental and marital guidance: "'You know, Thomas, so long as I am here in mamma's home, her child, it is to her that I owe obedience'" she explains to her fiancé, before promising: "'As soon as I shall be your wife, I shall owe it and give it implicitly to you'" (Wood, 1863a [n.d.]: 86). Never resentful or impatient, Ethel preserves her gentle manners while dealing with her capricious relatives and postpones her dreams of conjugal happiness to nurse her sister during a fever epidemic. In an ironic twist of the plot, however, she is unexpectedly infected and killed by the disease. In anticipation of Maria's self-induced illness narrated in a later episode, the fever Ethel contracts suggests that she is symbolically punished, rather than rewarded, for her intransigent self-restraint, which exposes her to contagion and death.

Only hinted at in Ethel Grame's brief tragedy, the distress caused by female self-repression is minutely rendered in other narratives, which confirm Wood's interest in the depths of female passion. Unlike many authors of domestic fiction, Wood portrays timid women assailed by strong emotions and sensual yearnings that they struggle to control and which, strikingly enough, never affect the purity of their conduct. A detailed scrutiny of this emotional excess is offered in *Lady Adelaide's Oath* (1867), where the shy Margaret Bordillion – "a delicately-looking woman of two or three and thirty" – falls utterly in love with "the gay and attractive George Lester" (Wood, 1867: I.197). Deluded by Lester's kind manners and by the strength of her own desire, Margaret falls prey to irresistible passions, which are described in an almost embarrassing crescendo of sensual details, such as the references to the "love [that] stirred within her at the gaze of him" or to her "wildly" beating heart (1867: I.202–203). Even stronger are the emotions to which she surrenders after learning about Lester's wedding with Adelaide Errol. Although she manages to control herself in the end, Margaret is physically overwhelmed by jealousy and rage, as suggested by the intensity of their somatic manifestations: "yet how subdue the agitation that gained upon her; how hide it? Her heart was beating in great thumps against her side; her face was white, her lips were dry" (1867: I.249). It is noteworthy, however, that Margaret is no sensation heroine. Her powerful emotionality does not affect her moral righteousness, which impels her to continue to look after Lester's children despite her bitter disappointment.

A similar anatomy of passions is found in *The House of Halliwell* (1890), which describes the "storm of despair" that shakes the sensitive Hester Halliwell after her fiancé, George Archer, abandons her for another woman (Wood, 1890 [1896]: 63). Her "wild desperation", her secret sobbing "when no eye could see" and her laying awake at night "battling with her unhappiness" (1890 [1896]: 63, 69) denote an emotional fervour strangely at odds with the self-composure she manifests to the world. Unorthodox is also the brief reawakening of her sentiments when her unfaithful fiancé reappears in her life as a married man some years later. Seriously ill and impoverished, Archer narrates to Hester his past misadventures and then kisses her hand "as fervently as he had kissed her own lips that night, years, years before" (1890 [1896]: 215). The kiss revives "a feeling, long buried, very like that forgotten *love*" in the woman who, after enjoying "a momentary sunshine on her heart", stifles the feeling by "laugh[ing] at herself for being a great simpleton" (1890 [1896]: 216). Apparently minor, this episode casts light on Wood's unconventional exploration of female feelings. Although she has learned to master her emotions, Hester temporarily yields to a desire for a married man that is inconceivable for respectable women. Yet, her rectitude seems unaffected by such moments of weakness: as shown in Chapter 1, the deep-feeling Hester develops into a wise and generous single woman who is the point of reference and the moral support of family and friends throughout the novel.

However varied their efforts and agonies, these impassioned but righteous women are not depicted as mere receptacles of unbridled feelings that necessitate external control. Their inner struggles configure them as desiring subjects who, rather than submitting to parental or conjugal guardianship, autonomously choose to manage their emotions. In many cases, moreover, their self-restraint is an excessive measure that unmasks some contradictions of Victorian normativity. This situation is well exemplified by Maria Godolphin, who is led to an untimely death by a disease engendered by self-repression. A similar process is described in *The Red Court Farm* (1868), in which Clara Lake dies of an illness caused by her mental torments. The wife of Robert Hunter, a careless man who has agreed to abandon his profession and live off on the Lakes' income, Clara is upset by her husband's fickleness, which becomes evident when he starts to flirt publicly with the attractive Lady Angeline Ellis. First haunted by a premonitory dream she interprets as a foreboding of her death (Wood, 1868b [1898]: 69), Clara is later assailed by jealousy and depression at watching the light-hearted conduct of her husband, who is overtly stigmatized as "[o]ne of those men who, wife or not wife, consider a flirtation with a pretty woman [...] a legitimate occupation in their idle life" (1868b [1898]: 101). In offering details of the woman's "wild jealousy" (1868b [1898]: 105), the narrator shows how her health is damaged by negative feelings. Even though she might be "predisposed" to consumption, an affliction that killed her mother and brother (1868b [1898]: 124), Clara is in fact crushed by the violent passions she strives to conceal from the world. A direct connection between illness and suppressed emotionality is drawn in the scene where she follows the two lovers and witnesses, unseen, to a "long and passionate kiss" between them in the garden (1868b [1898]: 111). Instead of giving vent to her rage, Clara stifles the emotions produced by this act of infidelity, but she develops an inflammation of the lungs immediately afterwards. Triggered by a cold caught during her espionage, her disease is accelerated by the painful images of the adulterous couple that keep haunting her mind. "[I]t was not precisely the way to get better" comments the narrator (1868b [1898]: 125), thereby offering a clue to the psychosomatic nature of her affliction. This interpretation is confirmed by a doctor who invalidates the suspicion of hereditary consumption and suggests that it is her mind that weighs upon her "healthy body": "'I cannot see why it should not have recovered; but the mind seemed to pull it backwards; two powers, one working against the other'" (1868b [1898]: 164).

The prolonged strife between body and mind is not relieved by Clara's late decision to reveal the source of her torments to her husband. Nor is she saved by his resolve to put an end to his flirtation. The second part of the novel opens with the laconic announcement of her death that happens off-stage: "Rushing through the streets of London, as if he were rushing for his life, went a gentleman in deep mourning. It was Robert Hunter" (1868b [1898]: 177). Instead of focussing on her passing away, the narrator situates the tragic event in a narrative gap between Parts 1 and 2 and, in opening the second part, brings the focus fully onto her mourning husband. The elliptical reference to her death is striking if we consider the central role that Clara plays in the first part of the novel. Her death gains meaning, however, if we analyse some polemical undertones of her self-induced disease. Particularly relevant is a narratorial comment on the woman's efforts to suppress her feelings after watching the adulterous kiss between Robert and Angeline:

> Clara Lake was not one of your loud women, who like their wrongs proclaimed to the world, and punished accordingly. In her sensitive reticence, she dreaded their betrayal more than any earthly thing. (1868b [1898]: 112)

Apparently orthodox in praising Clara's "sensitive reticence", the narrator seems to object to those "loud women" whom the reader is supposed to prefer. This conventional reading is however questioned by the painful details of the woman's sufferings provided in the following pages. By revealing the ominous effects that suppressed emotions may have on a healthy person, Wood attaches ironic connotations to the above-quoted comment. Betrayed by her husband, Clara is doubly victimized by her own decision to stifle her rage and leave her "wrongs" unproclaimed and unpunished. The negativity of her silence is confirmed by the marginality of her death. Deprived of the communicative energy of a "deathbed scene" which, in Peter Brooks's opinion, "stands as a key moment of summing-up and transmission" in Victorian literature (1984: 95), Clara can only speak somatically through her ailing body. Besides displaying the lethal consequences of her self-restraint, her long illness unveils the dangers inherent in a patriarchal system, which, as claimed by feminist theorists, justifies women's secondary social positions by containing them within frail, unruly bodies (Grosz, 1994: 13). Unlike those impassioned heroines who struggle with their emotions but manage to survive, Clara yields to an intense death wish, which progressively stifles her feelings. Her gradual renunciation to be a desiring subject during her illness becomes evident when Robert acknowledges his "passing folly" and asks for her forgiveness (Wood, 1868b [1898]: 166). Instead of responding emotionally, the ailing wife mentions her premonitory dream, a clear signifier of her self-destructive leanings (1868b [1898]: 168). By subduing all her feelings, Clara reveals the dangers of women's complicity with a system that encourages them to become socially 'invisible'. Her abrupt off-stage death is a symbolic warning against this kind of complicity, which condemns self-mortifying wives to be silently erased from the scene and rapidly replaced by other narrative actors.

As the examples above suggest, Wood attaches various meanings to the passions felt by sensitive women whose emotional freedom is often curbed by gender norms enforcing moderation and composure. A source of sufferings rendered in melodramatic details, female affect is also a means through which women are put to the test by the author, who connects the heroines' desiring impulses with their efforts (and, often, failures) to acquire more social autonomy. Heterogeneous in their personality and attitude, these heroines are generally portrayed as victims of their own psychophysical torments while the threat they pose to their family and social circles is shown to be slight.

More challenging is instead the function fulfilled by a second group of characters that manifest pathologized emotions, such as those emerging in hysteria and madness. In portraying women affected by various forms of insanity, Wood partly substantiates Victorian fears fuelled by the age's medical science, which defined female bodies as sites of instability that favoured mental disorders. Yet, she also questions these essentializing views by establishing thought-provoking links between these women's position of dependence and their propensity to commit violent actions.

Partly belonging to this second group of unruly women is Sibylla West, a controversial character of *Verner's Pride* (1863). Beautiful and capricious, Sibylla is ruled by two passions – "vanity and ambition" (Wood, 1863b [n.d.]: 91) – which make her pursue wealth and status through marriage. After a disastrous union with a man she loves, she manages to trap young Lionel Verner into a loveless match, which temporarily makes her the mistress of a grand local mansion. The couple's loss of privileges, which is consequent on a sensational chain of events, upsets Sibylla who becomes aggressive against her husband. Besides accusing him of a past crime, she holds him responsible for their socioeconomic fall and becomes pathologically jealous of his growing familiarity with young Lucy Tempest. Her hysterics turn into verbal aggression when she accuses Lucy and Lionel of adultery – an insult hurled with a violence that is also manifested somatically. "Body and mind were alike diseased", announces the narrator, before describing in a frightful crescendo Sibylla's growing inclination to be "cross, snappish, fretful", her tendency to fall into a "state of perfect fury", her frequent loss of temper and "wild fancies", and the bursting forth of her "pent-up anger" that makes her cheeks flame (1863b [n.d.]: 558, 561, 574). Unable to keep her excitement under control, Sibylla experiences the breaking of a blood vessel during a strife with Lionel who sees her suddenly "[lie] back gasping, the blood pouring from her mouth" (1863b [n.d.]: 565). Besides being a danger to herself, she comes to be perceived as a potential madwoman by her family and friends who progressively share the opinion held by Lionel's brother Jan, a young surgeon concerned over Sibylla's physical and mental health. "'I think you must be mad, Sibylla'", exclaims her husband, whose adoption of his medical brother's view is thus commented by the narrator: "The words Jan had used. If such temperaments do not deserve the name of madness, they are near akin to it" (1863b [n.d.]: 575).

Increasingly labelled as mentally unstable, Sibylla reaches a state of frenzy at a ball she joins despite the doctors' prohibitions. "'She is mad!'" exclaims Jan who is present at the party and overtly criticizes her disregard of medical instructions. Thin and wan because of a consumptive disease that is partly hereditary, partly self-induced, Sibylla resents being watched with pity and performs a last rebellious action: she launches into a frantic dance, "whirling round at a mad speed" until "a fit of coughing of unnatural violence" causes a new breaking of her blood vessel (1863b [n.d.]: 597–598). The fatal event, which leads her to a premature death, is repeatedly associated with her supposed mental unbalance. Explicitly mentioned by some characters – "'I always said there were moments when Sibylla's mind was not right', composedly observed John Massingbird" (1863b [n.d.]: 601) – insanity is also implied by her discomposed behaviour on her deathbed, as she strongly denies the inevitability of her fate and rejects a cooling drink by jerking her head away and spilling it (1863b [n.d.]: 603).

Still, these apparent symptoms of folly do not solve some puzzling elements of her characterization. Repeatedly associated with something "near akin to insanity", Sibylla is undoubtedly a hot-tempered woman whose lack of restraint is biologically inscribed in her highly sexual appearance (Mangham, 2007: 160ff). Yet, she is never officially diagnosed as mad by the novel's doctors, whose fretful judgments bring into question their professional reliability. Although she manifests signs of hysteria,[4] she is not the only unbalanced character featured in *Verner's Pride*. Before their wedding, Lionel himself is affected by a long, essentially feminine psychosomatic illness which confounds gender markers.[5] What is more, Wood connects Sibylla's growing embitterment with an external factor – her unexpected loss of wealth and status – that makes her repent her mercenary marriage. Morally questionable though it is, Sibylla's rage is an understandable response to the frustration of her selfish interests, baffled by adverse circumstances. A spoiled beauty rather than a deranged woman, Sibylla blurs the borders between morality and disease with her upsetting conduct, which casts a shadow onto the pathologization of female rebellion inherent in Victorian practices of moral management. The questions she poses are similar to those brought up in Braddon's *Lady Audley's Secret* (1862), whose eponymous heroine defies interpretation with her presumed but partly disproved insanity.[6]

Another thought-provoking aspect of Sibylla's portrayal is her taste for beauty and pleasures. Before developing her consumptive illness, the woman spends considerable time and money in the purchase of elegant clothes. Like the vain Selina Dalrymple in *Court Netherleigh* (1881), Sibylla behaves like a desiring subject that uses her shopping mania to escape her husband's control in two ways: by purchasing luxury items without his permission and by using these ornaments to be admired by other men in "innocent flirtations" (Wood, 1863b [n.d.]: 332). Considering this, her stubborn wish to participate in the fatal ball and be publicly admired is in line with her previous attempts to gain material pleasures and compliments. Driven by a burning energy that makes her deny the seriousness of her disease, she strives to beautify her wasting body by wearing ornaments that make her appear as a "bedecked skeleton" "in fairy attire", a dressed-up "ghost" and a "corpse bedizened with jewels" (1863b [n.d.]: 580, 583, 595). Grotesque and pitiful, these images evoke the gothic representation of Adeline de Castella's body exhibited at "the reception of the dead" in the eponymous tale (1855) and, later, in *St Martin's Eve* (1866). On close examination, however, it is possible to detect significant differences between the two episodes. While Adeline's beautifully attired corpse is a symbol of her passive submission to male decisions, Sibylla resists her victimization by making a last attempt to fulfil her desires. If it is true that her vanity is mortified by her ghastly appearance, it is also true that her last frenzied dance is an act of rebellion against social and medical prescriptions. This reading is validated by the fairy-tale intertextuality of the two novels, which are both strongly evocative of "Snow White". In ways similar to the eponymous heroine of the Brothers Grimm's tale, Adeline is a young woman victimized by adults, whose power continues to be exercised voyeuristically on her dead body. More ambiguous is instead the feminine model offered by Sibylla, who combines the cruel vanity and the decisional autonomy of the wicked stepmother[7] with Snow White's unconscious wish to be sexually attractive (Bettelheim, 1976 [1991]: 212). Although she is finally killed by her desires, Sibylla remains a potentially threatening figure as she strenuously resists against a system that aims to control her conduct and to define her sanity.

Defiant and vulnerable, exuberant and opportunistic, Sibylla West reveals the complexity of the novel's investigation of women's passions, which puzzlingly combines sociological considerations with notions drawn from the age's nascent psychiatry. Similarly rife with contradictions but more gloomily tinged is the characterization of some murderesses who play a central role in other Wood narratives. The ominous deeds committed by these women, who are driven to violence and crime by their intemperate nature, are partly explained by the symptoms of hysteria and mental derangement they display. There are, however, in their stories disquieting references to the influence exerted by contextual factors, which somehow challenge a purely medical interpretation.

As is well known, the Victorian gendering of insanity drew

scientific validation from medical hypotheses about women's biological vulnerability, which were inherited and further developed by Sigmund Freud. While madmen were presumed to suffer from an English malady produced by "intellectual and economic pressures", the female malady was specifically "associated with the sexuality and essential nature of women": "Women were believed to be more vulnerable to insanity than men, to experience it in specifically feminine ways, and to be differently affected by it in the conduct of their lives" (Showalter, 1985: 7). The period's constructions of hysteria confirm this approach. Etymologically derived from the Greek "uterus", "hysteria" became a catchall word for a wide range of psychic manifestations predominantly connected with the biological phases of women's lives. As gynaecologist Lawson Tait wrote in *Diseases of Women* (1877), adolescence was a dangerous phase of transition in which women of all classes could develop a "dormant tendency to mental disease": "I have several times seen girls so afflicted indulge in gestures and language which puzzled us to guess how the patients became acquainted with them, the girls were so young and had been so well brought up" (1877: 147). Criminal cases amply discussed in the press, such as the Road Hill House Murder (1860),[8] contributed to validating such medical theorizations and to inspiring narratives of pubescent women's assaults against the sanctity of the home.

Another alleged cause of female fury was sexual desire.[9] Journalistic accounts and literary versions of notorious murder cases, such as the 1857 trial of Madeleine Smith who was accused of poisoning her lover, show the extent to which medical and moral suppositions came to influence the legal approach to crimes triggered by female sexual appetites. Frustrated desire was equally believed to engender mental disorders, as evidenced by the century's tendency to represent spinsters as strange and mischief-making. All women, moreover, were deemed as liable to develop insanity during their menopause, which was conceived as a phase of worrying alterations in their personality. In Charles Dickens's *Great Expectations* (1861), both cases are exemplified by Miss Havisham, whose revengeful plot against men is connected with a mental instability produced by aging and frustrated love.

During their fertile stage, however, women were not immune to other risks. In addition to the dangers associated to adolescence and sexual desire, Victorian medical experts conceived the reproductive process itself as potentially destabilizing, and they classified different kinds of maternal manias. If pregnancy "was assumed to be imbued with [risks of violence]" by eminent psychiatrists like Jean-Étienne Dominique Esquirol, the puerperal state was believed to place a dangerous strain on women, and motherhood in general was viewed as an experience that could unsettle women's psychophysical balance (Mangham, 2007: 23–34). Fears of maternal violence were increased by the practice of baby farming that rose during the century, as well as by the high rate of child murders reported in the press. Although they were thought to prevail among the poverty-stricken, who were distressed by economic needs and problems of overpopulation (McDonagh, 2003: 97–104), these murders were also associated with forms of female insanity that transcended class borders. Crimes perpetrated within the family struck the imagination of popular novelists, who gave voice to circulating fears by portraying a host of biological and surrogate mothers charged with killing newborns or children. Recurrent, among these figures, are distressed unmarried mothers who commit infanticides, unfeeling stepmothers who endanger their husbands' offspring and careless nurses who are instrumental to the death of children entrusted to their care.

Closely connected with women's reproductive functions was also the problem of inheritance. Being a mother implied the possibility of transmitting disease, of passing onto one's children a vulnerability that would affect their mental and physical health. Although the Victorians did not exclude the transmission of various disorders through paternal lines, the medical literature of the time shows that "it was widely understood that mothers were more likely to bequeath insanity" (Mangham, 2007: 35). Daughters, in particular, were assumed to get madness from their mothers through female heredity lines that substantiated gender determinism.

The combined effects of medical theories and crime reports generated growing anxieties over female insanity. Reverberations of these anxieties are often found in Victorian literature, which offers various depictions of women driven to aggressiveness by inherited or developed impulses they are unable to control. In *Jane Eyre* (1847), for example, the fierce characterization of Bertha Mason threateningly combines racial prejudices with gendered views of hereditary madness. Some years later, sensation novelists drew largely on these anxieties. Besides responding to contemporary socio-medical concerns, these novelists used female violence both as a strategy to whet their readers' appetites for sensationalism and as a means to explore other sources of the phenomenon. In *Lady Audley's Secret*, notably, Braddon electrifies her readership with the portrayal of a potentially insane, fiendish beauty; but she also connects the heroine's loss of self-control with the socioeconomic threats posed to her life by the unexpected return of her first husband. Similarly, Wilkie Collins blends monomania with social determinism in *Man and Wife* (1870), when he describes the premeditated murder of a brutal husband by an oppressed low-class wife.

Female wild behaviour is similarly functionalized in Wood's oeuvre. Often used as a sensational device, it is attributed to a variety of factors rather than described in exclusively psychopathological terms. This complexity is most evident in *St Martin's Eve*, which pivots around different manifestations of female immoderacy. A combination of two early stories elaborated and merged together,[10] *St Martin's Eve* is equally composite in its treatment of female passions, ranging from simple emotionality to paroxysm, as well as of the consequences of women's lack of restraint, which reach their climax in a brutal episode of child murder. The latter crime is committed by the fascinating Charlotte St. John, née Norris, one of the novel's protagonists who perturbingly conflates ideas of female violence, insanity and victimization. A dark beauty with "raven-black hair" and "pale, regular features", Charlotte lacks the ideal qualities of Victorian marriageable heroines, but she is nonetheless considered a potentially good wife by two men of the St. John family, who are attracted by her "imperious, regal, haughty" appearance (Wood, 1866b [1893]: 7).

Early in the novel, her physical endowments make a strong impression on the widowed George Carleton St. John, who marries her one year after losing his first wife. Vainly opposed by her mother, whose secret motive is revealed much later in the novel, their union wreaks havoc on St. John's household. After giving birth to a little boy called Georgy, Charlotte develops a growing hostility toward her stepson, Benja who, in her view, attracts all his father's attentions. Her mounting rage results in verbal and physical aggressions against Benja. In one episode, for example, she strikes the boy with a violent blow before accusing St. John of being partial in his affections. The "strange, wild look" that appears on her face on this occasion is perceived as a potential sign of "madness" by her husband who is "too much scared, too terrified" by the sight (1866b [1893]: 44). But the spectre of insanity is partly neutralized by a description of St. John's attitude focalized through Charlotte:

> She had seen it all; the loving meeting with the one child, the neglect of the other. Passion, anger, jealousy, waged war within her. She could no more have controlled them than she could control the wind that was making free with her husband's hair. All she saw, all she felt, was that he had betrayed his ardent love for Benja, his indifference to *her* child. In that one moment she was as a mad woman. (1866b [1893]: 43)

Although they are excessive, the negative emotions that temporarily overcome Charlotte stem from her husband's disparity of treatment of the two children, as well as by his growing indifference to *her*, implied by the italicized possessive. The incipient mental disorder suggested by the adjective "mad" is here counterbalanced by the frustrating effects of the scene she observes from an open window, which is never said to be a delusive sight.

In subsequent pages, the narrator confirms the idea of St. John's responsibility for his domestic troubles. Assailed by remorse for forgetting his dead wife too soon and for ignoring her requests to find a good mother for their son,[11] he makes various mistakes in his second marriage, including his prolonged sojourns away from home to escape his difficult family life:

> Mr. Carleton St. John spent more time in London than was absolutely demanded by his parliamentary duties, frequently remaining there when the House was not sitting; and during his sojournings at the Hall, it seems that he never wanted an excuse for being away from home. [...] What his wife thought of these frequent absences cannot be told. A dark cloud often sat upon her brow, but things went on smoothly between them, so far as the servants knew. (1866b [1893]: 46)

Reticent and vague though it is, the narrator's comment on St. John's conduct reveals the frustrating effects it has on Charlotte who resents her husband's gradual estrangement. A second error is made by the man when he realizes that he is doomed to die prematurely of an inherited complaint. Worried about Benja's safety and rights, he adds a vexatious codicil to his will in which he leaves his estate to his firstborn and entitles Charlotte to remain as long as she acts as the boy's guardian. Instead of protecting Benja, however, the codicil paves the way to his destruction as it stirs more negative feelings in the dispossessed widow. Upset by what she defines "an infamous will" (1866b [1893]: 78), Charlotte strives to find consolation in the affection for Georgy, which becomes an all-absorbing passion "threatening to consume every healthy impulse" (1866b [1893]: 126).

A distorted version of maternal love, Charlotte's passion is not only described as an unquenchable inborn drive; it is also shown to stem from the loneliness of her widowed condition as well as from the sense of wrong she feels in living in her home as a guest. The frustration produced by the codicil repeats the negative experience made by Charlotte's mother at the death of her first husband, whose residence is inherited by a male heir of the family. "But ere she had well realized her position as a wife of a wealthy man, the mistress of a place so charming as Norris Court; almost ere her baby was born, Mr. Norris died, and the whole thing seemed to pass from her as a dream" (1866b [1893]: 24). In ways similar to Mrs. Norris, whose loss of Norris Court raises the question of "the intangibility of landed property for women" (Wynne, 2001a: 91), Charlotte is deprived of any control over her place of residence by a legal system that favours male primogeniture. What is more, despite her "indignation" and her perception of Benja "as a usurper", Charlotte initially manifests good intentions towards her stepson: "She deliberately intended to do right: but passion and prejudice are strong; unusually strong were they in her; and her mind was undisciplined and ill-regulated" (Wood, 1866b [1893]: 128). The narrator's reference to the inner strife between her well-meaning attitude and her emotional weakness partly absolves the woman from the responsibility of the terrible crime she commits a few pages later, when she locks the door of Benja's room during a fire, thus condemning him to an atrocious death.

By suggesting that Charlotte's impassioned nature is unrestrained by her defective education[12] and exacerbated by economic problems, Wood somewhat tempers the fiercest connotations of her murderous action. More sympathy for the character is aroused by her misadventures following Benja's murder. Oppressed by a sense of guilt that makes her look suspicious, Charlotte wanders throughout Europe with Georgy, unable to find rest and increasingly concerned over her son's wasting away.[13] The detailed references to the "torture" of her "troubled spirit", reinforced by somatic depictions of her torments – "her beautiful cheeks were haggard and crimson, her eyes had a wasting fire in them" – make her appear more as a victim than as a heartless villainess (1866b [1893]: 234, 238). The climax of her afflictions is reached with the premature loss of her son during their forced exile. Deprived of "the greatest treasure earth ever gave" her (1866b [1893]: 39–40), Charlotte also experiences the definitive loss of her landed property which, in the absence of direct male heirs, is inherited by the affluent Isaac St. John. Back in England, Charlotte is impelled to live on the generosity of Isaac who, attracted by her beauty, feels he has "committed a wrong" on her "by succeeding to the property" (1866b [1893]: 378). By emphasizing the limited rights of women in a society that privileges male inheritance, the author adds more weight to the "sympathy" for the anti-heroine aroused by her displayed sufferings – a sympathy that, in Wood's oeuvre, often "contradicts the overt moral message of the text" (Pykett, 1994: 66; 2004: xviii). As in *East Lynne*, in *St. Martin's Eve* a sinful woman goes through severe afflictions that make the reader feel strongly for her. Like Isabel Vane, moreover, Charlotte St. John is partly redeemed by her maternal role. A "demonic mother" to her stepson, whose murder reflects contemporary medical anxieties about "the impact of maternity on the female mind and body", Charlotte simultaneously incarnates a sacred Victorian ideal as she plays the role of a doting mother who loves her biological son "to excess" (Shuttleworth, 1992: 45). The contrast between the two maternal images is widened by her tragic loss of Georgy, to which she responds paroxysmally: "For a day or two, Mrs. St. John was almost unnaturally calm, but the second night, at midnight, her cries of despair aroused the house, and a violent scene came on" (Wood, 1866b [1893]: 327). Although it evokes the spectre of madness, Charlotte's nocturnal outburst of despair is also a melodramatic device that elicits sympathy for the bereaved mother, humanized by her heart-rending cries.

Drawing on her personal experience,[14] Wood created a picture of maternal distress that was supposed to mollify her female readers in an age marked by high rates of infant and child mortality. Despite the horrifying details of Benja's death, the characterization of his murderess evidences contradictions that confound the novel's moral message. Portrayed as a doting mother driven to crime by a combination of psychological and economic factors, Charlotte is partly a villainess, partly a victim. By killing a boy on whom she depends financially, she reveals the vulnerability of her condition within a system that denied women economic and social autonomy.

Equally rife with contradictions is the question of Charlotte's alleged madness developed on her return to England. Hosted by Isaac St. John, whom she seems willing to marry, she gradually recovers from her bereaved state: "In health she was perfectly well; all that dark time seemed to have passed away as a dream: she was better-looking than ever, and the inward fever that used to consume her and render her a very shadow, did not waste her now" (1866b [1893]: 378). Yet, the quiet of her new condition is marred by the presence of three people who somehow involve her in antagonistic relations: young Georgina Beauclerc, whom she sees as a rival in Isaac's affections; nurse Honour, who had previously accused her of Benja's murder and is now in service in Isaac's household; and Frederick St. John, who suspects her of madness and wishes to prevent her marriage with his stepbrother. Although they are unwilling antagonists, Georgina and Honour inspire anger and fear in Charlotte, who yields to temporary acts of violence that are first self-injuring[15] and later performed against the two women. In a gothic episode set outdoors at night, a dark-attired figure waiting in ambush for Georgina is scared away by

Frederick, who claims to have recognized Charlotte's features in the attacker (1866b [1893]: 429). A later episode describes Charlotte's aggression towards Honour. Stressed by people's suspicions, Charlotte locks herself up in her room to find some relief, but she is persecuted by relatives and acquaintances, who threaten to break the door open. When she finally comes out she has a paroxysmal crisis at the view of Honour, who reminds her of her past guilt, and she pounces upon the servant whom she bruises on her arms and bites on her cheek (1866b [1893]: 446).[16] The violence of the aggression, described as "a fight for dear life" (1866b [1893]: 446), connotes her as insane and paves the way to her permanent reclusion into an asylum with "*no* hope of her restoration" (1866b [1893]: 458). It is remarkable, however, that in narrating Charlotte's unladylike assault, Wood tries to explain the rationale behind her act and uses exclamations to arouse the reader's sympathy:

> Poor lady! What her thoughts had been during that self-imprisonment she alone knew. That they had tended rapidly to increase the mind's confusion, to speed her on to the great gulf of insanity, already so near at hand, perhaps to have been its very turning-point, there could be no doubt of. And it may be that the sight of Honour amidst her enemies, of Honour bearing a lighted candle, recalled her mind to that dreadful night not yet two years gone by. (1866b [1893]: 446)

Although she becomes insane in the end, Charlotte is partly excused for her aggression towards Honour, whose bearing a candle reawakens her remorse for Benja's death.

Benja's murder is described as not entirely her responsibility by her faithful servant Prance, who claims that her mistress "did not purposely set him on fire", that she is "not naturally cruel" but liable to "uncontrollable attacks", and that she committed the deed under the influence of "too much wine" (1866b [1893]: 450). Prance's confession, made when Charlotte is irremediably labelled as mad, casts doubt on the general interpretation of her mistress as incontestably insane and dangerous for the community. Further perplexities are aroused by Frederick St. John's conduct. In ways similar to Robert Audley, who in Braddon's *Lady Audley's Secret* spies on his aunt and conspires with a doctor to prove her insanity, Frederick obsessively watches Charlotte for signs of lunacy, becomes an amateur detective to find clues to her madness, and makes pressures on doctor Pym to reveal a family secret of Charlotte's: the mental disorder that killed her father, which the doctor fears might affect Charlotte herself. While Pym wavers in his convictions, however, Frederick wishes the woman to become mad and, through his persecution, he becomes instrumental to her derangement. The fact that Charlotte ultimately fulfils the two men's expectations casts a shadow on the reality of her disorder and, as Mangham claims, confirms "the text's dissent from the idea that female biology predisposed all women to the onset of aggressive mania" (2007: 77).

Further elements of confusion are the fact that Charlotte is supposed to have inherited her father's lunacy (a prospect that contrasts with Victorian expectations of female-to-female lines of heredity), and the vague clues to Frederick's own mental unbalance disseminated in the text.[17] Male propensity to mental disorders is indeed a recurrent topic in Wood's oeuvre. In addition to Frederick St. John, other men she portrays display symptoms of insanity or, more generally, of a mental weakness that makes them yield to destructive or self-destructive impulses. A sufficient example is the aforementioned tendency towards hysteria shown by Lionel Verner in *Verner's Pride*, the madness Adam Andinnian is supposed to have inherited from his mother in *Within the Maze*, the various forms of mental disturbance manifested by male characters in *Lady Adelaide's Oath*[18] and the almost comic mania that affects Captain Kerleton in *The House of Halliwell*, in which the apparently respectable officer makes compulsive marriage proposals as a consequence of an old injury: "*Captain Kerleton was a lunatic.* Some years previously, when in India, he had met with an accident which caused concussion of the brain, and he had never entirely recovered his intellect" (Wood, 1890 [1896]: 164). Congenital, inherited or induced by events, these disorders counterbalance dominant gender views, as they offer a varied picture of male psychic weakness that raises doubts about the age's construction of the "female malady".

In *St. Martin's Eve*, the idea of a daughter inheriting her madness from her father has similar disruptive effects. Without ever denying the reality of Charlotte's fall into insanity in the novel's conclusion, Wood uses camouflage strategies to contest the gendered biological determinism of her age. By showing that her anti-heroine's hysteria is progressively induced by social mechanisms, the author raises issues that would be explored and theorized by feminists one century later. A victim of socioeconomic inequalities, which she cannot question without upsetting the social order (Irigaray, 1977 [1985]: 185), Charlotte is also driven to hysteria by the strictures of a maternal role that prevents her from fulfilling her desires. The (female) reader's identification with the anti-heroine is also favoured by a crucial change Wood made to the novel: the deletion of a reference to a fierce case of domestic pyromania reported in *The Times* in 1845, which is evoked in the short version of "St. Martin's Eve" published in the *New Monthly Magazine* in 1853. The original story lays stress on Charlotte's cruelty by describing how the woman holds Benja in the fire untouched by his entreaties. A different impression is instead created by the novel's mention of the murderess's distance from the victim (Charlotte only locks the door) as well as by her haunting remorse (Mangham, 2007: 1–2, 72–73).

A woman of good social standing afflicted by maternal excess and hysteria, Charlotte St. John challenges dominant models of womanhood whose composure and self-control were assumed to guarantee social order.[19] Subject to a normativity that disempowers women at different levels, Charlotte is proof of the author's wish to explore the contradictions inherent in female desire. In addition to portraying gentlewomen driven to excess by frustrated aspirations, Wood suggests that similar emotions can rise in women belonging to all classes. In *Mrs. Halliburton's Troubles* (1862), for example, the author characterizes a governess, Bianca Varsini, who mistakenly kills the family's firstborn as an act of revenge against her deceitful lover. A liminal figure both socially and ethnically, Bianca commits her murder driven by frustrated yearnings for love and recognition which, as shown in Chapter 5, seem to offer a partial justification for her conduct.

Female sexual desire is also the trigger of violence in "The Mystery at Number Seven", a long tale divided in two stories: "Montpellier-by-Sea" and "Owen, the Milkman". First published in *The Argosy* in January-February 1877 and later collected in the sixth *Johnny Ludlow* series that appeared posthumously (1899), "The Mystery at Number Seven" is a sensational story of murder, mystery and detection that involves two housemaids, Jane Cross and Matilda Valentine, respectively in the roles of victim and murderess. Initially set in a coastal village and later in London, this long narrative combines domestic elements with the paraphernalia of a crime story. A sudden shift from the initial picture of provincial life is experienced when Jane is found dead in the home where she is employed, allegedly killed by a fall down the well of the staircase. Physical evidence of a fight, found on the girl's corpse and on the crime scene, makes the investigators conclude that Jane was not a victim of an accidental fall, but was murdered by someone present in the building. The police investigation and the inquest lead to no result. It is only in the conclusion that the apparently unsolvable whodunit ceases to be a mystery. The amateurish investigation of young Thomas Owen, and a fatal encounter – what the narrator calls the "thread of destiny" (Wood, 1899 [1901]: 48) – pave the way to the unmasking of the real culprit: Matilda. Confronted by Owen, who implicitly charges her with the crime, the young murderess experiences "a fit of passion" that turns her into "an insane woman", "her ravings interspersed with lucid intervals" during one of which "she disclose[s] the truth" (1899 [1901]: 50). The tale closes with Matilda's reclusion into an asylum, "likely to remain there for life" (1899 [1901]: 53).

The violent deed committed by Matilda is attributed to two main causes: her inherited fits of passion and her love for Owen, which turns into jealousy when he starts flirting with Jane. The spectre of hereditary madness, evoked late in the narration, is significantly combined with ethnic and gender prejudices in line with Victorian assumptions. Owen discovers that Matilda's mother was "a Spanish woman [...] of a wild, ungovernable temper, subject to fits of frenzy" (1899 [1901]: 46) that her daughter seems to have inherited. The question of madness is however left open to interpretation, as the fits that assail both the mother and the daughter "occur at rare intervals" and are followed by long periods of sanity. Matilda herself is supposed to have killed Jane during one of her crises, followed by a rapid sobering of her passion in which "her brain hastily concocted the plan she should adopt" (1899 [1901]: 52). The long-time success of her plan demonstrates the rationality of her actions, thereby challenging her depiction as an impulsive creature. Another element that raises doubts about the diagnosis of her insanity is the jealousy she feels as a result of her beloved's fickleness. In addition to flirting with both housemaids, Owen later becomes engaged to Matilda's cousin and provokes the murderess's collapse by announcing that he is going to get married. His insensitivity is contrasted with the pain felt by Matilda, with whom the narrator seems to sympathize: "If she had in truth loved Thomas Owen, if she loved him still, the announcement must have caused her cruel pain" (1899 [1901]: 50). Pity for the woman's suffering is also aroused by references to some bullying actions performed by Jane and other servants who, on two different occasions, mock Matilda for drafting a love letter to Owen (1899 [1901]: 36–37, 51). Persecuted by her social peers and afflicted by a remorse for her murder that gradually undermines her health, Matilda is partly turned into a victim by the narrator who repeatedly manifests his compassion for the "poor" housemaid: "Matilda was to be pitied"; "In my heart I could not help being sorry for her" (1899 [1901]: 34, 53, 27, 38). The cruelty of her fate is increased by her final incarceration as a madwoman, ironically juxtaposed with Owen's conjugal bliss: "Matilda Valentine is in an asylum, and likely to remain there for life; whilst Thomas Owen and his wife flourish in sunshine, happy as a summer day is long" (1899 [1901]: 53). Although they are gratified by the solution of the crime mystery, readers are left with a sense of bitterness for the unhappy destiny faced by Matilda who, far from being a cold-blooded murderess, appears as an "excellent servant" (1899 [1901]: 40) provoked to act violently by a combination of hereditary and circumstantial factors.

A different blend of hysteria, domestic murder and low-class female agency is offered in the short story "Hester Reed's Pills" and its sequel "Abel Crew" which, first serialized in *The Argosy* between August and September 1874, were later collected in the second series of the Johnny Ludlow stories (1880). What the two tales narrate is the mysterious poisoning of two baby girls who die after being administered pain-relief pills by their mother, Hester Reed. Their tragic death is followed by an investigation during which suspicions fall on Abel Crew, the herbalist who prepared the pills. Unable to prove his innocence, Crew is about to be condemned when a woman of the community, Ann Dovey, confesses to her husband that she might have been unwillingly responsible for the poisoning as she was carrying an anti-beetle powder in her gown-pocket. This prospect is cancelled by a final twist of the plot, which discloses that the babies' death was provoked by an unintentional exchange of pills made by a relative of their mother's, Cathy Reed.

Although it is proved to be accidental, the poisoning is

insistently associated with female figures. If Hester is initially suspected of having killed her own babies inadvertently, the roles played by Ann and Cathy are proof of the age's tendency to connect poisonous substances with women. A similar link is evoked by the imputation of the alleged crime to Abel Crew, who is feminized by his domestic leanings[20] and by his marginal status as a stranger of unknown origins: "Who he was, or what he was, or why he had come, or why he stayed, nobody knew" (Wood, 1880b [1905]: 42). Unlike Crew and the three women, the community men of all ranks act as investigators, judges and censors of the supposed crime. The gendered construction of the supposed poisoner is reinforced by the hysterical behaviour of Ann Dovey when she fears to be charged with murder: "She flung herself on the sofa when she saw us [...] and began to scream" (Wood, 1880a [1905]: 66). By conflating two dangerous aspects of femininity together, the author evokes circulating fears concerning domestic murderesses who, often driven by insanity, became the protagonists of notorious cases sensationalized in the Victorian press.[21]

With subtle irony, however, Wood challenges these very prejudices by concocting an unexpected solution for the crime that is discovered to be a "fatal mistake" (1880a [1905]: 74). Although the person responsible for the exchange of pills is a woman, her gendered status has little relevance to the chain of events leading to the babies' poisoning. By evoking expectations that are finally disproved by events, Wood obliquely hints at the limits of Victorian associations of domestic crime, and of poisoning in particular, with a female inborn disposition to violence. At the end of the sequel, the accidental death of the babies does not symbolize the potential dangers that women are supposed to pose to their homes and society. It is rather shown to be the unlucky result of fatal circumstances, while all the female suspects, including the feminized Abel Crew, prove to be honest, caring and well-meaning.

The final absolution of the suspects in the two short stories is one of the strategies Wood adopted to raise doubts about the Victorian stigmatization of female impulsiveness. Other characters examined above confirm that many impassioned women featured in her oeuvre are not tainted with immorality; they are rather encouraged to unleash their emotions, which, if stubbornly stifled, can dangerously affect their health. Even more provocative is Wood's characterization of women prone to hysteria and insanity. Although some of them commit terrible deeds, their mental disorders are never essentialized. Dominant medical presumptions are counterbalanced by detailed descriptions of the social constraints and adverse circumstances that affect these women's balance, turning them into objects of pity rather than loathing.

CHAPTER 4

The transgressive lady and the failings of patriarchy

Born into a family of entrepreneurs and married to a businessman, Ellen Wood came to embody two conflicting middle-class ideals in her adult life. The image of respectable matron she offered to the public was partly at odds with her successful literary career which, though increasingly tolerated during the century, jarred with the ideologeme of the separate spheres. The efforts made to reconcile domesticity with professionalism must have increased her awareness of the contradictions inherent in the middle-class gendering of roles, which she brought to the fore by representing the pitfalls of married life and the rigidness of social standards with which women had to comply. Although her loyalties lay with the Victorian bourgeoisie, Wood was not an uncritical champion of her class. Her fiction evidences her convinced celebration of bourgeois values such as self-help and perseverance, but it also exposes the strictures of a normative system that curbed women's wishes for happiness and self-development.

A similar complexity is found in her portrayal of upper-class people, especially women. Wood undoubtedly shared middle-class prejudices against the supposed parasitic leanings, the arrogance and the immoral proclivity of Victorian aristocrats, who were being superseded in their leading roles by the rising echelons of the bourgeoisie. Most women of gentle birth featured in her oeuvre bear evidence of these prejudices. Leisure-seeking, impassioned and inclined to transgress, these figures are generally depicted as the spoiled members of a class affected by moral and behavioural laxity. Yet, Wood generally avoids stigmatizing high-ranking women as irremediably sinful. What their characterization reveals is the author's wish to explore the troubles these women experienced at a time of unprecedented social mobility and changing behavioural norms.

A number of aristocratic women drawn by Wood are forced to marry below their rank by economic pressures. These characters face even greater challenges than those met by bourgeois heroines, as the more indulgent habits learned in their family of origin contrast with the stricter rules enforced by the new class they enter. By describing their efforts (and mainly failures) to perform successful domestic roles, Wood adds new perspectives to the reconsideration of the true yearnings of womanhood she encourages in her oeuvre.

Another effect produced by the agency of these downwardly mobile women is that of unveiling the failings of patriarchy across classes. Often compelled to enter mercenary marriages by the flawed conduct of their fathers, who incarnate aristocratic greed, improvidence and ambition, these women are in most cases disappointed by their husbands, who betray their expectations of a better life. Even when their partners are endowed with admirable qualities, their matches are marred by tensions and misunderstandings. A recurrent source of conjugal problems is the tendency of bourgeois men to give precedence to their professional occupations over their domestic duties. In some cases, this tendency has tragic outcomes for their marriage and family life. In other cases, a solution to domestic conflicts is found through a strengthening of traditional gender roles which, however, fails to dissolve the sense of frustrated female yearnings. If most male aristocrats combine tyrannical wills with symptoms of degeneracy, which include sexual licence and debauchery, bourgeois men waver among conflicting models of masculinity which they seldom manage to reconcile into a new convincing ideal. As shown in Chapter 1, Wood draws some compelling portrayals of aristocratic and bourgeois men who exhibit innovative traits, such as the reformed Lord Temple in *Danesbury House* (1860), the forbearing protagonist of *Verner's Pride* (1863), and the patient Francis Grubb in *Court Netherleigh* (1881). These portrayals suggest that the author wished to develop alternative models of being an ideal husband that might combine gentleness with resolution, domestic with public virtues. Still, there are in their characterization some elements that prevent them from being ideal mates for their women, who go through sufferings or have to relinquish their aspirations before achieving a relational balance. Furthermore, the promising role fulfilled by these characters is overshadowed by the agency of patriarchal figures belonging to both classes, such as upper-class tyrants and hard-hearted professionals, who generate tensions and despondency with their inflexible, authoritative conduct.

The best-known lady portrayed by Wood is Isabel Vane, the protagonist of the bestselling novel *East Lynne* (1861). The daughter of the spendthrift William Vane, Earl of Mount Severn, Isabel first appears on the scene as a young woman endowed "with a beauty that is rarely seen", whose sweet and delicate expression, mingled with a "sad, sorrowful look", captivates the ambitious lawyer Archibald Carlyle (Wood, 1861 [2000]: 49). After losing her home, purchased by Carlyle, she experiences the sudden death of her father, who leaves her destitute of any means. Her gratitude for Carlyle, who behaves affectionately to her, and the anxiety over her future convince the heroine to accept the lawyer's marriage proposal. Though attracted by the pleasure-seeking Captain Francis Levison, Isabel opts for the union with a wealthy man she respects and admires, but does not love. Her mercenary marriage soon proves to be a mismatch. Oppressed by Carlyle's domineering half-sister, Cornelia, a pragmatic middle-class woman who becomes "the bane of [their] household" (1861 [2000]: 236), she comes to resent her husband's professional occupations, which absorb most of his time and attentions. Owing to "her refined manners and her timid and sensitive temperament", Isabel is unable to contradict Cornelia (1861 [2000]: 236). Her domestic frustration is increased by the jealousy she feels at learning about Carlyle's frequent meetings with Barbara Hare, of which he refuses to speak for professional reasons. The widening gap between wife and husband reaches its climax when Levison reappears in Isabel's life. His flirtatious conduct and the cunning tricks he uses to fuel her jealousy convince the heroine to abandon her family and elope with him to France. The adultery she commits not only puts an end to her marriage; it turns her into a social outcast. Soon abandoned by her lover and divorced by her husband, she loses her illegitimate child in a train accident in which she is also believed to die. Apparently erased from the scene, she returns home disguised as a governess to take care of her children. She suffers greatly by witnessing the domestic happiness of Carlyle and his new wife Barbara, and dies of an illness triggered by overemotionality. Though recognized and forgiven by her husband on her deathbed, she is buried anonymously without regaining her lost identity and status.

Class differences play a central role in the tragic chain of events leading to Isabel's downfall. A woman of leisure who has learned to gratify her vanity as her surname ironically suggests,[1] Isabel lacks the pragmatism and propriety of middle-class women. Incapable of managing a household and too refined to compete for domestic power with her sister-in-law, she also lacks the self-restraint that Barbara develops after becoming Carlyle's second wife. An easy prey to passions, Isabel behaves like the impulsive aristocrat she is when she yields to jealousy and sensual drives. After her social indictment, she learns to reconvert her erotic desire into maternal affect, but she challenges the bourgeois virtue of measure by feeling excessively for her children. Her melodramatic embodiment of maternal love confirms her distance from bourgeois standards of femininity which, in the novel, are progressively embodied by her rival Barbara. Unlike the passionate mother in disguise, Carlyle's second wife has espoused domestic ideals of composure, which make her give precedence to her husband's needs over her baby's (1861 [2000]: 467). The emotional gap between the over-feeling Isabel and the almost emotionless Barbara confirms the former's inability to adapt to the behavioural standards of the class into which she has married but to which she never truly belongs. Isabel's social status is further complicated by her temporary impersonation of the role of employee which, as demonstrated in Chapter 5, conveys a disconcerting idea of class fluidity.

An elusive figure that confounds class barriers, Isabel Vane is perturbing from an ethical viewpoint too, as she arouses sympathy despite her adulterous conduct. As mentioned in Chapter 3, her melodramatic incarnation of suffering and guilt produces contradictory emotions in the reader, who wavers between stigmatization and pity. The complexity of her role is proof of the author's skilful combination of anti-feminist and proto-feminist attitudes. As Marlene Tromp suggests, *East Lynne* triggered a "schizophrenic response" in the Victorian press: while some reviews praised its brilliancy and charming style, others objected to its tactless characterization of an endearing heroine that violates the sacred bonds of marriage (2011: 258). A strong critique came from Margaret Oliphant who detected the most dangerous element of *East Lynne* in its daring portrayal of a fallen woman who, "[f]rom first to last", is the only figure "in whom the reader feels any interest" (1862: 567).

One century later, scholars have offered various interpretations of the novel's controversial heroine, thereby confirming that she is the pivot around which many problematic issues revolve.[2] Her class identity, in particular, has been debated as a crucial element in Wood's representation of thorny gender questions. A lady by birth, Isabel fails to become an ideal wife and mother after marrying Carlyle. Her transgressive sexuality is in line with

Victorian prejudices about upper-class immorality which, as Jessica Cox notes, contrasts with the middle-class abidance by "Victorian ethical standards of social behaviour" (2019: 39). Yet, the affective excess Isabel displays, as a jealous wife and an over-emotional mother, raises doubts about the patriarchal construction of female desire espoused by the rising bourgeoisie. Both distant from, and close to, Wood's target audience, the heroine of *East Lynne* bears witness to the author's use of camouflage strategies that were meant to mollify her orthodox readers while challenging some basic tenets of their class ethos. "The middle-class woman reader can simultaneously identify with Isabel as a woman and disavow that identification by constructing her as too aristocratic", observes Ann Cvetkovich, who also notices how the heroine's "melodramatic affects" are part of an aristocratic "cultural and emotional capital" needed by the Victorian bourgeoisie which, however, had to be purged of its excesses to suit middle-class ideals of "work and discipline" (1992: 108–109). This reading is validated by the fact that, though cleansed of its sexual connotations, Isabel's melodramatic tendency is still evident in the novel's closure, while Barbara Hare learns to curb her over-emotionality to "serve as an alternative locus of [middle-class] identification" (Cvetkovich, 1992: 109). Initially depicted as an impassioned young woman who dares to confess her love to Carlyle after his marriage with Isabel,[3] Barbara gradually develops into a model of self-restraint, which counterbalances the dangerous emotions associated with her upper-class rival. There are, however, in this combination of class status and female affect some elements that confound the novel's message. If it is true that Wood connotes Isabel's passions as dangerous for her domestic and social balance, it is also true that the coldness displayed by Barbara in her role of wife and mother casts a shadow onto the desirability of her model of womanhood. These perplexing aspects were noticed by Oliphant who lamented the fact that, while Isabel becomes "doubly a heroine" after her adultery, the virtuous Barbara is a woman "we should like to bundle to the door and be rid of" (1862: 567).

What *East Lynne* ultimately conveys is, thus, a double-bounded message that partly reassured, partly disturbed, its Victorian readership. As claimed by a number of scholars, Wood undoubtedly championed the values of her class by depicting "bourgeois men and women ousting and replacing the tired, incompetent (frequently dissipated) upper classes" (Wynne, 2001b: 66). If Carlyle supersedes dissolute male aristocrats like the Earl of Mount Severn and Levison,[4] Barbara offers an example of social rise "for readers' identification", as she replaces Isabel in the role of wife and humiliates her rival by becoming her temporary employer (Wynne, 2001b: 70). Together with her husband, Barbara emerges "as the ideal towards which the reader should aspire", an incarnation of the new middle-class liberalism on which the rising industrial capitalism of the age had founded its distinctive values (Kaplan, 1989: 48). At the same time, however, the characterization of Carlyle and his second wife reveals elements of ambiguity that confound the novel's morale. Rather unemotional in their family relations, the couple are disturbingly associated with notions of insincerity and gender inequality that raise pressing dilemmas. "Like Carlyle, Barbara adopts a kind of emotional distance toward questions of truth and disguise", writes John Kucich, who claims that, besides representing a "female adaptation to Carlyle's ethically fluid world", his second wife suggests that the pragmatic model of "new middle-class mother" she embodies is based on "a cold oversimplification" of female household priorities and that, not different from her rival, "she is still controlled by a man" (1994: 190, 193). Even though she thrives as mistress of East Lynne, Barbara needs to stifle her passions to become a suitable mate for Carlyle. The metamorphosis she experiences, by becoming a self-possessed wife and mother, does not turn her into a flawless icon of domesticity. Whilst Isabel challenges notions of moderation and is killed prematurely by her passions, Barbara evokes an impression of insincerity with her maternal tepidness, which prevents her from being an amiable figure despite her virtuous demeanour.

Both unsatisfactory as mothers, Carlyle's two wives are instrumental to the author's exposure of the limits of Victorian gender roles, which discouraged, rather than favoured, women's self-development. By juxtaposing Barbara's self-disciplined conduct with Isabel's impassioned nature, Wood suggests the difficulty of merely replacing old-fashioned models of femininity with new ideals which, though outwardly respectable, raise suspicions of hypocrisy and insensitivity. Another perturbing aspect of Isabel's characterization is the symbolic role she plays as a fetish-object exchanged among men – a role that, as Andrew Maunder contends drawing on Luce Irigaray's theories, makes her "a victim of the homosocial world of English society" (2000: 23). The striking beauty she is said to possess when she first appears on the scene suggests that, like the mansion purchased by Carlyle from her father, she can become part of a men-managed economic transaction that reifies her attractive body. Although she seems to decide to marry Carlyle autonomously, Isabel is actually performing an act determined by her father's profligacy, which has already caused the selling of East Lynne. Her marginality is confirmed by the fact that her fiancé conducts his marriage negotiations with her next of kin, the new Lord Mount Severn, who patronizingly orders Isabel to be "a good and faithful wife" to Carlyle, "for he deserves it" (Wood, 1861 [2000]: 187).[5]

Together with other anxieties, the novel also responds to Victorian fears of moral and mental degeneracy substantiated by contemporary medical literature. These fears are well rendered by Isabel's violation of sexual norms and her subsequent development of hysterical leanings, which enable us to read *East Lynne* also "as a text that concerns itself with policing and othering degenerate women" and to consider Wood "a guardian of bourgeois propriety" (Maunder, 2004: 69). Such interpretations are reconciled with the aforementioned exposure of the failings of Victorian gendering if we consider the double-bounded message conveyed by the novel.

By conflating orthodox and subversive views in one narrative, Wood explores the contradictions inherent in her age's conceptualization of femininity that celebrated ideals in contrast with women's true yearnings. From a generic viewpoint, moreover, *East Lynne* offers an early combination of sensationalism and domesticity, which enables its author to merge jarring forms and ideas together.[6] The impression that *East Lynne* is "an archetypal woman's novel" is substantiated by its frequent appeals to female readers, such as the famous warning against female impatience issued by the narrator, who exhorts an ideal "Lady – wife – mother" to "resist the demon that would urge you to escape" (Wood, 1861 [2000]: 334). Despite their conventionality, these appeals prove the centrality of a female-to-female discourse, which Wood strengthened in the volume edition by excluding an address to male readers present in the earlier serialized version (Wynne, 2001b: 61).

In ways similar to *East Lynne*, other Wood novels offer thought-provoking portrayals of transgressive ladies who raise thorny issues through their anomalous conduct. Quite heterogeneous in their psychophysical features, these ladies also differ in their class markers and loyalties. If many are born in the high ranks of society, others are socially mobile figures that have risen in status through marriage and have learned to imitate the old-elite lifestyle. The latter's experiences of gentrification are paralleled by experiences of embourgeoisement made by ladies like Isabel Vane, who join the rising middle classes by accepting a bourgeois husband. In representing these two-directional movements, which effectively render the complexity of the age's transformations, the author adopted no simplistic ideological stance. Although she shared her class's prejudices against the aristocracy, Wood did not always stigmatize the conduct of upper-class women as symptomatic of their class's moral decay. She rather made these women face similar challenges as those met by bourgeois women, thereby inviting a cross-class rethinking of the strict gender roles enforced by the Victorian ethos.

This is the case of the perplexing characterization of Adeline de Castella and Charlotte St. John in *St. Martin's Eve* (1866). As shown in Chapter 1, Adeline is a highborn French girl who initially rebels against her father's arrangements and attempts to marry a man of her choice. Her revolt is, however, followed by her resigned acceptance of the laws of patriarchy, which paves the way to her premature death. Another victim of male power featured in the novel is the passionate Charlotte St. John, who achieves upper-class status through marriage. Her violation of behavioural norms and the appalling murder she commits are attributed to more than one cause, including her hereditary insanity. But her characterization is not merely a response to circulating class prejudices. What Charlotte poses, in yielding to unladylike passions, are the problems of social and financial vulnerability faced by women of all classes who, as hinted in Chapter 3, enjoyed limited rights in the mid-1860s.

Despite the passing of the Married Women's Property Act in 1870, Wood continued to raise the issue of women's weak positioning within a male-dominated system in the following decade, as shown by her provocative representation of the snobbish aristocrat Adela Acorn in *Court Netherleigh*. A disobedient woman who violates many gender rules after her marriage, Adela is described as the worthy daughter of a profligate lord with whom she shares an inclination to live irresponsibly. As suggested in Chapter 1, however, her transgressive attitude is more than a cliché attached to her class of birth. By rebelling against the roles of wife and mother she is prescribed to embody after her arranged marriage, Adela fulfils a polemical function, as she exposes the reification of women in marriage transactions and their easy stigmatization as unruly when they refuse to comply with social expectations.

The complexity of the above-mentioned figures is not found in all the ladies portrayed by Wood, some of which are flat characters associated with upper-class flaws and incapable of development.

Laziness, vanity, sensuality, spendthriftiness, inconstancy and arrogance are the blemishes exhibited by these stereotyped upper-class women, who are often minor figures acting as foils for the bourgeois heroines' endowments and growth. Two examples of secondary characters that badly affect other people's lives are the hypochondriac Lady Oswald featured in *Oswald Cray* (1864), whose obstinacy and arrogance trigger a long chain of misfortunes including her own death, and the scheming Madam North in *Bessy Rane* (1870), who is a constant source of unhappiness for the demure heroine.

Equally troublesome and incapable of change is the eponymous protagonist of *Lady Adelaide's Oath* (1867). The daughter of a Scottish peer, Adelaide Errol is a pretty young lady who, after losing her parents, moves to Dane Castle to live with her next of kin. Attractive but untrustworthy ("her eyes roved about too much for true ones"), she is introduced as "one of the veriest, vainest coquettes" by the narrator, who remarks on her being "so innately selfish" (Wood, 1867: I.11, 16–17). While living with the Danes, Adelaide is courted by two young members of the family and flirts with both. The love triangle generates growing tensions that reach their climax in a gothic episode, in which one of the two rivals pushes the other down a cliff before the young woman's eyes. Unwilling to betray the man she loves, Adelaide declares that she saw nothing during the criminal investigation. Soon after giving her false oath, however, she rejects the murderer without explanations and accepts the marriage proposal of a third party, the dull-witted but titled Squire Lester. Their union gratifies Adelaide's vanity, but it proves to be a source of trouble for the Lester family. Capricious, selfish and craving luxury, the lady wastes part of her husband's wealth on clothes and ornaments, and she contributes to souring the squire's relations with his firstborn Wilfred. After a sensational twist of the plot – consisting in the homecoming of the presumed victim of the murder, Harry Dane – Adelaide is forced to confess her false testimony to the 'revenant', who scolds her by rephrasing the famous biblical motto from Galatians (6.7): "As we sow, so we must reap" (Wood, 1867: III.222). Adelaide owns to having been haunted by remorse and to having felt "humiliation", "pain" and "care" for years (1867: III.224). Yet, she entreats Harry not to disclose her secret. The man's acceptance of her request allows her to continue to enjoy her privileges, respected by a society that is unaware of her past deceit.

Adelaide visits Harry again when he is on his deathbed. Invited to throw her "hard selfishness" aside and develop "loving help and pity" by the dying man, she shows signs of repentance through "a sob", "unrest" and "miserable disquietude" (1867: III.301–302), but she still manifests her flaws. Long haunted by "[a]n awful fear of detection" (1867: III.221), she strives to exorcise this fear by beseeching Harry to keep her secret, thereby revealing a care for social recognition that is symptomatic of self-interest. The novel closes with a moral tone typical of Wood's endings; but no reference to a real change of heart of the protagonist is offered. The impression that Adelaide is more afraid of exposure than guilt-ridden is confirmed when she silently implores another victim of hers – Wilfred's wife Edith – not to disclose her mean conduct: "An uncomfortable feeling pervaded the room, and Lady Adelaide glanced at Edith, a pleading look on her burning face. It seemed to say, 'Do not, in pity, expose me'" (1867: III.290–291).

Rather static in her characterization, Lady Adelaide unquestionably sets a negative model of femininity. Besides fuelling disagreement in two families, she is described as a vain, deceitful and self-centred woman who gives flesh to circulating prejudices against her class of origin. If carefully examined, however, her figure proves to fulfil an important ideological function, as she brings to the fore the patriarchal tendency to attach moral bias to women, rather than men. This function is well explained by Andrew Mangham who analyses some key problems raised by "the intricate narrative structure of the text" (2007: 149). After explaining that *Lady Adelaide's Oath* expresses contemporary concerns about the destructive natures of women and the risks of making wrong marital choices, Mangham contends that Wood problematizes these concerns by suggesting that the troubles of the Dane and Lester families "also have a lot to do with the innate, self-destructive tendencies of men" (2007: 149). In both conversations he has with Adelaide, Harry Dane puts all the blame for the Danes' troubles on the deceitful lady. "'But for your conduct, Adelaide, […] that night's work had never taken place'", he exclaims when he learns about her false oath; in their following meeting, he confirms this idea by declaring: "'Ah, Adelaide, it is your own fault!'" (Wood, 1867: III.206, 301). With much irony, however, the plot contradicts these gender-biased statements. As Mangham convincingly argues, the sequence of events shows that the misfortunes of the Dane family are primarily the results of the actions performed by three neurotic men: the criminal Herbert Dane, who pushes his cousin down the cliff and usurps his estate; the temporarily insane Harry Dane, who lets his family believe that he was killed and washed out to sea; and the epileptic Mitchel, a coastguardsman who is assailed by panic after finding Harry's body and, seized by a fit, fails to provide precious information to rescuers (2007: 144–146). In a similar way, the main source of the problems within the Lester family proves to be Wilfred himself, whose impulsive conduct generates multiple tensions with his father and his young wife Edith.

By using facts to contradict Harry's view of Adelaide as the only blameable subject, Wood exposes the Victorian tendency to connote transgressive women as wholly responsible for the troubles and the moral degeneration of their environment. Exactly because she is flawed and fails to develop, the selfish lady brings these gender contradictions to the fore. If her partial guilt for the unhappiness of her family members is undeniable, the assumption of her full guilt is disproved by the misconduct of a group of men, which suggests the Victorian adoption of moral double standards in representing male and female wrongdoing.

Unlike *Lady Adelaide's Oath*, which questions gender stereotypes through the unfolding of events, other novels raise similar issues by representing socially mobile upper-class women who marry downwards into the bourgeoisie, contributing to developing alternative models of femininity. Often portrayed as self-assured characters, these ladies combine the relative autonomy enjoyed by upper-class women with bourgeois qualities typically attributed to men, such as resolution and initiative. This combination is evident in the characterization of Rebecca Copp in *The House of Halliwell* (1890). The descendant of a "noble and renowned and loyal house" that has lost its earldom and grandeur, Rebecca is "a wonderful woman, positive and contradictory in manner", "self-willed, [but] not disobedient", who married a captain beneath her social standing and is wont to accompany him on his voyages around the world (Wood, 1890 [1896]: 1, 3). Her travelling experiences and her exposure to the roughness of an embarked life increase her autonomy and self-reliance. Against dominant standards of femininity, she develops physical and decisional power, as evidenced by her clear-sightedness in practical and financial matters, by the courage she displays in moments of crisis, and by the explicit reference to "her strong arm" (1890 [1896]: 148). On her first appearance on the scene, for example, Rebecca proves to be more sharp-witted in business than her brother. Her ability to understand wrong investments is confirmed, a few pages later, by the financial bankruptcy of her brother's family, which ironically invalidates his prejudices against women "interfer[ing] in business matters" (1890 [1896]: 13). Resolute in practical matters, she displays unfeminine courage during a "disastrous" ship voyage when she witnesses the death of her husband and bravely accepts his burial at sea in conformity with marine customs (1890 [1896]: 135).

Despite some comic elements of her characterization,[7] Rebecca Copp sets an intriguing model of womanhood, which questions some basic tenets of the angel-in-the-house paradigm. A caring wife and mother, capable of playing both roles outside the domestic sphere, Rebecca gains further strength and autonomy after the death of two male family figures – her brother and her husband – whose loss turns her into an "odd" woman positioned "outside heteronormativity" (Liggins, 2014: 2). Besides enjoying the freedom of widowhood, she becomes a supportive aunt for her brother's family and, as such, she exerts a significant influence on her niece, Hester, who incarnates a positive model of spinsterhood, as shown in Chapter 1. The destabilizing function fulfilled by Rebecca is favoured by her display of self-help virtues associated with successful masculinity, such as sharp-wittedness and resolution, which are reinforced by her upper-class strength of will. Together with her class mobility, Rebecca's unwonted combination of male and female qualities becomes a vehicle for a subtle critique of social categories, including gender ones. What is suggested by her striking agency is the provocative idea that "woman" is not an essence, but a construct within patriarchal culture – an idea that would be developed and theorized by Simone de Beauvoir in the following century (1949 [2011]: 283). The proto-feminist insights of Rebecca's characterization are confirmed by an interesting parallel between her sea adventures and a story reported in *Women and Work* (1857) by Barbara Leigh Smith Bodichon, who tells the heroic tale of Mrs. Patton – a captain's wife who travels with her husband and manages to command the ship in a moment of crisis – to illustrate "the power evinced by women" in "unusual directions" (1857: 32–34).

If Rebecca Copp challenges gender assumptions with her energetic attitude, other aristocratic women portrayed by Wood expose the consequences of women's inactivity and subjection to men's tyrannical will. This is the case of two women featured in *The Red Court Farm* (1868): Clara Lake and Angeline Ellis. The gender questions raised by their characterization merge with specific issues concerning "the social and cultural competition between gentility in decline and, conversely, upstart vulgarity" (Wagner, 2008: 200). By representing this competition, Wood not only articulates contemporary class anxieties; she also demonstrates that the social mobility of the age offers unequal opportunities of self-development to men and women. Whereas men are challenged to negotiate new identities within a rapidly changing system, women of all classes achieve status through marriages that limit their autonomy, making them liable to psychophysical disorders provoked by ennui and emotional frustration.

Such disparity is well rendered by the unhappy marriage of Robert Hunter and Clara Lake in *The Red Court Farm*. The daughter of "an old-fashioned man who had once worn a pig-tail", Clara is a woman of aristocratic background who dies prematurely of a broken heart (Wood, 1868b [1898]: 15). Her physical and emotional vulnerability is significantly associated with her genteel status which, as seen in Chapter 3, prevents her from giving vent to her rage when she discovers her husband's infidelity.

Whereas Clara represents the fading aristocratic world with her ultra-refined fragility, Robert is a rising professional associated with progress and upward social mobility. Temporarily lured by the privileges of the leisured classes, whom he joins through marriage, he quickly tires of his laziness and resorts to flirting to escape boredom. Deprived of money and possessions by his wife's premature death, he is forced to resume his engineering profession and to rethink his class identity.[8] The second half of the novel describes his successful building of a professional career. Instead of regretting the loss of his upper-class wife, status and privileges, Robert connotes this loss in salvific terms: "'I am *saved*! I shall go to work now'" (1868b [1898]: 177). The novel closes with the announcement of his future marriage with another high-ranking woman, Mary Anne Thornycroft; but the conditions of his second union are different from those of his first marriage. Instead of joining the leisured classes and adopting their lifestyle, Robert is now a successful professional who has achieved status and autonomy through his work. The bourgeois ethic he has espoused not only "saves" him from an idle life; it also offers his wife-to-be a potential escape from her corrupted family and, by extension, from her declining class of birth. Although Wood invests some members of the elites with "sympathy and even virtue",[9] the novel's emphasis is laid on the self-help virtues rediscovered by Robert who, after his early marriage into the aristocracy, experiences a liberating return to his class of origin, which paves the way to his socioeconomic, professional and moral growth.

The class discourse revolving around Robert is reinforced by the story of Angeline Ellis (née Finch), who repeatedly crosses the male protagonist's path. A scheming woman with limited means and "a propensity for living beyond [her] income" (1868b [1898]: 188), Angeline is compelled to work twice in her life. First employed as a companion to a lady in India, she later serves as the Thornycrofts' governess. On both occasions, she uses her occupations to secure a wealthy husband and exorcise the spectre of poverty, which she is said to dread "as a nightmare" (1868b [1898]: 189). After marrying "an old man in his dotage" (1868b [1898]: 189) in India and becoming his widow, she returns to England where she captivates Robert. Fascinated by her "handsome" features and her sensuality (1868b [1898]: 64–66), the married man flirts with her unashamedly, thereby breaking his wife's heart. Rejected by Robert after Clara's death, Angeline marries Squire Thornycroft and becomes mistress of Red Court Farm. But she achieves no happiness through her new social rise. Forbidden to move freely inside and around the castle by the squire's firstborn, Richard,[10] she is also precluded from managing the household routine and, growingly afflicted by ennui, she develops a "grave inward disorder" (1868b [1898]: 244) that causes her premature death. In her last meeting with Robert during her illness, Angeline is shown to have undergone a significant change of heart, as she repents living as "a vain, worldly, selfish woman" (1868b [1898]: 345–346) and asks for forgiveness.

Alongside its religious undertones, Angeline's last speech sheds light on the cross-class experiences made by Robert, which are similar to her own. Two high fliers who climb the social ladder through marriage, they are both frustrated by the idleness of their new leisured life. What differs in their experiences, however, is that fact that Angeline marries again after losing her first husband. Frightened by poverty and by the prospect of working to earn her bread, she seduces Squire Thornycroft and becomes the mistress of a gothic castle where she develops her lethal complaint. Whereas Robert prospers by losing caste, the ambitious woman is killed by her efforts to be part of the social elite. Imbued with bitter irony, the obstinacy with which she pursues her objective reveals her error of judgment. Unlike the rising engineer, who gains new status by espousing bourgeois values, Angeline fails to understand her changing world and continues to aspire to marry into a declining class.

The cross-class mobility associated with Robert and Angeline reveals the social uncertainty of an age that compels people to rethink their class loyalties and their sense of belonging. But the different choices they make in their widowhood also evidences the unequal opportunities offered to Victorian men and women. Whereas men can rise by developing their skills, women are expected to achieve status through marriage. Unlike Robert, Angeline has no chances to become a successful professional as she lives in a society that stigmatizes upper-class female work. Rather than facing the hard life of a governess, she thus strives to acquire social and financial privileges by becoming a genteel wife.

Another interesting aspect to consider is the fact that, being a parvenu, the woman needs to learn to impersonate a lady. Like other ambitious heroines portrayed by sensation novelists,[11] Angeline displays remarkable acting abilities that enable her to play the role of an aristocratic lady. Beautified by her use of cosmetics and her ability to dress "youthfully" (1868b [1898]: 65), she has acquired charming manners that lure the owner of Red

Court Farm into her matrimonial trap: "And Justice Thornycroft was becoming fascinated. He began to think there was not such another woman in the world" (1868b [1898]: 192). An ambitious woman capable of fashioning herself into a lady, Angeline not only poses the ethical problem of faking one's identity, but she also conveys subtly provocative views of class and gender, as the ease with which she embodies the ladylike ideal suggests the constructedness of the age's dominant categories.

More deeply ironic is the exposure of the constructedness of social roles in *Elster's Folly* (1866). An understudied novel pivoting around ideas of performativity, *Elster's Folly* challenges the assumed naturalness of class and gender roles by revealing their fluidity and potential reversibility. This provocative function is fulfilled by two bizarre figures: Lady Kirton, a countess-dowager that questions upper-class and women's social models with her eccentric behaviour, and Val Ester, the weak and feminized Earl of Hartledon, who becomes a victim of the countess's plots. Their complex relational dynamic is skilfully developed to intimate the artificiality of the roles they play, both as representatives of an upper class traditionally associated with refinement and self-assurance, and as foils for dominant gender models. As will be shown, the two characters exhibit features that are at odds with their high-ranking status and complicate their social belonging. In similar ways, their looks and behaviour clash with their assumed gender identities. If Lady Kirton exhibits typically masculine volition and self-confidence, Val is initially docile and feminized and, after developing a more self-assured attitude, he is still impelled to negotiate his newly acquired role with the strong-willed woman. What their agonistic relations demonstrate is the fundamental instability of Victorian gender boundaries which, constantly blurred and redrawn by the two characters' actions, are shown to depend on acquired, rather than inborn, elements.

The unwonted portrayals of Lady Kirton and Val suggest Wood's intuitive perception of notions that would be developed and theorized by twentieth-century feminists, such as Beauvoir's differentiation between sex as biological facticity and gender as cultural interpretation of that facticity (1949 [2011]). By revealing how the characters' actions continuously reshape their identities, moreover, Wood suggests an idea that would be systematized in the late 1980s, when Judith Butler would demonstrate that "gender is in no way a stable identity or locus of agency from which various acts proceed; rather, it is an identity tenuously constituted in time – an identity instituted through a *stylized repetition of acts*" (1988: 519). As we will see, the anomalous characterization of Lady Kirton and Val not only implies the fickleness of class belonging, but it also vaguely evokes an idea of "performative fluidity" of genders, showing that, far from being "univocal signifiers", the essentialist notions of femininity and masculinity are social constructs which are "stabilized, polarized, rendered discrete and intractable" to serve "a social policy of gender regulation and control" (Butler, 1988: 528).

The "folly" mentioned in the novel's title is an anticipation of Val's swerving from normativity. A man of "good birth and breeding" endowed with "a most attractive face", the eponymous protagonist violates dominant assumptions of class and gender with the "sweet expression" of his face, his "utter want of resolution" and his "extreme sensitiveness as to the feelings of other people, let them be his equals or his inferiors" (Wood, 1866a [1903]: 4, 8). Neither masculine nor haughty, he is "unfit [for] the battle with life" and fails to play the role of Earl of Hartledon convincingly when he happens to inherit the title. The difficulties posed by his weak personality are increased by the agency of Lady Kirton who, firmly resolved to find a good match for her daughter Maude, hatches a plot against the unassertive earl. Manipulated by the cunning woman, Val betrays the girl to whom he had previously proposed, Anne Ashton, and marries Maude in a secret ceremony into which he is beguiled, feeling "convicted of utter cowardice" (1866a [1903]: 199). His inability to avoid the "burlesque of a marriage" concocted by the scheming Lady Kirton is the climactic manifestation of his "known irresolution" (1866a [1903]: 200), which is patently at odds with the model of male aristocrat he is expected to embody.

Equally swerving from the norm is Val's antagonist. "The wife of a very poor and improvident Irish peer, who had died early, leaving her badly provided for" with "a whole troop of children", Lady Kirton is introduced as an "utterly unscrupulous" woman soured by unfavourable circumstances (1866a [1903]: 43). Determined to see her daughter Maude become Lady Hartledon, she uses all her skills to set a clever matrimonial trap for the weak-willed Val and continues to intrude into the couple's life after their wedding. Much more resolute than her son-in-law, Lady Kirton not only questions Victorian gender expectations, but she also challenges class markers with her flamboyant style and her lack of taste. A corpulent woman "as broad as she was high" who makes an excessive use of cosmetics and wears garish clothes and ornaments, she nonetheless displays her aristocratic arrogance by always "carr[ying]" her "snub nose [...] in the air" (1866a [1903]: 47). The gap between her high-class status and her unrefined appearance is widened by her unrestrained consumption of food and drink. Decidedly unfeminine, Lady Kirton's alimentary practices are ridiculed in different episodes, in which she is described eating with too much relish, "speaking with her mouth full of high-seasoned maccaroni" and showing her nose "scarlet with the wine" she copiously drinks (1866a [1903]: 142, 442). Such descriptions destabilize the Victorian use of food images to articulate class and gender lines. A sign of low-class status visibly in contrast with aristocratic refinement, Lady Kirton's ravenous appetites also clash with the gender prescriptions of the age, which idealized nonappetitive and insubstantial women (Cozzi, 2010: 60, 72). Additionally vulgarized by her corpulence and, possibly, by her Irish origins, the eccentric woman challenges the very ideal of motherhood by displaying little affection for her children, whom she uses as pawns in her unscrupulous games.

A gargantuan, affectless and voracious mother belonging to the high ranks of society, Lady Kirton challenges the idea that taste "helps to shape the class body" and that gender distinctions are strictly determined by "divisions of foods between the sexes" (Bourdieu, 1979 [2010]: 188, 190). Instead of being a habitus that demonstrates the position she occupies within the social system (Probyn, 2000: 29), her unruly body suggests the fluidity of her identity markers that upset social expectations. The elusiveness of her characterization is further increased by the insanity associated with the frantic "war-dances" she performs when she is enraged (Wood, 1866a [1903]: 196, 442). The convulsive dance she executes in the climactic episode of the novel, in which she discovers Val's secret bigamy, is perceived as madness by the young man, whom she shocks with her fury: "'Madam! [...] Are you mad?'" (1866a [1903]: 442). Even more disquieting is that fact that Lady Kirton is neither punished for her villainy nor subjected to moral management. After pestering Val into an unpleasant confession, she abuses him for breaking Maude's heart and for wrecking their children's lives with the shame of illegitimacy. Entreated by the earl to keep his shameful secret, she obtains from him a yearly allowance of "port wine" together with a good income that enables her to live in "a nice little place in Ireland" (1866a [1903]: 454). Pleased by the transaction, she appropriately melts into tears, making her face "stripy" with cosmetics and receiving a soothing hot tea with some "brandy in it" (1866a [1903]: 454). Her appeasement and gratification pose further interpretative problems. A theatrical, eccentric and intemperate matron, she does not meet the exemplary punishment reserved to Victorian transgressive women but is rather rewarded with material benefits. A key to her puzzling characterization can be found by taking two elements into consideration: her embodiment of what Mikhail Bakhtin defines as "the carnivalesque principle" – the liberating potential of the grotesque bodily lower stratum (1965 [1968]) –

and her antagonistic relationship with Val.

Let us first focus on the subversive implications of her displays of excess and grotesqueness which, in ways similar to the carnivalesque, create alternative social spaces of freedom. An obese woman with an abnormal appetite, Lady Kirton eludes categorization with her excessive corporeality and manners. High-ranking in status but low-class in impulses, she disquietingly combines male voracity with feminine greed. Her anomaly is increased by her unconventional maternal role.[12] An insatiable mother, who symbolically feeds on her offspring rather than nurtures them, she uses Maude to gain personal advantages, as evidenced by the food and drinks she avidly consumes in her daughter's household. By conflating different ideas of transgressiveness together, Lady Kirton fulfils two important functions. First of all, she exposes the limits of Victorian gender norms, which confined women to the narrow roles of ambitious mothers and mercenary daughters. Provocatively epitomized by her gluttony, the materialistic drives inherent in the age's modelling of femininity are confirmed by Maude's disposition to become an object of transaction in the marriage market. On a symbolic level, moreover, Lady Kirton shows the possibility of overcoming such gender constraints. Despite her caricatural aspects, she incarnates the liberating potential of Bakhtin's carnivalesque principle with her corporeal and behavioural excess.[13] More protean than the low-class Mother Pepperfly analysed in the following chapter, Lady Kirton levels social differences and frees femininity from conventional restrictions, thereby giving flesh to an ideal of "performative fluidity" that makes her figure difficult to classify.

Another source of contradiction is her antagonistic relationship with Val. Despite his titular prominence, the male protagonist of *Elster's Folly* is no hero. Totally devoid of "what may be called moral courage", he is skilfully manoeuvred by the cunning Lady Kirton, who takes advantage of the "bane" of his life: "irresolution" (Wood, 1866a [1903]: 8, 68). The result is a strange reversal of the patriarchal power structure. Instead of being an authoritative man who manages women, Val becomes "a very reed in the hands of the old woman", who exerts her influence upon him as a mighty matriarch (1866a [1903]: 45–46). This anomalous imbalance of power is favoured by their long-term acquaintance, which has enabled Lady Kirton to embody an awe-inspiring role: "He felt afraid of her, he bent to her will. The feeling may have had its rise partly in the strange fear of her instilled into his boyhood, and partly in the yielding nature of his disposition" (1866a [1903]: 46).

After marrying Maude, Val faces some problems that weigh on his mind, slowly changing his disposition. His secret bigamy, in particular, becomes a source of fear, which triggers a more aggressive, resolute attitude soon detected by Lady Kirton: "He was no longer the puppet in her hands that he had been; the day had gone by for ever" (1866a [1903]: 310). As a consequence, the cunning lady modifies her attitude to Val. She first strives to keep her rage under control in his presence. When she learns about Maude's sudden death, however, she manages to exert new power on her son-in-law by reviving her aggressiveness, "rav[ing] about the house in an unseemly fashion, abusing him for his meanness and want of respect to his dead wife" (1866a [1903]: 372–373). A further change of strategy occurs when Val marries again. In order to boycott his union with Anne Ashton, Lady Kirton fuels her grandchildren's jealous rivalry with the couple's children and secretly supports their rebellion against their father and stepmother:

> The real moving spring in the feeling was the countess-dowager. She it was who excited in secret the passions of the elder against their little brothers and sisters; but so craftily, so cautiously was her work done, that Anne could never lay hold of anything tangible to remonstrate against. (1866a [1903]: 410)

Lady Kirton's ability to produce resentment within Val's household is highlighted by the narrator, who later shows how these tensions are instrumental to the woman's negotiations of a good income and other benefits. By "craftily" and "cautiously" manipulating her grandchildren, Lady Kirton puts the *pater familias* under pressure and, after discovering an incriminating letter, she makes him surrender to her will. Her final victory proves that Val's metamorphosis is insufficient to upset the power hierarchy established by the woman, who continues to exert a steady influence upon him.

The disruptive energy manifested by Lady Kirton is not interpretable in purely negative terms. Although she is accused of being an uncaring mother and grandmother (1866a [1903]: 455), the woman is no stereotypical villainess. Occasional references to her sufferings counterbalance her callous disposition, thereby adding more shades of meaning to her thought-provoking portrayal. This is the case in regards to a sympathetic comment made by the narrator who, while ironizing on the woman's self-interest in the novel's conclusion, refers to the unhappiness "really" experienced by "the poor old creature" (1866a [1903]: 454). On a moral plane, moreover, Lady Kirton is less blameable than Val, if we consider his "folly" in exposing his family to the stigma of an invalid union. During their last confrontation, moreover, she rightfully reproaches the earl for his children's illegitimacy and shows a "wrath" that makes her temporarily superior to the irresponsible father (1866a [1903]: 452). These relational details complicate the moral interpretation of her exuberant figure. A Machiavellian schemer, comic in manners and endowed with remarkable psychological skills, Lady Kirton is a complex character that cannot be encompassed within rigid categories. Neither a female caricature nor a consistent villainess, she transgresses multiple boundaries with her irrepressible energy and, in so doing, she raises thorny questions about the class and gender boundaries set by conservative Victorians.

As shown above, the carnivalesque principle she embodies with her vulgar manners and grotesque corporeality challenges social distinctions. Even more disruptive are the energies unleashed by her combative relationship with Val, whom she controls as a powerful matriarch. The censorious and authoritative role she plays, when she accuses her son-in-law of wrecking the life of his family, unveils a main failing of patriarchy: the rigidity of a law that stigmatizes children born out of wedlock. By attributing the problematic status of her grandchildren to their father's lack of responsibility, Lady Kirton suggests that Val has misused the patriarchal power that enables men to appropriate their progeny through the marriage contract.

The idea that Val deserves the blame for the situation is confirmed by the unconventional solution offered to the problem of his children's illegitimacy. Whereas his son dies of scarlet fever and is appropriately erased from the scene, his daughter survives and is raised as a highborn lady in defiance of social norms.[14] The difference in the two siblings' fate is noted by Jessica Cox who, in examining the novel's "significant absence of gender division when it comes to punishing characters' sins", detects a "potential for disruption" in the girl's irregular status as a would-be-lady (2008: 239–240). Besides posing a threat to a patriarchal system that indicts illegitimacy, the girl's survival casts light on the troublesome relation between Val and Lady Kirton. If the failing Val is punished with the suppression of his (irregular) patrilinear descent, the eccentric countess-dowager passes her transgressive legacy on to her illegitimate granddaughter, thereby establishing a female line of descent that is prospectively liberating.

Cross-class, extravagant and masculine in her demeanour, Lady Kirton fulfils an important textual function, as she questions the presumed immutability of Victorian hierarchies. Nominally a lady but unrefined in manners, she resembles other lawbreaking upper-class women portrayed by Wood, but she plays a more disturbing role with her grotesque corporeality and her total lack of restraint.

Besides violating the rigidity of the Victorian class system, Lady Kirton interrogates dominant gender categories. Her agonistic relationship with the feminized Val, who fails to quench her overflowing energy, questions the age's belief in male superiority and offers glimpses into the performativity of social roles, which appear constructed rather than inborn. More eccentric than other high-ranking women portrayed by Wood, Lady Kirton bears evidence of the author's interest in different aspects of the Victorian female condition. Instead of blindly espousing her class's prejudices against the aristocracy, Wood explores the yearnings and frustrations felt by upper-class women, who experience similar sufferings as bourgeois women even though they are sometimes allowed a larger autonomy of action.

CHAPTER 5

Unconventional low-class women

In the course of the nineteenth century, male-controlled domains of knowledge produced a variety of gendered discourses on what it meant to be a woman. Unstable and contradictory though they were in conceptualizing femininity, these proliferating discourses revolved around a common assumption: the inferiority of women's physical and mental development. As we have seen in the previous chapters, biomedical theories like Tait's and Esquirol's validated the idea of the inherent weakness of the female body. Mainly defined in terms of reproduction, women's corporeality was essentialized in sexual terms to justify the separate-spheres doctrine and the many constraints women suffered in socioeconomic, political and legal matters.

Some inconsistencies of these Victorian discourses emerge in the imbrication of gender, class and racial categories. As Lyn Pykett notes, "[w]oman's inferiority to man" was insistently linked to her presumed "similarities to children, the subordinate classes, and to 'inferior' or 'primitive' races"; but those very similarities threatened to contaminate the "white and middle-class" ideal of domesticity whose respectability could be reasserted only by making bourgeois women "different from (and usually superior to) working-class and aristocratic women, and African and Oriental women" (2001: 80). Victorian literature bears witness to the stridency produced by such conflicting views. Fictions written by women, in particular, reveal the extent to which female identity became a site of socio-discursive contests between patriarchal conceptions and attempts to rethink femininity through a (more or less conscious) reconsideration of its assumed frailty, imperfection and unruliness.

Noteworthy, in this regard, were some difficulties that bourgeois novelists met in reconciling dominant gender models with gripping class anxieties. As suggested by Pykett, arguments about women's natural inferiority implied that bourgeois women (including writers) had much in common with the female members of those low ranks by whom the middle class felt menaced. Another source of anxiety was the threat to class distinctions posed by the rising numbers of middle-class working women who, by challenging the bourgeois indictment of female employment, risked being confounded with the vulgar labouring classes. Victorian novelists were increasingly forced to cope with the necessity of female occupation and, confronted with the consequent anxieties of class volatility, they reshaped their views accordingly. Besides characterizing middle-class heroines employed in non-domestic activities, these novelists showed a growing sympathy for the hardships faced by working-class women, conceived models of shabby-gentility and, in some cases, questioned the negative stereotyping of low-class female corporeality.

Evidence of this reshaping process can be found in narratives by Ellen Wood, whose representation of low-class women is still largely unstudied. Wood was undoubtedly a champion of the English bourgeoisie, which is portrayed in full detail in her oeuvre. As shown in Chapter 4, moreover, she was keen to explore the world of the aristocracy. Haughty, inclined to transgression and often degenerate, the upper-class people featured in her works are also instrumental in reflecting on the condition of all Victorian women, as they throw into sharp relief some contradictions inherent in the bourgeois habitus and values. More open to interpretation, contrastingly, is Wood's interest in the lower ranks of Victorian society. The paucity of biographical documentation is certainly an obstacle to determining her socio-political views. As we have seen in the Introduction, Wood was fretfully defined as a benevolent conservative by her son Charles, who claimed that her far-reaching sympathies for the marginalized did not shake her belief in a God-ordained social hierarchy. Equally vague are most observations by later scholars, who tend to share Charles's views. In Rolf Burgauer's opinion, for instance, Wood was a novelist who never questioned class differences: compassionate to the poor, she nonetheless believed that they should live within their predestined class and objected to any forms of rebellion against the status quo, such as factory strikes[1] and cross-class marriages (1950: 42–45).

Wood's fiction seems to confirm her conservatism. Characters belonging to the lower classes rarely feature in prominent roles and, when they do, their portrayal is often contradictory or imbued with irony. In describing cross-class unions, moreover, Wood is generally wary of women of working-class origins who dare to rise above their station through marriage. More sympathetic is her attitude to those women who, independently from their class of origin, are forced to work in order to earn their living. Such an attitude is evident in her characterization of governesses. As will be shown, these governesses share one important element: they are all liminal figures wavering between classes, whose identity problems unveil the gender and social challenges Victorian women faced in a society dramatically divided between tradition and change.

The variety of all these figures suggests that Wood was curious about the hardships and potentialities of women ranking below the middle class. Most challenging is the role played by a group of female characters analysed in the last part of this chapter. All born in the lower social strata, these characters represent the wide range of working-class and indigent women who performed menial jobs, lacked means and were threatened by dangers of physical and moral degeneration that the Victorians associated with the miserable conditions of the poor.[2] In addition to household servants, socially below governesses, Wood's fiction offers interesting portrayals of nurses, employees of manufacturers and farmers, destitute housewives, prostitutes and poverty-stricken women starving in the streets. These figures rarely play a major role in the texts, but the function they fulfil is worth exploring. First of all, they raise thorny class issues that problematize Wood's conservative attitude. While believing in a God-ordained social structure, Wood also displays a Christian sympathy for the sufferings of the dispossessed, which are pitifully described in her narratives. In some cases, moreover, her low-class women perform a decidedly subversive role, as they are endowed with moral and behavioural qualities that make their feminine models admirable.

Let us start with two narratives that exemplify Wood's reservations about low-class women seeking social elevation through marriage. In the sequence consisting of "Major Parrifer" and "Coming Home to Him", two stories that appeared in the first series of *Johnny Ludlow* (1874), the conjugal sufferings of young Cathy Reed stem from her ambition to marry a higher-class suitor. A gardener's daughter "trained to idleness" (Wood, 1874b [1895]: 49), Cathy marries Major Parrifer's son in secret; but she tragically loses her husband and her son, is abandoned by her in-laws and condemned to a life of poverty. The two stories undoubtedly offer a critique of the haughty Parrifers. Their unfeeling attitude is coupled with their tendency to degeneracy, epitomized by the dishonourable conduct of Cathy's husband, who dies in jail accused of wilful murder. While criticizing upper-class flaws, however, Wood exhibits a conservative attitude toward Cathy. A social climber who has "acquired a distaste for work", the young woman has received an education that has triggered her vanity: "Cathy could idle away her time at the glass" (1874b [1895]: 50). The second story closes with her bitter regret for her cross-class marriage, announced by a narrator who gives voice to Wood's conservative creed: "Better that she had married an honest day-labourer: and Cathy knew it now" (1874a [1895]: 79).

Besides Cathy Reed, other social climbers featured in Wood's oeuvre are punished for violating class borders and endangering the position of high-class men. A case in point is the serial *Parkwater*. First published in the *New Monthly Magazine* in 1857, refashioned for serialization in *The Argosy* in 1875 and later reprinted in volume form by Bentley (1876), *Parkwater* narrates the tragic story of Sophia May, a working-class girl reared above her station, who is involved in two clandestine relationships with socially superior men and murders her illegitimate child to avoid scandal and exposure. The brutality of her crime reinforces the vulgarity of her nature, which she vainly strives to hide behind a mask of performed gentility. Sophia's innate coarseness and the tragic consequences of her class transgression prove Wood's conservative views. Yet, as Janice Allan observes, this novel also "engages with a range of contemporary anxieties, relating to the permeability of class boundaries and the possibility that class (and gender) identities are merely performative" (2011: 9). Like other Wood texts, *Parkwater* reveals the author's use of subtle strategies, as it both confirms and destabilizes orthodox discourses on class and gender.

As mentioned above, Wood was less critical of working women who moved across classes, such as governesses. Quite different in their origins and personal histories, the many governesses she characterizes go through a variety of experiences that challenge their classification into a single category. Sometimes portrayed as impoverished women of upper- or middle-class birth who might regain their original status, they are other times conceived as low-ranking women partly refined in their manners and aspiring to climb the social ladder. In some cases, moreover, Wood draws more disquieting pictures of governesses who, independently from their high- or low-class origins, socially decline or become involved in upsetting violent actions. Both typologies reflect Victorian concerns over the much-debated question of redundant or surplus women, as well as the age's prejudices against women working for their living, who were assumed to be "morally bankrupt" (Armstrong, 1987: 78). The anomaly of the governess's position in a household was further increased by the conflicting roles she played as surrogate mother/servant and surrogate mistress/employee. In addition to blurring the confines between domestic bourgeois respectability and paid labour, this figure was affected by psychophysical stress resulting from her occupational duties (long hours of teaching, disobedient pupils to manage, etc.). As scholars have amply demonstrated, moreover, the governess raised fears of class erosion mixed with gender anxieties, as she posed a potential danger to the family's stability with her sexuality (Peterson, 1973; Poovey, 1989; Hughes, 1993). A number of Victorian novels, including Wood's, focus on the problematic presence of a refined young employee in the household, who might exert sexual attraction on the family men and be involved in dangerous cross-class or adulterous relations.

Owing to these contradictions, the governess became pivotal in those mid-Victorian novels that aimed to explore various forms of women's discontent. As shown by the eponymous heroine in *Jane Eyre* (1847), the particular imbrication of gender and class anxieties that distinguished the governess's status enabled novelists to represent alternative female roles within a heteronormative society dominated by bourgeois values. By laying emphasis on the sufferings and frustration of this occupational group, moreover, Victorian writers added new shades of meaning to the literary expression of female affect which, as Ann Cvetkovich clarifies, was a strategy used either to resist, or to enforce, dominant structures of power (1992: 42).

In the wake of Charlotte Brontë, Wood experimented with the female bildungsroman to create a romanticized typology of the governess who experiences socioeconomic hardships before rising in status through a love marriage. A gentlewoman by birth, this figure is often an orphan forced to work by unfavourable circumstances but endowed with bourgeois virtues that finally enable her to get her reward. Unlike Jane Eyre, however, Wood's romantic governess tends to be a less resourceful and autonomous woman, as evidenced by the protagonist of two short stories published in the third series of *Johnny Ludlow* (1885): "Janet Carey" and "Dr. Knox". Arranged in a sequence that rewrites the Cinderella tale from a modern angle, the two stories tell the misadventures of Janet Carey, a young woman of bourgeois origins compelled to work by her orphaned condition. After teaching in a school, Janet is employed as nursery-governess by Mrs. Knox, a distant relative. During her service, however, she is wrongly accused of theft by her mistress, who is worried about the tender friendship between her employee and her stepson, Dr. Arnold Knox. After conducting a long detection, Knox manages to prove Janet's innocence and marries her. Their wedding not only lifts the former governess to a superior class status; it also confirms that she deserves her embourgeoisement, as she has previously been shown to possess the diligence lacking in her lazy mistress: "Mrs. Knox had no talent for management, and was frightfully lazy besides; and Janet, little foreseeing what additional labour she would bring on herself, took to remedy as far as she could the shortcomings and confusion. Mrs. Knox saw her value, and actually thanked her. As a reward, she made Janet her own attendant, her secretary, and partly her housekeeper" (Wood, 1885b [1899]: 117–118).

The first aspect worth considering is the fairy-tale intertextuality. Skilfully embedded into two quietly sensational narratives, the Cinderella motif is modernized and used to question the fixity of Victorian class identity, as shown by the substitution of the fairy-tale's prince with Arnold Knox, a middle-class professional. Secondly, the false accusation suffered by Janet and her later rehabilitation suggest that women can legitimately aspire to climb the social ladder if endowed with admirable bourgeois qualities. These provocative elements are, however, counterbalanced by two conformist facts: Janet is 'rescued' by her would-be husband and restored to her class of origin through marriage.

Similarly dependent on male guidance is the eponymous heroine of *Anne Hereford* (1868), an understudied novel by Wood with a strong Brontëan intertextuality. An orphan of high birth and little means,³ Anne temporarily works as governess for an exploitative mistress who makes her toil but fails to pay her wages. After leaving her position for a new occupation as lady's companion, she finds herself trapped in a country mansion where she falls in love with the family's heir, Harry Chandos. Unable to leave the place because she is penniless, Anne gets involved in the family's secrets and becomes the protagonist of sensational adventures modelled on the gothic sub-plot of *Jane Eyre* and seasoned with scary elements drawn from the fairy-tale tradition (as discussed in Chapter 2, there are many intertextual references to "Little Red Riding Hood" and "Bluebeard"). Although she is endowed with courage and self-reliance, Anne readily accepts Harry's guidance and protection. The traditional role of helper played by the young man is evident in several episodes in which he forbids her from entering a mysterious wing of the house, asks her to trust him blindly and protects her from external dangers (i.e., an angry dog and her wolfish uncle). In a scene imbued with erotic undertones, Harry embraces Anne to shield her from some mysterious peril that is later found to be a dark family secret:

> Mr. Chandos's heart was beating more violently than is common to man, and as the steps went by, he clasped me with an almost painful pressure: so that to look up, had I been so inclined, was impossible. […]
> "But what was the danger?" I took courage to ask.
> "A danger that you may not inquire into". (Wood, 1868a [1896]: 299)

The sensuality of his action, which limits Anne's cognition, evokes the biblical link between forbidden sexuality and the interdiction of female knowledge. Variously reworked by the Western literary tradition, this link is here recast in perplexing terms as the violence implied by the "almost painful pressure" of the embrace both enforces patriarchal strategies of control and raises doubts about their desirability.

Harry's action takes place just after Anne has confessed to the reader her own attraction for the young man. Expressed in strongly physical terms,[4] her love for him partly aligns her with other impassioned heroines depicted by Wood who, as we have seen in Chapter 3, challenge the domestic novel tradition with the intensity of their feelings. This disruptive potential is, however, stifled by Anne's decision to respect Harry's prohibition. By accepting the guidance of her lover without making inquiries, the protagonist performs an act of female obedience that preludes to her later transformation into a model wife. What Wood offers here is a double-bounded view of female affect which, transgressively expressed in the form of unrestrained passion, is gradually contained by the heroine's submission to masculine directions. If Anne's development into an upper-class wife legitimizes the containment of women through marriage, the implications of Harry's violent embrace are not dispelled. A vague sense of danger is confirmed, in the novel's closure, by a strange offer the heroine receives from her (partially reformed) uncle, Edwin Barley, who announces that she will have a permanent "refuge" in his home should she "find herself less happy as Lady Chandos" and that she will "be amply provided for at [his] death" (1868a [1896]: 449–450). Though implying another form of male protection, Barley's offer casts a shadow onto the conjugal expectations of his niece and, more generally, of all those women who willingly submitted to patriarchal rules. His promised legacy, moreover, brings into focus the thorny question of women's legal disadvantages, as it grants Anne a financial autonomy that was hard to attain by law before the Married Women's Property Act of 1870.

More disturbing than this romanticized figure is Wood's characterization of a second typology of governess whose class identity and morality are dramatically put to the test. A villainous governess is Miss Howard, portrayed in *The House of Halliwell* (1890). Hired to take care of Dr. Matthew Goring's children, Miss Howard flirts unashamedly with the housemaster until she is dismissed by Hester Halliwell, the housemistress's sister. Soon after her departure, however, the doctor's wife dies poisoned by strychnia, and is soon replaced by the scheming governess in the role of wife and stepmother. Although the culprit is never found, suspicions are aroused by the doctor and his new spouse, who appear to Hester in a sequence of frightful dreams: "I see Miss Howard standing, barefooted, by a bedside, on which lies a happy wife, sleeping calmly. I see her leaning over a small table, with a phial in her hand, [...] And I have noted the form of Dr. Goring hovering near, and sometimes he seems to look on approvingly through all" (Wood, 1890 [1896]: 305). These oneiric clues are an effective device through which the author casts doubt on the couple without bringing their supposed guilt to light. While giving voice to conservative fears about the disruptive agency of social interlopers like governesses, Wood avoids exposing the terrible crime committed by an intrusive employee and a *pater familias* whose complicity destabilizes the peace of a Victorian family.

Decidedly more complex and perplexing is the agency of the governess in disguise who plays a central role in *East Lynne* (1861). As shown in Chapter 4, Isabel Vane's homecoming under the assumed identity of Madame Vine poses gender and class questions that were widely debated at the time. Apart from revealing the limits of a mercenary marriage and the separate-spheres doctrine, this character comes to embody a disconcerting idea of class fluidity when, after her adultery and her social disgrace, she returns to her conjugal home to serve her former family as governess. Her uncanny performance of multiple roles in the same household (as former earl's daughter, former bourgeois wife and mother, and present employee in disguise) enables the author to represent "the paradox of the position of governess during the nineteenth century" as Isabel is a "hired woman", "situated in the home yet outside its domestic bliss" (Losano, 2004: 107–108). This paradoxical position is made more perturbing by the spectacle of Isabel's intense sufferings, which aroused the sympathy of nineteenth-century readers. Stigmatized by such reviewers as Margaret Oliphant (1862), who objected to the redemption-through-pain parable of an adulteress, the heroine's torment was not only offensive to orthodox Victorians because of its sexual implications. Her suffering also conveyed a potentially unsettling view of class borders, as it exposed the progressive downgrading of a highborn woman who becomes an unhappy bourgeois wife before experiencing the hardships of the lower ranks of society. Differently from Janet Carey and Anne Hereford, moreover, Isabel enjoys no social rise in the novel's conclusion. The unredeemable reality of her status, with which she comes to terms before her melodramatic death,[5] reflects the class anxieties facing Wood's middle-class female readers who were threatened by the spectre of becoming redundant and losing caste.

The irony of living in a mobile society that offered limited opportunities for self-development to women is palpable in *Lord Oakburn's Daughters* (1864), in which two female characters symbolically exchange social roles. One of them is Miss Lethwait, a clergyman's daughter hired as governess by Jane Chesney. Gifted with magnificent "dark eyes and hair" and elegant in manners (Wood, 1864a [1872]: 200), she fascinates the earl and accepts his marriage proposal that makes her the Countess of Oakburn. Although she consciously opts for a mercenary marriage that fulfils her social aspirations, Miss Lethwait proves to be a good wife and stepmother, thereby suggesting that she could legitimately aspire to social elevation. Her self-possession is evident in the words she utters just before receiving the earl's proposal: "'I was not made to live out my life in dependence, in servitude: every hour of the day I feel that I was not. I feel that my mind, my heart, my intellect, were formed for a higher destiny'" (1864a

[1872]: 236). Worth noticing, moreover, is the fact that she has been trained to her profession since an early age: "She [...] had been educated for a governess. Her father had judged it better to give his children an education by which they might make their way in the world" (1864a [1872]: 200–201). In describing how work facilitates her rise in station, Wood seems to echo Barbara Leigh Smith Bodichon's proto-feminist praise of paid occupation for women, especially for the daughters of the lower middle class, who needed to be taught how to turn labour into money, as work done gratuitously was a mistake that lessened dignity (1857: 48–49). The subversive implications of Miss Leithwait's training and ambitions are made more acceptable by the fact that she is the daughter of a churchman who gives spiritual validation to her life choices.

Quite different is the experience of Clarice Chesney, one of Lord Oakburn's daughters who becomes a governess against her father's will before the earl's unexpected inheritance of lots of money and his title. With an act of filial disobedience, Clarice leaves her home and goes into service for a while before disappearing mysteriously. Her sensational story, which is reconstructed in the novel's conclusion, includes a secret marriage, the birth of a son and her murder committed by her own husband, who has meanwhile fallen in love with her sister, Laura. If compared with Miss Leithwait's rise, Clarice's descending parable poses interesting questions of class and women's labour. A high-class (albeit impoverished) woman, Clarice falls in status by stubbornly pursuing a paid occupation for which she lacks training and parental permission. Her limited experience in professional and life matters makes her easy prey for an adventurer like Dr. Lewis Carlton, who is similarly rash in action and improvident. Besides reflecting anxieties about potential husbands' unreliability and violence, her story suggests that most high-ranking women were unprepared for a life of labour that exposed them to difficult social tasks and relations. By concocting a terrible punishment for the rebellious young lady, Wood seems to indict her cross-class transgression and filial disobedience. Her conservative view is, however, counterbalanced by a symbolic act of justice made by a group of lower-class women. As will be shown later in this chapter, the unmasking of Clarice's Bluebeard-like husband is achieved through the deeds and testimonies of a servant, a nurse and two widows whose discovery of Lewis Carlton's murder of his wife amounts to a collective action of class and gender revenge. If Clarice proves unfit for a life below her status by birth, the actions taken by the sisterhood of amateurish detectives and witnesses who avenge her murder suggest the porosity of Victorian class borders and the possibility of developing female solidarity across those borders.

Anxieties about cross-class mobility take a different form in *Mrs. Halliburton's Troubles* (1862), which narrates the vindictive course of action chosen by a foreign governess, Mademoiselle Bianca Varsini. An Italian woman with "strange eyes" and a fine figure, Bianca is the daughter of an actress who sent her to a French convent to be educated as a governess (Wood, 1862 [1897]: 227). Not of respectable origins and racialized as a fiery-tempered Mediterranean woman, Bianca falls in love with Herbert Dare, her employer's second-born, who flirts with her without reciprocating her sentiments. Driven by jealousy and revenge, Bianca stabs her employer's firstborn, Anthony, by mistake and lets his brother be suspected and jailed for the murder. Later in the narration, she reappears on the scene to reveal her crime before dying prematurely. Yet, she shows no deeply felt repentance for her crime and continues to be resentful against her lover. "'He used me ill; yes, he used me ill, that wicked Herbert! [...] He told me stories; he was false to me; he mocked at me! [...] He had but amused himself – pour faire passer le temps!'" she bursts out, before adding: "'It was the right man who lay in prison for it'" (1862 [1897]: 439, 441). The negative passions to which she gives vent offer two important clues to her unsettling narrative function. In addition to being instrumental to the punishment of a gendered betrayal that was often tolerated at the time (Victorian men were less criticized than women for being fickle in love), the governess gives voice to a polemical discourse against the ill usage of female employees in well-to-do households. What Bianca performs, by destroying the life of the two male heirs of the family, is a symbolic act of rebellion against class, gender and racial barriers, as she vindicates her right to punish an insensitive man of leisure who has humiliated her. As is often the case in her narrative, Wood uses subtle strategies to convey a heterodox message here. The questionable sides of Bianca's characterization – as a foreign, fierce woman of low origins – enable the author to weave her social critique obliquely. At first sight, Wood seems to espouse conventional views by portraying a transgressive female figure that is not 'one of them'. Yet, exactly because she is diminished in status, the racialized governess can convey a message of radical justice without disturbing orthodox readers. Her liability to stigmatization gives her a certain freedom of action and speech, while her demands for fairer social relations is covertly legitimized by the wicked, unredeemable portrayal of the two Dare brothers.[6]

If the Victorian governess was a liminal figure wavering between classes, those belonging to the lower ranks by birth represented the 'Other' that faced the bourgeoisie within an inequitable social structure. As mentioned above, Wood rarely turned low-class characters into the protagonists of her fiction but she nonetheless drew some admirable portraits of them. Despite some recurrent comic traits, such as their lack of taste and refinement, these figures emerge as paragons of virtue or are endowed with Smilesian qualities that make them prevail over higher-class individuals. Two telling examples are the black servant Pompey in *Lord Oakburn's Daughters* and the self-possessed Richard Ravensbird in *Lady Adelaide's Oath* (1867). A target of irony for his funny manners and his broken English, Pompey is a racialized servant of African origins, who bears the earl's bad manners with patience and a subservient attitude. His unshaken affection for his master is evident in the grief he feels at the earl's deathbed: "'Never a better massa! never a better massa! Pompey like to go with him'" (Wood, 1864a [1872]: 239). A victim of colonial policies that turn him into a comic enslaved 'Other', Pompey is also a means through which Wood exposes the arrogant ways of Lord Oakburn, an upper-class Englishman who tyrannizes both his daughters and his faithful servant. A similar relation is represented in *Lady Adelaide's Oath* in which Richard Ravensbird, another racialized foreigner of unclear ethnicity, is put to a hard test. Insistently represented in terms of strangerhood, Ravensbird is assimilated to non-European ethnic groups by his physical description as "a dark, sallow-complexioned, stern-looking man, ugly at the first glance", but he is nevertheless endowed with an "honest" face, "a kindly expression in the penetrating black eyes" and a strong loyalty to his master (Wood, 1867: I.24, 26, 181). In the course of the narration, he not only proves to be an affectionate servant of Captain Dane's; he also reveals self-assurance, honesty and ability in managing his business after his master's presumed death, thereby providing an unusual model of Smilesian self-help that questions ethnic and class prejudices. Both dark-complexioned and both involved in difficult master-servant relations, Pompey and Ravensbird exhibit a potential for humanization that was uncommonly attributed to low-ranking people in Victorian literature, and especially to racialized people, who were generally sketched as indistinct figures in the background.

A different group of marginalized subjects are the female servants featured in Wood's oeuvre. Unlike the two male figures examined above, whose social inferiority derives from a combination of class and ethnic elements, these women are doubly marginalized on the basis of their gender identity, which adds to the stigma of their class belonging. In addition to unveiling mechanisms of social oppression, their characterization offers chances to explore unconventional models of femininity, as some of them possess qualities that enable them to act more freely and innovatively than high-class women.

The key function fulfilled by such figures in sensation fiction has been recently acknowledged by Elizabeth Steere who, in commenting on the genre's subversive treatment of class, observes that "many of the most shocking and extreme reversals of class status involve female servants" whose crucial role has escaped critical attention (2013: 9, 3). Steere gives a few effective examples from Wood, mostly drawn from *East Lynne*, *Mrs. Halliburton's Troubles* and *Verner's Pride* (1863). But more thought-provoking figures can be added to Wood's selection to determine her particular functionalization of female servants. An important aspect to consider before delving into our analysis is the fact that such figures belong to three main occupational groups that are directly in contact with their employers and, as such, more likely to be involved in relations that bring thorny social issues to the fore. Besides the governesses analysed previously, Wood represented a number of maidservants who interact closely with their mistresses, and a range of nurses employed to breastfeed, care for babies or assist doctors in patient-treatment.

Varied in their typology and occupational duties, the nurses characterized by Wood bear evidence of her refashioning of a traditionally stereotyped figure imbued with prejudices. A recurrent type in her fiction is the wet nurse, who became an object of growing anxieties during the century. Mostly working-class, poor and uneducated, wet nurses were at the bottom of the hierarchy of servants. In the 1860s, they came to be viewed as dangerous for babies' physical and mental health owing to their predisposition to drunkenness and petty crime (McBride, 1978: 46–52). These class prejudices were increased by the fear of employing fallen women who could jeopardise the purity of the household by transmitting diseases and vices to children (Mangham, 2007: 29). For these reasons, bourgeois mothers were increasingly encouraged to breastfeed and take an active part in raising their children – a social demand that, as shown in Chapter 1, contributed to further limiting their movements outside the home.

Wood responded to these circulating anxieties by portraying wet nurses and nannies that somehow imperil the family's well-being, but she also wove a discourse of affect around these figures that both contained resistance and questioned the equity of class and gender categories. An early example is found in *Danesbury House* (1860), where the drunken Glisson accidentally poisons the baby she nurses and, in so doing, triggers a chain of dramatic events leading to her mistress's death and the family's deterioration. What is noteworthy in the portrayal of this dangerous nurse is the fact that she is never demonized but rather described as a victim of alcohol dependency and social inequalities. Dismissed by her new mistress, Glisson comes to play a central role in a sub-plot set in the London underbelly, in which she vainly strives to help the family of her alcoholic brother. The dreary connection between urban dirt, poverty and addiction drawn in this sub-plot arouses the reader's pity. Although she explores the tragic consequences of drinking in all classes, Wood declares that intemperance is "the curse of England's poor" (Wood, 1860 [n.d.]: 71), thereby expressing social preoccupations that were at the basis of the Temperance Movement during the nineteenth century (Brian Harrison, 1971). This view is confirmed by Glisson's pathetic death. Fatally ill and poverty-stricken, the former nurse repents the problems created by her addiction on her deathbed; but she also describes the squalid slums of London, dominated by "poverty, and ruins, and rags, and famine" that increase the temptation of losing oneself in the "flaring gin-shops" (Wood, 1860 [n.d.]: 88). If it is true that her downfall and death parallel similar experiences made by some intemperate members of the Danesbury family, it is also true that her pathetic characterization questions the fairness of class privileges. This subversive function emerges in a confrontation with the new Mrs. Danesbury, whose vexatious conduct has caused

Glisson's relapse into her vice. Harshly reproached for drinking in service, the nurse has the courage to retort the accusation against her own mistress: "'You have your strong ale, ma'am, and you can take your spirits after it: sometimes it's gin, and sometimes it's brandy; but you don't go to bed without one of 'em. It's shameful, is it, for a poor hard-working servant? What is it for you, ma'am? Where's the difference?'" (1860 [n.d.]: 64). Even though she is a minor figure, Glisson is animated by a rebellious spirit that, appropriately softened by her pitiful misfortunes, interrogates the pretensions of the higher classes who are not immune from the same vices they blame in their social inferiors.

Similar effects are produced by the agency of two nannies in *St. Martin's Eve* (1866). The first part of the novel focuses on the negative effects of the disagreement between two household nursemaids: the high-principled Honoria Tritton (called Honour), who is hired to take care of Mr. St. John's firstborn, Benja, and the ambiguous Prance, who serves St. John's second wife Charlotte and nurses the couple's son Georgy. An arrogant figure with morbid leanings, Prance is instrumental to Charlotte's murder of Benja, as she fuels the many tensions in the house and stubbornly protects her insane mistress to the end. For her part, Honour develops a strong dislike for Charlotte and Prance, which contributes to destabilizing the household relations. Even more disconcerting is Honour's unintentional ability to trigger the lady's violent outburst analysed in Chapter 3. Suspicious of her mistress since Benja's murder, the nurse gradually becomes a mirror for Charlotte's guilty conscience. By simply reappearing on the scene after a long absence, she provokes a brutal reaction in her former mistress who, in attacking her 'persecutor', reveals her long-concealed madness: "She eluded him with a spring, pounced upon the unsuspecting and terrified Honour, and in another moment was grappling with her, a fight for dear life. [...] Honour was released, terrified nearly to death, bruises on her arms, and a bite on her cheek, of which she would never lose the mark" (Wood,

1866b [1893]: 446). Apart from suggesting the oppressiveness of master-servant relations, the mark left on Honour's cheek hints at a symbolic reversal of class distinctions. While Charlotte yields to feral instincts generally attributed to the lower orders, the nurse becomes instrumental to the disclosure of the lady's dangerous leanings, thereby playing a role that is both 'honourable' (as her name suggests) and socially unsettling.

Another occupational figure stigmatized in nineteenth-century literature was the sickroom nurse. Traditionally caricatured as an elderly, corpulent, unrefined working-class woman with a predisposition to drunkenness, this figure appears in such novels as Dickens's *Martin Chuzzlewit* (1843) and Brontë's *Jane Eyre* (1847), which express class and sexual anxieties about women working in contact with dangerous forms of corporeality. The nurse's closeness to abject bodies – like those of diseased people – was not only at odds with the purity and sensitivity associated with ideal femininity, it also evoked the spectre of sexual impropriety owing to her proximity to male patients and doctors. These fears account for the literary caricatures of early-nineteenth-century nurses: their advanced age was a deterrent against sexual promiscuity, and their contact with corporeal abjection was made less offensive by their working-class roughness. Things started to change around the middle of the century, when the professionalization of nursing became an important topic of debate. Thanks to the pioneering work of Florence Nightingale, who strove to reconcile the maternal sides of caretaking with new professional challenges, nursing slowly became a proper occupation for educated middle-class women.[7]

The transformation of old-style into new-style nursing was not devoid of contradictions and it raised manifold fears that were widely represented in mid- to late-Victorian fiction. Sensation novels, in particular, responded to the clamours for recognition of this occupational group by questioning two traditional prejudices: the bias against women's employment in promiscuous or socially degrading environments, and the tendency to represent women either as disembodied angels or as earthly magdalens overdetermined by (their or others') physicality. In Wood's oeuvre, nurses are yes-no figures that encompass divergent behavioural models and are interpretable in light of Julia Kristeva's theory of "non-disjunction" (1968), as figures that resolve contradictions by connecting opposites. A combination of old-style and new-style aspects of nursing, their portrayals evidence Wood's use of strategic indirection in characterizing this occupational group, which is both ridiculed for preserving old-fashioned traits and praised for its professional and moral attitudes. This odd combination is well exemplified by Nurse Chaffen in *Within the Maze* (1872). Hired to assist a young mother who is ill after giving birth prematurely, the nurse proves to be a competent professional in fulfilling her duties, even though she likes to "indulge in unlimited gossip, and loved a glass of beer when she could get it" (Wood, 1872 [1891]: 279).

A bigger impression is left by the portrayal of Nurse Pepperfly in *Lord Oakburn's Daughters*. One bizarre protagonist of the novel's sub-plot pivoting around unconventional low-class women, Pepperfly is an ageing fat matron with inelegant manners, an abnormal appetite and a weakness for beer and gin. Introduced to the reader as "a short, stout barrel of a woman, with grizzled hair and black eyes" and "attired in a light-coloured print gown", Pepperfly is insistently represented as a disorderly figure prevented from keeping a dignified, tidy appearance by her "extraordinary rotundity" (Wood, 1864a [1872]: 16, 73). In many episodes, the nurse is reproached for drinking – "'Mother Pepperfly […] has her besetting sin, drink'" (1864a [1872]: 55) – while her gluttonous leanings are described in highly comic tones. Her relish for meat and heavy foods, in particular, deserves attention. In an apparently insignificant scene, the woman is asked to stop eating in order to join the doctor at her patient's bed: "Mrs. Pepperfly, fond of her supper at least in an equal degree with the widow, resented the suggestion, and held up her plate, in defiant spirit, for more bacon" (1864a [1872]: 41). Markedly, there is here an association between "bacon" and "defiance" that attaches subversive connotations to her figure.

The nurse's questionable taste in clothing, eating and drinking – three aspects closely connected with her corporeality – helps shape her inferior "class body" as it functions as "an incorporated principle of classification" (Bourdieu, 1979 [2010]: 188). In addition to embodying her low-rank habitus, her coarseness poses a serious challenge to dominant gender models. Too corpulent to fit patriarchal tropes of female beauty and self-restraint, Pepperfly confirms her gender anomaly by revealing an immoderate appetite for heavy aliments and a special craving for meat (the "bacon") which, in Bourdieu's view, is the masculine food par excellence (1979 [2010]: 190). In addition to evoking the lower bodily stratum, her over-eating is associated with a maternal role that reinforces the idea of monstrous female corporeality (she is often addressed as "Mother"). Configured as a grotesque mother prone to swallowing all sorts of victuals and drinks, Pepperfly appears as an incarnation of the carnivalesque that poses a threat to society with its uncontainable excess (Bakhtin, 1965 [1968]).

Unlike Lady Kirton analysed in Chapter 4, however, Nurse Pepperfly is no treacherous mother who symbolically feeds on her progeny. Despite her comically grotesque traits, she is a rather benevolent maternal figure that cares for her patients, is good at her job, and keeps faithful to her principles in adverse circumstances. An early recognition of her professional abilities is made by Judith Ford, a maidservant working for the Chesneys, who contends: "'But she has her wits about her; provided she keeps sober there's not a better nurse living'" (Wood, 1864a [1872]: 21). While mentioning the problem of Pepperfly's liking for alcohol, Judith praises the nurse's professional attitude which, in her view, is not significantly affected by her drinking habits. Another quality of Pepperfly's comes to the fore after her patient, who is later found to be Clarice Chesney, is murdered. Questioned by the coroner during the inquest, the nurse refuses to validate a lie told by Dr. Carlton who is trying to concoct an alibi for himself. In so doing, the woman exhibits her fundamental honesty and, although unknowingly, she protects her dead patient's interests. When she later reappears on the scene, Pepperfly invites a doctor to visit an ill boy, thereby proving instrumental to the discovery of an important clue to the murder (the boy is discovered to be Clarice's child during the visit). Even though she plays a minor role, the nurse makes her small contribution to unmasking the deceitful Carlton. On a symbolic plane, moreover, she fulfils an important subversive function with her grotesque body, which combines two non-traditional images of femininity: the hungry woman and the fat woman. Both viewed as projections of "male fear and disgust" during the nineteenth century (Cozzi, 2010: 79), these two images are made less frightening by the compassionate characterization of Mrs. Pepperfly, who provides a caring, albeit imperfect, model of maternity. Her challenge to traditional gender stereotypes is increased by the contrast between her honesty and Carlton's villainy. By suggesting that a grotesque plebeian woman is morally superior to a respectable-looking male rogue, the novel indirectly questions the reliability of patriarchal conceptions of femininity which, founded on sexualized and aestheticized constructions of the body, were meant to contain heterodoxy and "to establish an identity for women in essentialist, ahistorical, or universalist terms" (Grosz, 1994: xiv). Though partly inspired by old-style models of nursing, this grotesque figure does not enforce conservative views of femininity; she rather questions gender, class and professional hierarchies as, despite her coarse appearance, she proves to be a righteous person in comparison with Carlton, a male professional who has betrayed his family and his deontological duties.

In Nurse Pepperfly's case, social boundaries are blurred by her corporeality that defies simplistic classification. On other occasions, it is the woman's actions that question the supposed immutability of those interpersonal relations on which Victorian society was founded. The latter case is well exemplified by some female servants portrayed by Wood, who surpass their masters in skill, conscientiousness and initiative. A telling example is found in *Lord Oakburn's Daughters,* in which the shrewd Judith discovers Carlton's guilt. Described as a "sensible-looking young woman" (Wood, 1864a [1872]: 5) who cares for the mysterious Mrs. Crane (the false identity assumed by Clarice Chesney), Judith combines loyalty and compassion with powerful intuitive skills. In comparison with most of the novel's high-class characters, who are either flawed or deceitful, she appears as a trustable, affectionate and intellectually bright woman whose agency destabilizes gender and class stereotypes. The innovativeness of her role emerges in the second half of the novel in which she acts as amateur detective. Keenly interested in the murder, she develops growing suspicions about Carlton and, when she re-encounters two widows who used to know the victim (Mrs. Smith and Mrs. Gould), she offers an important clue to the mystery, helping to establish justice. In a later chapter, moreover, Judith reveals her intuitions to the Chesneys and to Frederick Grey. Significantly titled "Judith's Story", this chapter is inherently subversive as it gives an authoritative voice to a low-class woman who informs her social superiors of important facts concerning their family. It is also worth noting that Judith adds a class critique to her talk:

> "I did not dare to speak", was Judith's answer. "Who was I, a poor humble servant, that I should bring an accusation against a gentleman – a gentleman like Mr. Carlton, thought well of in the place? Nobody would have listened to me, sir. Besides, in spite of my doubts, I could not believe he was guilty. I thought I must have made some strange mistake. And I feared that the tables might have been turned upon me, and *I* accused". (1864a [1872]: 457)

Although she admits to having been uncertain about her interpretative skills, Judith is strongly polemical in her answer and insists on the inequalities of a social system that impelled low-ranking people to submit silently to the powerful. Her provocative view of social disparities is confirmed during Carlton's trial, when the defence lawyer charges her with telling a story of "pure invention" and hints at the possibility that she herself poisoned the victim. "'I feared that I should not be believed'", Judith replies before complaining that the lawyer's manipulation of facts against her is exactly the danger she had foreseen: "'I feared the very suspicion might be turned upon me; as you are now trying to turn it'" (1864a [1872]: 484). The class discrimination implied by her words is validated by the lawyer himself who, in addressing the magistrates, depicts the witness in strongly prejudiced terms: "'You cannot condemn a man like Carlton upon the sole testimony of an obscure witness; a servant girl who comes forward with a confession of things that, if true, should have been declared years ago'" (1864a [1872]: 485).

The lawyer's manipulative speech is disproved by two documents: a letter and a marriage certificate. The latter is discovered through the agency of one of the widows Judith meets, Mrs. Smith, who is so entirely convinced of Mr. Carlton's guilt that "if she could have genteely appended the surgeon with one of her silk pocket-handkerchiefs to any convenient beam, she had hastened to do it, and not waited for the delay and intricacies of the law" (1864a [1872]: 473). One of the women who contribute to Carlton's conviction, Mrs. Smith becomes instrumental to the solution of the heinous crime, thereby giving indirect support to Judith's testimony. By portraying a group of strong-willed avenging 'sisters' who arouse the reader's sympathy, the novel questions those gender prejudices that limited the female sphere of action to the domestic realm. Even more unsettling is the lower-class identity of these women who, by unearthing the secret guilt of a middle-class man, pose a serious threat to the stability of Victorian social hierarchies.

A similar function is fulfilled by Fanny Jelly in *Bessy Rane* (1870). An inquisitive servant "called by her latter name" by her employer and acquaintances (Wood, 1870 [1872]: 24), Jelly relentlessly investigates two crimes committed by an apparently respectable doctor: Oliver Rane. The crimes are an anonymous slanderous letter that causes the death of one of the defamed people, and a financial fraud suspiciously connected with the sudden death of Dr. Rane's wife. As I demonstrate elsewhere, in acting as an amateur detective, Jelly not only arouses Victorian anxieties of household espionage, she also proves to be a skilful sleuth, who dares to investigate the suspicious deeds committed by an esteemed professional, rightly interprets the clues and is not intimidated by the suspect's higher status (Costantini, 2015: 268–271). These actions have important social implications. A first element to consider is the idea of power associated with her cleverness. In a dialogue she has with a man wrongly suspected of writing the slanderous letter, Jelly asserts her different interpretation with a self-assured laugh: "Not a loud laugh, was it, but rather derisive, and full of *power*" (Wood, 1870 [1872]: 225). Italicized in the text, the power she gains through her hermeneutic skills is reflected in the fears assailing Dr. Rane, who feels threatened by someone doubly inferior to him from a socio-sexual perspective (1870 [1872]: 226).

In addition to investigating the epistolary slander, the curious maid plays a central role in solving the mystery of the sudden death and hurried burial of Bessy Rane. Convinced of having seen a ghost when she catches glimpses of the dead Mrs. Rane, Jelly stubbornly pursues her detection: she convinces the law to intervene and order an exhumation of the body, thereby paving the way to the unveiling of the fraud. What the exhumation reveals is that there is no body in the coffin: Mrs. Rane is alive and has connived with her husband to organize the fraud (her existence was an obstacle to her husband's cashing in the proceeds of a tontine – a particular form of investment). In the end, Jelly hands her enquiry over to a police detective, Inspector Jekyll, a "red-faced" man "experienced in crime" (1870 [1872]: 406) whose name interestingly puns on the maid's. Nonetheless, her amateurish investigation is essential to unmasking the ambiguous conduct of two professional men, the deceitful Dr. Rane and Lawyer Dale, the local coronet who would rather "have remained quiescent, and consigned the doctor to his conscience" (1870 [1872]: 376). The maid's initiative is crucial to the discovery of the truth. Besides interrogating the limits of female professionalism, her agency as amateur investigator conveys an important ethical message, as it suggests that the morality of people's conduct is independent from their social and occupational status.

Probably influenced by an earlier figure portrayed by Wilkie Collins – the eponymous low-class protagonist of the short story "The Diary of Anne Rodway" (1856) – the strange female sleuth characterized in *Bessy Rane* fulfils two important functions: she proves the relevance of Wood's experimentation with crime (and detective) fiction that would make Wood one of the genre's "mothers" (Sussex, 2010: 4); and she evidences the extent of the novel's interrogation of Victorian social boundaries. The latter function is suggested by the fact that, instead of enforcing the double marginality of plebeian women, *Bessy Rane* features a detective maid endowed with intellectual abilities that are used to challenge the privileges of higher-ranking characters. From this perspective, it is hardly surprising that Wood attributed to the maid some comic elements that were meant to mollify her subversiveness. In addition to falling prey to supernatural fears, Jelly is said to have an improper "love of admiration" that makes her choose younger suitors she can patronize (Wood, 1870 [1872]: 119). Decidedly unladylike in her selection of male admirers, she stays unmarried until the end of the story when, after being abandoned by a faithless suitor, she accepts the courtship of another young man. The novel closes with an image of Jelly "ruling" the household where she is employed, "giving her opinion, unasked, in a free and easy manner" and receiving the attentions of a head gardener whom she controls (1870 [1872]: 448). By attaching comic undertones to the maidservant's lack of restraint and by suggesting her distance from middle-class ideals of femininity, *Bessy Rane* confirms the secondary role played by Jelly both socially (as a low-class woman) and diegetically (as a minor character). Such an ironic description must have reassured the novel's conservative readership. If carefully compared with the novel's protagonists, however, Jelly offers a double-bounded model of femininity that invites scrutiny. Apparently norm-enforcing as a grotesque low-class figure, she nonetheless exhibits a sharper mind and a stronger sense of justice than most middle- and upper-class characters. Independently from their gender, most high-class characters featured in *Bessy Rane* are in fact flawed or prone to vice. The eponymous heroine herself betrays a questionable morality when she accepts to play a part in her husband's fraud. By implying that a servant might surpass the higher ranks in talent and morality, Wood covertly questions the solidity of the very class hierarchies she seems to validate.[8] Similarly provocative is the final reference to Jelly's autonomy of speech, action and sexuality that, despite its comic undertones, points to new paths of freedom for women in an age that identified the yearnings of womanhood solely with marriage and domestic subservience. An analogous function is fulfilled by Mary Barber, a young woman with visionary powers featured in *Dene Hollow* (1871). As Alison Jaquet argues, Mary is an anomalous female figure, as she rejects the path of marriage, shuns male protection and freely chooses the life of a servant to gain economic independence. Unlike her mother, who married an incapable man, Mary "presents an alternative and influential model of femininity", which is enhanced by Wood's use of feminine supernaturalism "as an avenue for power and understanding" (Jaquet, 2008: 253, 256).

The characterization of maidservants endowed with qualities lacking in the higher classes is a subtle strategy of critique adopted by Wood. Without openly defying her bourgeois readership, the author showed her alertness to some cracks that were appearing in Victorian society and her wish to explore the tensions produced by emerging forces. Such a heterodox approach is confirmed by her sympathetic portrayal of some foreign maids who embody marginality at three different levels. In *Within the Maze*, for instance, Lucy Cleeve's French maid Aglaé saves her mistress's life by an act of volition, as she gives precious information to Lucy's suitor in defiance of the family's prohibition. Even more troubling to Victorian class conventions is the function fulfilled by Sophie Deffloe, a French maid in the service of the eponymous heroine in *Lady Adelaide's Oath*. Despite her supposed inferiority of class, gender and ethnicity, Sophie provides an imitable behavioural model and feels indignation at witnessing the deceitful conduct of her mistress, who flirts with two suitors and lies to protect a supposed murderer. Apart from symbolizing the stifled voice of Adelaide's conscience, the French maid embodies an innovative female role as she is bold in her utterings and authoritative in her actions. A further element of novelty is her successful marriage with Ravensbird whom she chooses as life- and business-mate. In the course of the narration, the couple sets a compelling example of affection and dignity, while their class superiors fall prey to deceit, cruelty and self-delusion. The fact that they are both foreign increases the unsettling effects of their characterization, as they surpass all the British characters in truthfulness and generosity.[9]

Although not all the maids portrayed by Wood are endowed with admirable qualities (a malevolent figure, among others, is that of Tiffle in *Lady Adelaide's Oath*), their class belonging frees them from the strictures of bourgeois normativity. Owing to this freedom, their characterization becomes a vehicle for alternative femininity, as it offers a dynamic spectrum of new attitudes that women could adopt if they lived in a less constraining social system.

More stereotypical is, instead, Wood's depiction of destitute women belonging to the lowest orders of society. Several novels lay bare the author's conservative, albeit compassionate, approach to these women, who are only occasionally differentiated from the uncouth masses inhabiting the London underbelly, the industrial slums or the nation's impoverished farming areas. What dominates in such representations is generally a patronizing notion of the poor's co-responsibilities in their sufferings. As Burgauer observes, most working-class women portrayed by Wood are charged with the task of keeping their homes comfortable despite their deprivations – a task that, generally unaccomplished, is viewed as a main cause for their men's drunkenness and moral laxity (1950: 44–45). Such a reactionary view is evident in novels like *Danesbury House* and *Mrs. Halliburton's Troubles*, both of which insist on the female poor's responsibility for the hygienic and moral degradation of their families. Even though she acknowledges class disparities and manifests an evangelical pity for the dispossessed, Wood tends to show a disparaging attitude towards these women's hardships. What she blames is their inability to improve their condition by adopting a Smilesian model of self-help founded on perseverance and physical work.

In line with dominant Victorian prejudices, moreover, Wood often associates low-ranking women's corporeality with illicit sexuality, even though she questions the naturalness of this link by hinting at some social causes of their unchastity. Her divided attitude is evident in her treatment of prostitution. A notable example is found in *Mrs. Halliburton's Troubles*, where the story of a working-class victim of seduction, Caroline Mason, is effectively juxtaposed with the tragedy of an unnamed fallen woman, probably induced to prostitution by poverty. In neither case is the woman's loss of dignity, due to her fall, justified. Seduced by a wealthy rogue, Caroline becomes a social outcast after her fall and is forced to walk the streets. Quite unexpectedly, the novel closes with her reformation through the agency of Charlotte East, a compassionate friend who offers her a job and support against social censure. But Caroline's lack of discernment is insistently stigmatized in the text that attributes her fall to her inability to resist seduction. Less clear is instead the responsibility of the unnamed daughter of Widow Booth, who is briefly mentioned in the novel's opening pages. A pale figure in the background "dying from famine [...] in a dreadful state of exhaustion" (Wood, 1862 [1897]: 17), the starving girl is not spared moral criticism by Jane Halliburton's mother, who describes her as "sinful, ill-doing" and unworthy of compassion (1862 [1897]: 17). Pitiful though she is, the fallen girl's condition reveals Wood's conservative attitude in dealing with the problem of prostitution. While exposing the possible social causes of the dying creature's fall, the author warns women against falling into an abyss of sin from which they are seldom rescued.

More pitiful and unorthodox is instead Wood's attitude towards the social problem of incest produced by poor housing and promiscuity. A rare case of her treatment of this tabooed topic is found in *Verner's Pride*. Summoned to visit Alice Hook, the daughter of a poverty-stricken family who had a miscarriage and lies very ill, Jan Verner generously assists the "miserable castaway" disparaged by local people (Wood, 1863b [n.d.]: 381). In a conversation with his sister-in-law, the young surgeon defines Alice as a victim of family conditions that reflect the miserable state of the nation's dispossessed: "'Suppose you and I had to sleep in a room of few feet square, no chimney, no air, and that others tenanted it with us? Girls and boys growing up – nay, grown up, some of them; men and women as we are, Sibylla. The beds huddled together, no space between them; sickness, fever –'" (1863b [n.d.]: 392). Interrupted by his interlocutor, Jan adds more clues to the picture by referring to the lack of moral sense resulting from the Hooks' promiscuity: "'And therefore their perceptions of right and wrong are deadened. The wonder is, not that Alice Hook has lost herself, but that –'" (1863b [n.d.]: 392). Although the second ellipsis leaves the sentence unfinished, the hint at the family's immorality evokes the spectre of incest among the poor, a scandalous topic surrounded by "a conspiracy of silence" at the time (Wohl, 1978b: 200). What is noteworthy in this passage is Jan's perception of Alice as a victim of specific social problems rather than a sexualized diseased body bearing the stigma of declassed femininity. The surgeon's refusal to essentialize his patient in terms of abject corporeality is proof of the subtle strategies Wood used to interrogate gender stereotypes. Yet, these strategies emerge only occasionally in her portrayals of low-ranking women, which generally validate the notion of social determinism espoused by Victorian elites. If the poor are trapped in their degenerate environment, more opportunities of improvement are offered to women of humble origins who possess talents, inclinations and an honest disposition that protects them from lures of illicit sexuality.

An unsuccessful specimen of this kind is Rachel Frost, a labourer's daughter who becomes maid and protégée of a lady in *Verner's Pride*. "A very beautiful girl" with delicate features and "refined as any lady", Rachel attracts men belonging to different classes, including her mistress's sons, one of whom she secretly loves (Wood, 1863b [n.d.]: 12). In an early dramatic episode, Rachel's body is found floating in a local pond and the mystery of her death remains unsolved until the novel's final pages, when she is discovered to have been driven to suicide by unwanted pregnancy and unrequited love. What Rachel epitomizes are the difficulties facing working-class women who fight against class determinism. Despite her remarkable beauty and manners, she has no chaste disposition and is therefore punished for her ambition to rise in station. This reading is confirmed by her early erasure from the scene that prevents her from arousing the reader's compassion.

Quite different is, instead, the destiny of Charlotte East featured in *Mrs. Halliburton's Troubles*. A glovemaker condemned to long hours of manual work, Charlotte provides an intriguing study of working-class self-help that mirrors the Smilesian model offered by

Jane Halliburton, the novel's shabby-genteel heroine. As we have seen in Chapter 1, Jane moves across classes without losing her perseverance, which enables her to fully develop her talents. On a slightly lower scale, Charlotte reduplicates Jane's industry and wisdom. A hard-labouring woman who never yields to despair, she is not distracted by trifles but invests her little free time in the embellishment of her home: "How she did her house-work no one knew. Not a woman married or single, got through more glove-sewing than Charlotte. Not one kept her house in better order" (Wood, 1862 [1897]: 111). Although it might appear unrealistic, the reference to the order in which she keeps her house is important to set an admirable model of low-class femininity. Praised for the cosy household she creates despite her fewer means, Charlotte is also a prudent woman who has limited ambitions and keeps distant from dangerous men. Her prudence in love matters is rewarded with a happy marriage and a new comfortable, though still low-rank, position.

Heterogeneous, class-biased but also thought-provoking, Wood's characterization of low-class women bears witness to her exploration of feminine roles and identities that were not encompassed within essentializing bourgeois models. Her interest in the hardships and innovative potentials of some women belonging to the lower ranks is in line with her sympathy for cross-class figures like governesses, who, as shown above, challenge bourgeois norms with their paid occupation and liminal status.

Like Frances Trollope, Sarah R. Whitehead and other mid-Victorian writers, Wood was influenced by the early-century evangelical movement that encouraged a serious treatment of the social problems faced by the dispossessed, including prostitution (Mitchell, 1981: 22). This evangelical pity is evident in her portrayals of reformed prostitutes, suffering drunkards and victimized employees discussed above; but the sympathy aroused by such portrayals was more than an example of high-class benevolence. If Wood's conservatism is undeniable, we should also consider that her professed acceptance of social hierarchies coexists with her skilfully concealed curiosity about the subordinate classes. The characterization of low-rank women evidences Wood's adoption of clichés, such as vulgarity and ignorance, which were commonly applied to the lowest orders. In her works, however, such clichés are perplexingly combined with innovative views of femininity that question dominant stereotypes. In addition to portraying conscientious and truthful figures, Wood endows some low-class women with unfeminine qualities, such as perspicacity and initiative, which are positively connoted rather than stigmatized. The sharp-witted detective-maids analysed above are proof of her interest in women's potentiality for self-development, as their invasion of typically male spheres of action paves the way to justice making and law-enforcement.[10] Even more compelling is Wood's association of women's abnormal corporeality with likeable traits which, as exemplified by the honest and gargantuan Pepperfly, confound traditional views of female excess and unruliness.

Conclusion

A self-assured professional and an icon of domesticity, Ellen Wood is still an object of debate among scholars, who are challenged to interpret the apparently irreconcilable ideas underlying her writings. Drawing on a selection of feminist theories, this study shows that many contradictions of her personal history and works are due to her deep interest in Victorian gender practices, and especially in the age's modelling of women's roles, which she strove to represent in their lights and shadows. Although she was a champion of bourgeois values, Wood used camouflage strategies to question the strictness of those social norms that limited women's self-development, such as the separate-spheres doctrine and the indictment of female labour. Conservative in her sympathies, innovative in her exploration of women's hardships and potentialities, she created effects of epistemic stridency in her narratives, which often puzzled Victorian reviewers. Having faded into obscurity in the post-Victorian age, Wood has been rediscovered in the last few decades, but she still elicits diverse critical responses that complicate her positioning within the newly canonized genealogy of popular women writers.

Instead of forcing Wood into single critical categories, this book acknowledges the complexities of her professional experiences and writing practices. Particular attention has been paid to her constant wavering between anti-feminist and proto-feminist ideas, which emerges in her oblique critique of Victorian gender orthodoxy. As shown in Chapters 1 and 2, her representations of women's roles within the marriage contract bear evidence of her distinctive blend of conservatism and innovation. While drawing pictures of domestic life that seem to enforce middle-class ideology, Wood unveils the strictures of a marriage institution that tends to curb women's aspirations to happiness and activity. The suffering wives she portrays raise thorny questions about the desirability of conjugal and maternal bonds celebrated by conduct books and fairy tales, whose ideals of female forbearance is often shown to frustrate the heroines' real yearnings.

Also thought-provoking is Wood's depiction of female immoderacy analysed in Chapter 3. In contrast with bourgeois models of self-restraint, Wood avoids stigmatizing female passions and impulsiveness. In depicting women's psychophysical disorders, moreover, she questions essentializing notions of inborn female hysteria validated by Victorian medical science, as she unveils many social triggers of her heroines' problems. Sensational in their actions, which sometimes pose serious threats to others, the impassioned women featured in her oeuvre are often characterized as victims of a social system that strives to repress their emotional freedom. Besides arousing sympathy for these transgressive women, Wood offers unorthodox pictures of men who, feminized by their tender disposition, their weak personalities or their psychophysical ailments, confirm the author's subtle critique of Victorian gender assumptions.

Another discourse imbricated with these gender issues is the one on class. If it is true that most of Wood's protagonists belong to the Victorian bourgeoisie and embody its values, such as respectability and self-help, it is nonetheless true that daring models of alternative femininity are offered by characters ranked higher or lower than the author's class. In portraying upper-class women, for instance, Wood was not immune from dominant prejudices against the parasitic leanings and the immoral proclivity of the aristocracy. Yet, she drew on these prejudices to conceive prospectively liberating models for women who, like the adulterous

Isabel Vane or the eccentric Lady Kirton analysed in Chapter 4, enjoy some autonomy of action and emotional freedom. Even more provocative are the cross-class and low-ranking figures examined in Chapter 5. In addition to characterizing destitute gentlewomen who lose status and are forced to work by adverse circumstances, Wood portrayed women born and positioned in the lower orders of Victorian society, who are endowed with uncommon perspicacity and initiative.

Largely understudied by scholars, these low-class minor figures are here paid critical attention as they bear evidence of the author's innovative stance. Exactly because of their marginal narrative role and social status, characters like the sharp-witted detective-maid Jelly and the gargantuan Nurse Pepperfly perform a potentially liberating function as they violate gender constraints that few bourgeois heroines are allowed to challenge. The processes through which Wood shaped these unconventional women also shed light on the narrative experiments she conducted by merging conflicting narrative modes and genres together. Viewed as offensive by orthodox reviewers, these experiments were nonetheless essential to her literary success as they appealed to a large cross-class audience. As Andrew Maunder suggests, "Wood's fusion of decorum and daring" allowed "her readers to glimpse the gaps within contemporary ideology" as she used conventions to thinly veil "things readers would rather not hear about middle-class life" (2000: 24). If her characterization of low-class women threw into relief some questionable aspects of bourgeois femininity, her unsettling combination of highbrow and lowbrow forms, domesticity and sensationalism, posed a similar challenge to the gender models validated by serious literature. The heterogeneous, cross-class nature of her prose is confirmed by the history of the stage adaptations of *East Lynne* which, after becoming a Victorian bestseller, inspired a variety of performances including plays produced for working-class theatres (Maunder, 2006). Although Wood had no part or share in these adaptations, their history suggests that there were, in her novel, lowbrow elements typical of melodrama that could be easily appropriated and refashioned for a working-class public.

Wood's combination of philistine and low-class elements was criticized by Victorian reviewers, who snobbishly objected to the distastefulness and the ideological stridency of her literary hybrids. In 1866, the vulgarity of her writings was lamented by Eliza Lynn Linton, who expressed her perplexity about their popularity (117). Yet, what fascinated the public were exactly those commonplace aspects condemned by Linton and her fellow critics. In ways similar to other women writers, Wood experimented with declassed forms and modes drawn from lowbrow literature, such as the Gothic, sensationalism and crime fiction. These generic combinations not only favoured her extraordinary popularity during the Victorian age. They also enabled her to develop narrative forms that could articulate her experiences and, especially, offer glimpses into some contradictions of contemporary discourses of femininity that she perceived but was still unable to systematize and resolve.

Notes

Introduction

1. Feminist theorists like Annis V. Pratt and Mary Daly consider "methodolatry" particularly dysfunctional as, in their view, the insistence upon a single method is distinctive of patriarchal disciplines (Ruthven, 1984: 25).
2. Her deformity seems to have contributed to her death, which her son attributes to the combined effects of a respiratory infection and the pressure upon her heart provoked by her inward curvature (Charles Wood, 1894: 302).
3. These prejudices are manifest in her late novel *Court Netherleigh* (1881), in which the invalid Alice Dalrymple renounces to marry her beloved in a melodramatic scene of self-sacrifice.
4. "Under Wood's ownership *The Argosy* achieved an average monthly circulation of 20,000" (Maunder, 2000: 29).
5. Novelist Caroline Norton accused Wood of plagiarizing her in 1871. Yet, she found "a formidable opponent" in her fellow novelist, who retorted that *East Lynne* had been "taken partly from [her] own imagination, partly from a romance enacted in real life, some of whose actors were living still" (Sussex, 2010: 105). Accusations of plagiarism against women novelists were frequent. Another well-known case is the charge brought against Mary Elizabeth Braddon by a *Pall Mall Gazette* article, which accused her of plagiarizing Octave Feuillet's play *Dalila* in her 1867 novel *Circe* (Beller, 2012: 50).
6. Charles specifies that she used to work "from nine until six" at times of extreme pressure, but she adopted a strict routine of writing at other times, regularly devoting four hours a day to her professional duties. He also observes that she considered her deadlines "sacred and binding" and "never kept anyone waiting an hour for any manuscript" (Charles Wood, 1887: 432).
7. Growing attention has been lately paid to Wood's editorial experiences. It suffices to consider Beth Palmer's comparative study of Wood, Braddon and Florence Marryat, three women authors and editors who made successful careers in a male-dominated magazine market but also faced gender-biased opposition (2011).
8. Attacked as "a purveyor of immoral fiction", Braddon was also criticized for her unorthodox life choices. In the early years of her career, she "defied the conventional path of life for a middle class girl by becoming an actress and

eventually deciding to live as the common law wife of the publisher John Maxwell" (Carnell, 2000: 1–2).
9. Even though she was "not avowedly evangelical" and despite her early experience of "high-church cathedral life", Wood read the commercially successful evangelical publications of her age, and she appropriated the rhetoric of what was considered a "religion 'of the heart'" (Palmer, 2011: 87–88).
10. "*The Times*, in reviewing *East Lynne*, said they had never before met an authoress so capable in delineating with a few strokes of the pen the portraits and characters of men, and of *noble* men" writes Charles Wood, who attributes this skill to the model of "refinement and intellectual attainments" provided by Thomas Price (1894: 16).
11. Translated into many languages, *East Lynne* became a bestseller in Europe, the United States and the colonies. The magnitude of its success was proved by its many stage adaptations on both sides of the Atlantic soon after its publication.
12. An example of oversimplification is Nicholas Rance's definition of Wood as a "conservative" sensation novelist who, unlike Collins, Braddon and other "radical" representatives of the genre, used sensational elements for moral purposes (1991: 5).
13. For an insightful comparison of the two essays see, among others, Millett (1970).
14. Despite her conservatism, Oliphant uses irony to dismantle the traditional marriage plot in novels like *Miss Marjoribanks* (1865–66) and *The Curate in Charge* (1875–76). For an in-depth analysis of these contradictions see, among others, Sanders (1996) and Wagner (2009).
15. Delivered as a speech before a branch of the National Society for Women's Service in 1931, this essay was published posthumously in *The Death of the Moth and Other Essays* in 1942.
16. The combination of apparently irreconcilable discourses, such as those of evangelicalism and sensationalism, is analysed by Beth Palmer (2008), who offers convincing textual examples and a cogent analysis of the cultural context in which Wood produced her works.
17. This idea was further developed by Jonathan Culler, who influenced later approaches to the question of "reading as a woman" (1983: 43–64).
18. To say this does not mean that Wood made her readers fully aware and critical of the male-centred culture of their age. In ways similar to Valerie Sanders, I think that such a programme was too extreme for a number of Victorian women. But I am also convinced that the idea of "resistance" can be consistently applied to Wood, as the thorny issues dramatized in her fiction encourage her readers to "resist a blanket application of cultural, gender-based expectations" (Sanders, 1996: 53).

Chapter 1. The necessity and traps of Victorian marriage

1. The companionate ideal became "a common aspiration by the dawn of the 19th century" when marriage, no longer viewed simply as "a transaction between

families", came to be "imagined as a union of companions who were supposed to emotionally enrich each other's lives" (Phegley, 2012: 2). While "gesturing towards equality between the sexes", however, this ideal clashed with the reality of many Victorian marriages, which were often contracted for material purposes and required the "submission" of wives criticized by J. S. Mill and other champions of women's enfranchisement (Phegley, 2012: 7, 26–27).
2. Nineteenth-century literature was marked by the gradual disappearance of traditional gothic spaces, such as castles or abbeys, which embodied the power of the aristocracy and the *ancien regime*. These spatial paraphernalia were increasingly replaced by urban and homely contexts, which expressed a wide range of anxieties concerning the bourgeois family and its values (Botting, 2014: 104–105ff).
3. Frances endures social ostracism for her rebellious marriage but she is rewarded with a companionate union with a gentlemanly lower-class partner. For her part, Anne loses her autonomy through love, as she accepts guidance from a man who, as shown in Chapter 5, asks her to perform multiple acts of female obedience.
4. At the *fin de siècle*, Charlotte Perkins Gilman described female consumption as "luxurious and enervating", and connected to women's "false economic position" in a society in which they were "debarred from any free production, unable to estimate the labor involved in the making of what [they] so lightly destroy[ed]" (1898: 120). This comment suggests that women's dependence on men came to be viewed as a disabling factor by early feminist authors.
5. On the economic and socio-sexual implications of this scene, see Lysack (2008: 1–2) and Marroni (2017: 22–24).
6. Drawn from folklore, "Beauty and the Beast" was first published by Gabrielle-Suzanne Barbot de Villeneuve in 1740 and later reprinted in an abridged version by Marie Leprince de Beaumont. In the mid-nineteenth century, the tale appeared in English translation, as evidenced by its inclusion in the volume *Four and Twenty Fairy Tales* (Planché, 1858: 225–328). Though not attested, it is likely that Wood read it either in English or in its French original. Her description of a young woman monetarized to pay off her father's gambling debts seems to anticipate postmodern rewritings of the fairy tale, such as Angela Carter's "The Tiger's Bride" (1979), which opens with the sentence: "My father lost me to The Beast at cards" (1979 [2006]: 56).
7. In the last part of the novel, Grubb inherits his title from Margery Upton, thereby getting back the legacy he had lost owing to his mother's rebellious marriage.
8. Margaret Oliphant was one of these trenchant but influential critics. She objected to many appealing portrayals of transgressive women offered by sensation novelists, including the sympathetic characterization of Isabel Vane in *East Lynne* ([Oliphant], 1862).
9. Wood adapts the fairy tale to the context of Victorian bourgeois capitalism. In the original tale, Beauty's father is a merchant partly debased by his trading

profession in comparison with the aristocratic Beast. In *Court Netherleigh*, instead, the plebeian Grubb is endowed with gentlemanly qualities and finally elevated to an upper-class role, while the high-ranking Lord Acorn is prey to vices suggesting moral and financial degeneration.

10. Initially frustrated by pregnancy – described as a period of restricted "liberty" and poor health (Wood, 1881 [1898]: 81) – Adela is further upset at the prospect of nursing: "'But the trouble! – and the sacrifice. Oh, how cross and contrary the world sometimes is!'" (1881 [1898]: 89). Rather than revealing "perversity", this exclamation suggests that the young woman perceives herself as the victim of a society that forces her into a role she has not freely chosen. The idea that she is neither cruel not unnatural is confirmed by "the spark of tenderness" (1881 [1898]: 84) she feels for the baby, whom she later accepts to breastfeed.

11. "In her inner purity, her sensitively refined nature, she could not bring herself to speak openly to her husband upon topics of this unpleasant kind" (Wood, 1872 [1891]: 163). The pretty woman is Rose Turner, the wife of Karl's brother Adam. The couple secretly lives in the cottage to escape the Law after Adam broke out from the prison where he was convicted for killing a rival in love. Even though Adam deserved his sentence to life imprisonment, Karl cannot deny his help to his criminal brother.

12. For this concept, see the Introduction.

13. Like Wood, the novel's heroine studies the classics and receives a wide-ranging education from her father. Both of them earn money through their intellectual work after becoming wives and mothers, and both pursue their careers without leaving the domestic sphere.

14. On the Victorian fascination with Mormon beliefs and practices see, among others, Lecourt (2013).

15. A good example is the melodramatic story "The New Man (A Fragment from the Romance of the Near Future)" appeared in *Punch* in October 1849. See MacDonald (2015: 16ff).

16. By the late-Victorian period, proto-feminist demands and pressing social issues led to a rethinking of traditional forms of masculinity. One of the "deep roads [...] made into patriarchal power" was the discrediting of male sexuality consequent on concerns over public health and morality (Tosh, 1999: 153–154). The 1890s, moreover, witnessed the emergence of "sensitive, nurturing, domestic" New Men, who incarnated "specific embodiments of the Victorian gentleman" (MacDonald, 2015: 3).

17. Jocosely defined a "famous [nurse]" by his wife, the reformed lord applies the epithet "nurse" to himself when he indulges his baby's whims to prevent him from crying (Wood, 1860 [n.d.]: 236, 241).

18. The novel's digressive structure is due to the author's embedding of various texts. Besides expanding an early story published in 1853 with the same title, Wood interpolated into the novel an 1855 story, entitled "The Reception of

the Dead". See Pykett (2004: xxxiii) and Pires (2008: 179, 183). As publisher William Tinsley noted, Wood devised "an ingenious system of novel-writing": she often wrote short stories "complete in themselves" but with "connecting links" that she could later arrange to work "groups of stories together into full-length books" (Newbolt, 2001: 82). This writing strategy is confirmed by Elwin (1934: 236–237).

19. *The House of Halliwell* was one of those works "offered to Bentley and other publishers [...] unsuccessfully" which "appeared only after [Wood's] fame, or posthumously" (Sussex, 2010: 111). Its early composition is confirmed in a note to the reader that defines it as "the earliest of Mrs. Henry Wood's works", "written some years before 'EAST LYNNE'" (Wood, 1890 [1896]: v).

Chapter 2. Variations of the Griselda theme

1 The young bride is actually the couple's daughter whom Gualtieri falsely announced to have put to death some years earlier. Conceived as a further test of Griselda's patience, the arranged wedding has worrying incestuous connotations, which reinforce the oppressive role of fathers and husbands in patriarchal societies.

2. Unlike Mrs. Hare, Barbara is neither afraid of her father nor willing to justify his domestic tyranny. Her rebellious attitude emerges in a conversation she has with her shy mother, during which she calls the *pater familias* "pig-headed" (Wood, 1861 [2000]: 284).

3. Charlotte Brontë made a large use of direct address in her novels, most famously in *Jane Eyre* (1847), thereby establishing a sort of intimacy with her readers. This strategy of communication was recurrent in Victorian fiction, especially in women's writing.

4. Widely read by middle- and upper-class women, Victorian conduct books offered a variety of teachings and advice: from household management, as famously exemplified by *Mrs. Beeton's Book of Household Management* (1861), to moral standards and social duties. Well-known examples are Sarah Stickney Ellis's *The Women of England: Their Social Duties and Domestic Habits* (1839) and Florence Hartley's *The Ladies' Book of Etiquette, and Manual of Politeness* (1860).

5. In this essay, Linton laments the demise of the "fair young English girl" of the past, an "ideal of womanhood" described as "a creature generous, capable, modest; something franker than a Frenchwoman, more to be trusted than an Italian, as brave as an American but more refined, as domestic as a German and more graceful". Immodest and unreliable is, instead, the emerging "fast girl", who imitates "the *demi-monde* in dress", talks boldly, loves luxury and pleasures, and aims to make a mercenary marriage, driven by "the desire of money before either love or happiness" (Linton, 1868: 339–340).

6. Anorexia nervosa was recognized as a disorder in the second half of the nineteenth century, when two physicians, William Withey Gull and Ernest-Charles Lasègue, offered detailed descriptions of cases and symptoms. For an early entry of the

term "anorexia", defined as "loss of appetite for food", see an 1861 glossary by Alexander Henry (12).
7. Often reproached for her unfeminine activities, Charlotte is the object of awful predictions by people who foresee that "'She *will* be killed, [...] some day, with those horses of hers'" (Wood, 1863a [n.d.]: 223). Quite ironically, no accident involves the bold driver in the course of the narration while it is the inactive Maria that faces a tragic death.
8. This comment anticipates a similar idea expressed by Linton in "The Girl of Period": "But she [the Girl of the Period] does not marry easily. Men are afraid of her; and with reason. They may amuse themselves with her for an evening, but they do not readily take her for life" (1868: 340).
9. In Mangham's opinion, Wood's contradictory views of gender are further evidenced by the ambiguous characterization of Lady Godolphin. A modern wife endowed with autonomy and self-will, Lady Godolphin uses her own money to build the Folly and freely makes her domestic arrangements. Yet, she also contributes to bringing down the family as she convinces her husband to ignore the curse and move into the modern building – an act that triggers the Godolphins' tragic demise.
10. The refused inheritance is from Lady Oswald, who is unwillingly killed by Davenal's assistant, Markus Cray, during surgery. Although he is not responsible for the accident, Davenal keeps the secret of Markus's guilt and is consequently assailed by remorse.
11. While Sara is denied disclosure, the reader knows Oswald's secret. What he is ashamed to reveal is the fact that he had suspected Dr. Davenal of being responsible for Lady Oswald's death and that he had decided to abandon Sara driven by his pride.
12. In the novel's conclusion Anne learns that, when Maude died of a heart attack, Alice Waterlow, with whom Val had previously contracted an irregular Scottish marriage, had also passed away after spending some years in an asylum affected by mental illness (Wood, 1866a [1903]: 443–449).

Chapter 3. Desiring subjects and the effects of immoderacy
1. See, among others, Phyllis Chesler, who examines the repressive function of asylums in *Women and Madness* (1972). For a brief illustration of different theoretical approaches to female mental disorder, see Quay (1996: 212–213).
2. In "Sorties", Cixous celebrates women's madness as a source of energy and a means to contest patriarchal order. Yet, she also considers the extent to which the overflowing nature of femininity tends to be perceived as unruly and dangerous: "An outpouring that can be agonizing, since she may fear, and make the other fear, endless aberrations and madness in her release" (Cixous, 1975 [1986]: 91).
3. See Chapter 2, note 4.
4. Besides her bursts of anger, Sibylla behaves hysterically during a thunderstorm when, terrified by the "peals of thunder", she "bur[ies] her head amidst the soft

cushion of a chair" (Wood, 1863b [n.d.]: 408–409). It is noteworthy, however, that her over-emotional response to the storm is an endearing element that humanizes her figure. Lionel himself is moved by this sight and forgives her previous brusqueness while holding her in a patient, soothing embrace.

5. Triggered by a sun-stroke, Lionel's illness is complicated by social, financial and sentimental problems that weigh on his mind. The psychosomatic nature of his affliction is suggested by Jan Verner: "'Is there anything on your mind that's keeping you back?'" (Wood, 1863b [n.d.]: 160). On the idea that Lionel's malady is "essentially feminized" as it "bears all the hallmarks of hysteria", and on "how central such 'fears' were to the construction of the 'gentlemanly' ideal", see Mangham (2007: 166, 168).

6. As scholars have amply recognized, Braddon's novel raises doubts about Victorian medical diagnoses that confounded madness with immorality. This problem is evident in Dr. Mosgrave's analysis of Lucy Audley's symptoms: "'The lady is not mad; but she has the hereditary taint in her blood. She has the cunning of madness, with the prudence of intelligence. [...] She is dangerous'" (Braddon, 1862 [1987]: 379).

7. In the Brothers Grimm's tale, the cruel Queen is also killed in a frenzied dance. There is however an important difference between the two texts. While Sibylla West dances as an act of volition, the fairy-tale stepmother experiences a reduction of her decisional power, as she is forced to wear red-hot iron shoes that make her dance until she drops dead. What the fairy tale envisages for the Queen is an exemplary punishment that is meant to curb her dangerous female agency and reaffirm traditional gender roles.

8. Widely covered in the Victorian press, the case caused much stir as it involved the brutal killing of a child by his sixteen-year-old half-sister, Constance Emily Kent, who confessed the murder in 1865, but kept silent about the motive.

9. As Pamela Gilbert notices, in Victorian novels desire, and especially "illicit desire", is "alienating, because in desiring an Other, one moves toward transgression". Yet, desire also produces restraining forces as it "must be 'contained' by law and custom, or sublimated" (2005: 42–43ff).

10. See Chapter 1, note 18.

11. The man is connoted as fickle by the repetition of a sentence uttered by the first Mrs. St. John on her deathbed: "'To remain faithful to the dead is not in man's nature'" (Wood, 1866b [1893]: 4, 11).

12. Charlotte's "undisciplined" mind is indirectly explained by her being a spoiled child, the object of her mother's "inordinate" love and "care" (Wood, 1866b [1893]: 19, 23).

13. Though hereditary, Georgy's consumption is also connected with the tragic loss of his stepbrother. "George St. John was in a decline – the same disease that had killed his father. [...] The puzzle was – *what* had harmed him? Had he taken too much? [...] Had he suffered a shock from the fright?" (Wood, 1866b [1893]: 234–235).

14. Ellen Wood lost a daughter during her French sojourn. Both versions of Charles Wood's biography mention the girl's death of scarlet fever and the blame Wood put on French doctors for the wrong treatment of her child (1887: 264; 1894: 51–52).
15. In a moment of jealousy, for instance, Charlotte crushes a crystal chessman in her hand and is wounded by the impulsive action, but she immediately recovers from her emotion and appears "calm, sweet, impassive" (Wood, 1866b [1893]: 413).
16. On the class implications of this attack, see Chapter 5.
17. Temporarily questioned by some people during his obsessive investigation, Frederick's mental balance is shown to break down when he falls prey to rage and disfigures the portrait of Adeline de Castella (Wood, 1866b [1893]: 301). On the latter episode, see Chapter 1.
18. *Lady Adelaide's Oath* offers different examples of mentally weak men, such as the epileptic Mitchel and the impulsive Wilfred Lester. For details, see Chapter 4.
19. On the conflation of such contradictory roles in Charlotte's characterization, Pykett notices: "If the maternal woman lies at the heart of [the nineteenth-century feminine ideal], then Charlotte's madness is both a symptom or expression of femininity and its negation" (2004: xx).
20. Crew is described as an erudite stranger who lives alone in his cottage, "cooking his food and waiting on himself", and pursuing domestic activities that are more typical of women, such as selling honey, growing herbs and preparing home-made medicaments (Wood, 1880b [1905]: 42–43).
21. The domestic scene and the threat posed by women evoke notorious Victorian murders, such as those committed by serial poisoner Mary Ann Cotton (tried and executed in 1873) and the Road Hill House infanticide (see note 8).

Chapter 4. The transgressive lady and the failings of patriarchy

1. Intimated by the phonic pun *vane-vain*, Isabel's inclination to vanity is criticized when she dresses too elegantly for a concert (Wood, 1861 [2000]: 119, 123).
2. Unlike most Wood characters, Isabel Vane has attracted the attention of feminists like Elaine Showalter (1977) and E. Ann Kaplan (1989), and is still the object of critical attention. See, among many others, Pykett (1992), Shuttleworth (1992), Kucich (1994), Maunder (2000), Wynne (2001a), Tromp (2011), and Simpson (2012).
3. "Barbara Hare's temper was not under strict control", announces the narrator, before describing how the woman gives vent to her jealousy and reminds Carlyle of the time when he had been "more intimate with [her] than a brother": "'If *she* had not come between us, should you have loved me?'" (Wood, 1861 [2000]: 211, 213).
4. In addition to purchasing the earl's property and (symbolically) his daughter, Carlyle beats Levison in local elections and becomes instrumental to his social downfall.

5. Lord Mount Severn performs a strict paternal role again when he reproaches the adulterous Isabel for betraying "an upright and good man" like Carlyle (Wood, 1861 [2000]: 360).
6. Victorian domestic fiction fulfilled a didactic function as it focused on the daily lives of women, especially middle-class girls. Quite different was the effect produced by sensation fiction, which unveiled the secret crimes and the hypocrisy of apparently respectable members of the Victorian bourgeoisie.
7. Besides playing a main role in the comic episode of Captain Kerleton's compulsive marriage proposals mentioned in Chapter 3, Rebecca is ironized in some passages that focus on her bizarre volition and her over-emotionality. Yet, these humorous tinges hardly affect her function of caring, strong-willed and autonomous woman, whose model is imitated and further developed by Hester Halliwell.
8. Being childless, Robert loses "the house and income" to which he was entitled by marriage and begins life anew by starting his engineering career "lower than where he had left off" (Wood, 1868b [1898]: 177–178).
9. Wood displays some fondness for the "shabby-genteel" that complicates the novel's depiction of class relations. Worthy of notice is her ambivalent portrayal of the aristocratic Thornycrofts, whose criminal leanings are partly redeemed by two late events: the discovery of the illegitimacy of the delinquent firstborn and his brother Isaac's marriage with the "shabby-genteel" Anna Chester, who becomes "the rightful mistress of a reconstituted Red Court" (Wagner, 2008: 214).
10. Both prohibitions are due to the smuggling activities performed at Red Court Farm. Richard Thornycroft strives to protect his criminal deeds by forbidding his stepmother to enter the "shut-in rooms" he inhabits and walking around the property at night (Wood, 1868b [1898]: 215, 219). This interdiction, resonant with echoes from "Bluebeard", is combined with the typical gothic legend of a ghost haunting the premises at night, which is also used to keep nosy people away.
11. The best-known case is that of Braddon's Lady Audley, who proves that "[b]eing a lady is a matter of performance" (Lysack, 2008: 61). A similar idea is expressed by Magdalen Vanstone, the controversial heroine of Wilkie Collins's *No Name* (1862), who suggests the possibility of feigning gentility when she trains her maid to impersonate herself: "'Shall I tell you what a lady is? A lady is a woman who wears a silk gown, and has a sense of her own importance'" ([1994]: 503).
12. Victorian conduct books stigmatized female appetites, especially in maternal figures that were supposed to nurture rather than devour. An interesting example is offered by Isabella Beeton, who describes the pains suffered by an infant owing to its wet-nurse's consumption of food that should be avoided while breastfeeding (1861: 1023).
13. Lady Kirton's obesity and eccentricity are evocative of Count Fosco, featured in Wilkie Collins's *The Woman in White* (1860), another sensational aristocrat who challenges Victorian customs with his unorthodox behaviour.

14. Even though the irregular situation of Maude remains a secret at the heart of the family, the high-ranking status she is granted neutralizes a basic law of patriarchy. Like Wood, Wilkie Collins exposed the problem of children's vulnerability to illegitimacy in novels such as *The Woman in White* and *No Name*.

Chapter 5. Unconventional low-class women

1. Wood is overtly critical against trade union activism in novels like *A Life's Secret* (1862) and *Bessy Rane* (1870), in which the workers' strikes are shown to have dramatic consequences upon the protesters and their families.
2. For a reflection on the links between poverty, filth, disease and moral contagion in Victorian culture and literature see, among others, Gilbert (2005: 38–41).
3. Her elusive status emerges in her reflection on what dress code to adopt as hired companion of Emily Chandos: "My birth entitled me to [dress as a lady]; but did my position?" (Wood, 1868a [1896]: 153).
4. When she first acknowledges her love, Anne uses references to touch to convey the physicality of her love: "the bliss of feeling his hand on me" (Wood, 1868a [1896]: 304). In later passages, she describes the bodily sensations felt in receiving his "impassionate kisses" which cancel all her moral restraints – "I fear I did not think whether it was right or wrong"; "I lifted my eyes and stole my hand into his. Down came his kisses upon my lips by way of sealing the compact" (1868a [1896]: 338, 383).
5. Overwhelmed by her resentment for Barbara, the disguised Isabel dares to remind Carlyle that his wife is not his children's mother. His haughty retort "'You speak hastily, madame'" is followed by her bitter reflection on her inferior position in the household: "The reproof beat upon her heart, and she remembered who she was; remembered it with shame and humiliation. She, the governess!" (Wood, 1861 [2000]: 584).
6. Both arrogant, violent, deceitful and inclined to debt, Anthony and Herbert Dare are two flawed characters that contrast with the novel's paragons of male virtue incarnated in the young Halliburtons.
7. The idealized image of nursing was largely influenced by Nightingale and her staff's participation in the Crimean War as medical attendants. On her return, Nightingale established a nursing school, trained a body of professional caregivers and used her writings to create a sympathetic audience. Her essays, and particularly *Cassandra* (1859), describe the emptiness of women's domestic life and represent social service as a better alternative. On these topics see, among others, Bailin (1994) and Judd (1998). For specific representations in sensation fiction, see Costantini (2015: 330–336).
8. The novel's challenge to class hierarchies is confirmed by the positive characterization of Mrs. Gass, a housekeeper of "neither birth nor breeding" who makes "an advantageous match" by marrying her master and exhibits "many good qualities" that make her popular and respected (Wood, 1870 [1872]: 12).

9. The French origins of this figure might have contributed to enhancing her positive function. Wood was particularly delighted by the "sunny" and "constant" temperament of the people she met in France (Charles Wood, 1894: 78). Yet, she also disliked specific aspects of French culture, such as its Catholic fanaticism (Pires, 2008). What is undeniable is that France was to Wood an important "contact zone" which, as I demonstrate elsewhere, enabled her to widen her cultural experiences and to develop alternative models, such as the one embodied by Sophie Deffloe (Costantini, 2019).
10. Detective-maids like Judith Ford and Fanny Jelly undoubtedly embodied the age's anxieties aroused by servant surveillance (Trodd, 1989; McCuskey, 2000). Yet, Wood decreased these anxieties in two ways: she justified the maids' detection by exposing the undeniable guilt of middle-class lawbreakers; and she represented these employees as inherently loyal to their household, as they are not in the suspects' service.

Works Cited

Alcoff, Linda, 1995. "Cultural Feminism versus Post-Structuralism: The Identity Crisis in Feminist Theory", in Nancy Tuana and Rosemary Tong (eds.), *Feminism and Philosophy: Essential Readings in Theory, Reinterpretation, and Application*. Boulder and San Francisco: Westview Press, pp. 434–456.

Allan, Janice M., 2011. "A 'base and spurious thing': Reading and Deceptive Femininity in Ellen Wood's *Parkwater* (1857)", *Critical Survey*, 23, 1, pp. 8–24.

Armstrong, Nancy, 1987. *Desire and Domestic Fiction: A Political History of the Novel*. New York and Oxford: Oxford University Press.

Bailin, Miriam, 1994. *The Sickroom in Victorian Fiction: The Art of Being Ill*. Cambridge and New York: Cambridge University Press.

Baker, Ernest, 1950. *A History of the English Novel*, vol. 9. New York: Barnes and Noble.

Bakhtin, Mikhail, 1965 [1968]. *Rabelais and His World*. Trans. Helene Iswolsky. Cambridge, MA: MIT Press.

Beauvoir, Simone de, 1949 [2011]. *The Second Sex*. Trans. Constance Borde and Sheila Malovany-Chevallier. New York: Vintage Books.

Beeton, [Mrs.] Isabella, 1861. *The Book of Household Management*. London: S. O. Beeton.

Beller, Anne-Marie, 2008. "Suffering Angels: Death and Femininity in Ellen Wood's Fiction", *Women's Writing*, special issue: "Ellen (Mrs. Henry) Wood", edited by Emma Liggins and Andrew Maunder, 15, 2, pp. 219–231.

-----, 2012. *Mary Elizabeth Braddon: A Companion to the Mystery Fiction*. Jefferson, NC, and London: Mcfarland.

Bettelheim, Bruno, 1976 [1991]. *The Uses of Enchantment: The Meaning and Importance of Fairy Tales*. London: Penguin.

Boccaccio, Giovanni, 1353 [1973]. "Novella Decima", in Giovanni Boccaccio, *Il Decameron*, edited by Carlo Salinari, 2 vols; vol. 2, Roma and Bari: Laterza, pp. 758–778.

[Bodichon], Barbara Leigh Smith, 1857. *Women and Work*. London: Bosworth and Harrison.

Botting, Fred, 2014. *Gothic: The New Critical Idiom*. London and New York: Routledge.

Bourdieu, Pierre, 1979 [2010]. *Distinction: A Social Critique of the Judgement of Taste*. Trans. Richard Nice, with an introduction by Tony Bennett. London and New York: Routledge.

Braddon, Mary Elizabeth, 1862 [1987]. *Lady Audley's Secret*, edited by David Skilton. Oxford and New York: Oxford University Press.

Bronfen, Elisabeth, 1992. *Over Her Dead Body: Death, Femininity and the Aesthetic*. Manchester: Manchester University Press.

Brooks, Peter, 1984. *Reading for the Plot: Design and Intention in Narrative*. Cambridge, MA, and London: Harvard University Press.

Burgauer, Rolf, 1950. *Mrs. Henry Wood: Persönlichkeit und Werk*. Zürich: Juris-Verlag.

Butler, Judith, 1988. "Performative Acts and Gender Constitution: An Essay in Phenomenology and Feminist Theory", *Theatre Journal*, 40, 4, pp. 519–531.

Calder, Jenni, 1976. *Women and Marriage in Victorian Fiction*. London: Thames and Hudson.

Carnell, Jennifer, 2000. *The Literary Lives of Mary Elizabeth Braddon: A Study of Her Life and Work*. Hastings: The Sensation Press.

Carter, Angela, 1979 [2006]. *The Bloody Chamber and Other Stories*, with an Introduction by Helen Simpson. London: Vintage.

Chesler, Phyllis, 1972. *Women and Madness*. New York: Doubleday.

Cixous, Hélène, 1975 [1986]. "Sorties: Out and out: Attacks/Ways out/Forays", in Hélène Cixous and Catherine Clément (eds.), *The Newly Born Woman*. Trans. Betsy Wing. Minneapolis and Oxford: University of Minnesota Press, pp. 63–132.

Collins, Wilkie, 1862 [1994]. *No Name*, edited by Mark Ford. Harmondsworth: Penguin.

Costantini, Mariaconcetta, 2015. *Sensation and Professionalism in the Victorian Novel*. Bern: Peter Lang.

-----, 2019. "Challenging Encounters: The Cultural Presence of France in Victorian Sensation Fiction", in Maria Micaela Coppola, Francesca Di Blasio, and Sabrina Francesconi (eds.), *Contact Zones. Cultural, Linguistic and Literary Connections in English*. Trento: Università degli Studi di Trento, pp. 163–180.

Cox, Jessica, 2008. "'A touch of in'nard fever': Illness and Moral Decline in *Elster's Folly*", *Women's Writing*, special issue: "Ellen (Mrs. Henry) Wood", edited by Emma Liggins and Andrew Maunder, 15, 2, pp. 232–243.

-----, 2019. *Victorian Sensation Fiction*. London: Red Globe Press.

Cozzi, Annette, 2010. *The Discourses of Food in Nineteenth-Century British Fiction*. New York: Palgrave Macmillan.

Culler, Jonathan, 1983. *On Deconstruction: Theory and Criticism after Structuralism*. London and Melbourne: Routledge and Kegan Paul.

Cvetkovich, Ann, 1992. *Mixed Feelings: Feminism, Mass Culture, and Victorian Sensationalism*. New Brunswick, NJ: Rutgers University Press.

Elwin, Malcolm, 1934. *Victorian Wallflowers*. London: Jonathan Cape.

Fetterley, Judith, 1978. *The Resisting Reader: A Feminist Approach to American Fiction*. Bloomington: Indiana University Press.

Gardiner, Judith Kegan (ed.), 2002. *Masculinity Studies and Feminist Theory*. New York: Columbia University Press.

Gilbert Pamela K., 2005. *Disease, Desire and the Body in Victorian Women's Popular Novels*. Cambridge: Cambridge University Press.

----- (ed.), 2011. *A Companion to Sensation Fiction*. Malden, MA, and Oxford: Wiley-Blackwell.

Gilbert, Sandra M., and Susan Gubar, 1979 [2000]. *The Madwoman in the Attic: The Woman Writer and the Nineteenth-Century Literary Imagination*. New Haven and London: Yale University Press.

Gilman, Charlotte Perkins, 1898. *Women and Economics: A Study of the Economic Relations Between Men and Women as a Factor in Social Evolution*. Boston: Small, Maynard and Company.

Greimas, Algirdas Julien, 1983. *Structural Semantics: An Attempt at a Method*. Trans. Daniele McDowell, Ronald Schleifer, and Alan Velie. Lincoln, NE: University of Nebraska Press.

Grosz, Elizabeth, 1994. *Volatile Bodies: Toward a Corporeal Feminism*. Bloomington: Indiana University Press.

Gruner, Elisabeth Rose, 1997. "Plotting the Mother: Caroline Norton, Helen Huntington, and Isabel Vane", *Tulsa Studies in Women's Literature*, 16, 2, pp. 303–325.

Harrison, Brian, 1971. *Drink and the Victorians: The Temperance Question in England, 1815–1872*. London: Faber & Faber.

Harrison, Kimberly, 2011. "'Come buy, come buy': Sensation Fiction in the Context of Consumer and Commodity Culture", in Pamela K. Gilbert (ed.), *A Companion to Sensation Fiction*. Malden, MA, and Oxford: Wiley-Blackwell, pp. 528–539.

Hendershot, Cyndy, 1998. *The Animal Within: Masculinity and the Gothic*. Ann Arbor: The University of Michigan Press.

Henry, Alexander, 1861. *A Glossary of Scientific Terms for General Use*. London: James Walton.

Herndl, Diane Price, 1996. "Invalidism", in Elizabeth Kowaleski Wallace (ed.), *Encyclopedia of Feminist Literary Theory*. London and New York: Routledge, pp. 214–215.

Hughes, Kathryn, 1993. *The Victorian Governess*. Rio Grande, OH: The Hambledon Press.

Irigaray, Luce, 1977 [1985]. *This Sex Which Is Not One*. Trans. Catherine Porter and Carolyn Burke. Ithaca, NY: Cornell University Press.

Jaquet, Alison, 2008. "The Disturbed Domestic: Supernatural Spaces in Ellen Wood's Fiction", *Women's Writing*, special issue: "Ellen (Mrs. Henry) Wood", edited by Emma Liggins and Andrew Maunder, 15, 2, pp. 244–258.

Johnson, Joseph, 1862. *Clever Girls of Our Time: And How They Became Famous Women*. London: Darton and Hodge.

Jordan, Jane, 2011. "The Law and Sensation", in Pamela K. Gilbert (ed.), *A Companion to Sensation Fiction*. Malden, MA, and Oxford: Wiley-Blackwell, pp. 507–515.

Judd, Catherine, 1998. *Bedside Seductions: Nursing and the Victorian Imagination, 1830–1880*. Basingstoke: Macmillan.

Kaplan, E. Ann, 1989. "The Political Unconscious in the Maternal Melodrama: Ellen Wood's *East Lynne* (1861)", in Derek Longhurst (ed.), *Gender, Genre and Narrative Pleasure*. London and Boston: Unwin Hyman, pp. 31–50.

Keddie, Henrietta [Sarah Tytler], 1911. *Three Generations: The Story of a Middle-Class Scottish Family*. London: John Murray.

King, Alice, 1873. "Female Suffrage", *The Argosy*, 15 (March), pp. 191–195.

Kristeva, Julia, 1968. "Problèmes de la structuration du texte", in Michel Foucault, Roland Barthes, Jacques Derrida, *Théorie d'ensemble*. Paris: Éditions du Seuil, pp. 297–316.

-----, 1980 [1982]. *Powers of Horror: An Essay on Abjection*. Trans. Leon S. Roudiez. New York: Columbia University Press.

Kucich, John, 1994. *The Power of Lies: Transgression in Victorian Fiction*. Ithaca, NY, and London: Cornell University Press.

Langbauer, Laurie, 1990. *Women and Romance: The Consolation of Gender in the English Novel*. Ithaca, NY, and London: Cornell University Press.

Lecourt, Sebastian, 2013. "The Mormons, the Victorians, and the Idea of Greater Britain", *Victorian Studies*, 56, 1, pp. 85–111.

Lévi-Strauss, Claude, 1949. *Les structures élémentaires de la parenté*. Paris: Presses universitaires de France.

Liggins, Emma, 2001. "Good Housekeeping? Domestic Economy and Suffering Wives in Mrs. Henry Wood's Early Fiction", in Emma Liggins and D. Duffy (eds.), *Feminist Readings of Victorian Popular Texts: Divergent Femininities*. Aldershot and Burlington: Ashgate, pp. 52–68.

-----, 2014. *Odd Women: Spinsters, Lesbians and Widows in British Women's Fiction, 1850s-1930s*. Manchester and New York: Manchester University Press.

Liggins, Emma, and D. Duffy (eds.), 2001. *Feminist Readings of Victorian Popular Texts: Divergent Femininities*. Aldershot and Burlington: Ashgate.

Liggins, Emma, and Andrew Maunder (eds.), 2008. *Women's Writing*, special issue: "Ellen (Mrs. Henry) Wood", 15, 2.

[Linton, Eliza Lynn], 1866. "*Elster's Folly*", *Saturday Review*, 22 (July), pp. 117–118.

-----, 1868. "The Girl of the Period", *Saturday Review*, 25 (March), pp. 339–340.

-----, 1875. "The Philosophy of Shopping", *Saturday Review*, 40 (October), pp. 488–489.

Longhurst, Derek (ed.), 1989. *Gender, Genre and Narrative Pleasure*. London and Boston: Unwin Hyman.

Losano, Antonia, 2004. "*East Lynne, The Turn of the Screw*, and the Female Doppelgänger in Governess Fiction", *Nineteenth-Century Studies*, 18, pp. 99–116.

Lysack, Krista, 2008. *Come Buy, Come Buy: Shopping and the Culture of Consumption in Victorian Women's Writing*. Athens, OH: Ohio University Press.

MacDonald, Tara, 2015. *The New Man, Masculinity and Marriage in the Victorian Novel*. London: Pickering & Chatto.

Mangham, Andrew, 2003. "'I see it; but I cannot explain it': Female Gothicism and the Narrative of Female Incarceration in the Novels of Mrs. Henry Wood", in Karen Sayer and Rosemary Mitchell (eds.), *Victorian Gothic*. Leeds: Leeds University, pp. 81–98.

-----, 2007. *Violent Women and Sensation Fiction: Crime, Medicine and Victorian Popular Culture*. Basingstoke and New York: Palgrave Macmillan.

-----, 2008. "Life after Death: Apoplexy, Medical Ethics and the Female Undead", *Women's Writing*, 15, 3, pp. 282–299.

Marroni, Francesco, 2017. "Unweaving the Oriental Rainbow: Charlotte Brontë and the Byronic Paradigm", *Rivista di Studi Vittoriani*, 44, pp. 7–30.

Massé, Michelle A., 1992. *In the Name of Love: Women, Masochism and the Gothic*. Ithaca, NY: Cornell University Press.

Maunder, Andrew, 2000. "Ellen Wood Was a Writer: Rediscovering Collins's Rival", *Wilkie Collins Society Journal*, 3, pp. 17–31.

-----, 2004. "'Stepchildren of nature': *East Lynne* and the Spectre of Female Degeneracy, 1860–1861", in Andrew Maunder and Grace Moore (eds.), *Victorian Crime, Madness and Sensation*. Aldershot: Ashgate, pp. 59–71.

-----, 2006. "'I will not live in poverty and neglect'. *East Lynne* on the East End Stage", in Kimberly Harrison and Richard Fantina (eds.), *Victorian Sensations: Essays on a Scandalous Genre*. Columbus, OH: The Ohio State University Press, pp. 173–187.

McAleavey, Maia, 2015. *The Bigamy Plot: Sensation and Convention in the Victorian Novel*. Cambridge and New York: Cambridge University Press.

McBride, Theresa, 1978. "'As the twig is bent': The Victorian Nanny", in Anthony S. Wohl (ed.), *The Victorian Family*. London: Croom Helm, pp. 44–58.

McCuskey, Brian W., 2000. "The Kitchen Police: Servant Surveillance and Middle-Class Transgression", *Victorian Literature and Culture*, 28, 2, pp. 359–375.

McDonagh, Josephine, 2003. *Child Murder and British Culture 1720–1900*. Cambridge and New York: Cambridge University Press.

Mill, John Stuart, 1869 [1870]. *The Subjection of Women*. London: Longmans, Green, Reader, and Dyer.

Millett, Kate, 1970. "The Debate Over Women: Ruskin versus Mill", *Victorian Studies*, 14, 1, pp. 63–82.

Mitchell, Sally, 1977. "Sentiment and Suffering: Women's Recreational Reading in the 1860s", *Victorian Studies*, 21, 1, pp. 29–45.

-----, 1981. *The Fallen Angel: Chastity, Class and Women's Reading, 1835–1880*. Bowling Green, OH: Bowling Green University Popular Press.

Nemesvari, Richard, 2015. "Manful Sensations: Affect, Domesticity and Class

Status Anxiety in *East Lynne* and *Aurora Floyd*", in Phillip Mallett (ed.), *The Victorian Novel and Masculinity*. Basingstoke: Palgrave Macmillan, pp. 88–115.

Newbolt, Peter, 2001. *William Tinsley (1831–1902): "Speculative Publisher"*. Aldershot and Burlington: Ashgate.

[Oliphant, Margaret], 1858. "The Condition of Women", *Blackwood's Edinburgh Magazine*, 83 (February), pp. 139–154.

[-----], 1862. "Sensation Novels", *Blackwood's Edinburgh Magazine*, 91 (May), pp. 564–584.

Palmer, Beth, 2008. "'Dangerous and foolish work': Evangelicalism and Sensationalism in Ellen Wood's *Argosy Magazine*", *Women's Writing*, special issue: "Ellen (Mrs. Henry) Wood", edited by Emma Liggins and Andrew Maunder, 15, 2, pp. 187–198.

-----, 2011. *Women's Authorship and Editorship in Victorian Culture: Sensational Strategies*. Oxford and New York: Oxford University Press.

Peterson, M. Jeanne, 1973. "The Victorian Governess: Status Incongruence in Family and Society", in Martha Vicinus (ed.), *Suffer and Be Still: Women in the Victorian Age*. Bloomington and Indianapolis: Indiana University Press, pp. 3–19.

Phegley, Jennifer, 2005. "Domesticating the Sensation Novelist: Ellen Price Wood as Author and Editor of *The Argosy Magazine*", *Victorian Periodicals Review*, 38, 2, pp. 180–198.

-----, 2012. *Courtship and Marriage in Victorian England*. Santa Barbara, Denver and Oxford: Praeger.

Pires, Matthew, 2008. "'Boulogne-sur-Mer, of all places in the world!': France in the Works of Ellen Wood", *Women's Writing*, special issue: "Ellen (Mrs. Henry) Wood", edited by Emma Liggins and Andrew Maunder, 15, 2, pp. 169–185.

Planché, J. R. (trans.), 1858. *Four and Twenty Fairy Tales: Selected from Those of Perrault and Other Popular Writers*. London: Routledge.

Poovey, Mary, 1989. *Uneven Developments: The Ideological Work of Gender in Mid-Victorian England*. London: Virago Press.

Price, Cheryl Blake, 2016. "Medical Bluebeards: The Domestic Threat of the Poisoning Doctor in the Popular Fiction of Ellen Wood", in Louise Penner and Tabitha Sparks (eds.), *Victorian Medicine and Popular Culture*. Pittsburgh: University of Pittsburgh Press, pp. 81–93.

Probyn, Elspeth, 2000. *Carnal Appetites: FoodSexIdentities*. London and New York: Routledge.

Propp, Vladimir, 1928 [1968]. *Morphology of the Folktale*. Trans. Laurence Scott, with an Introduction by Svatava Pirkova-Jakobson. Austin: University of Texas Press.

Pykett, Lyn, 1992. *The "Improper Feminine": The Women's Sensation Novel and the New Woman Writing*. London and New York: Routledge.

-----, 1994. *The Sensation Novel: From* The Woman in White *to* The Moonstone. Plymouth: Northcote.

-----, 2001. "Women Writing Woman: Nineteenth-Century Representations of Gender and Sexuality", in Joanne Shattock (ed.), *Women and Literature in Britain 1800–1900*. Cambridge and New York: Cambridge University Press, pp. 78–98.

-----, 2004. "Introduction" and "A Note on the Text", in Andrew Maunder (ed.), *Varieties of Women's Sensation Fiction: 1855–1890*, 6 vols.; vol. 3, Ellen Wood, *St. Martin's Eve*, edited by Lyn Pykett, London: Pickering & Chatto, pp. vii-xxii and xxxiii-xxxiv.

Quay, Sara E., 1996. "Insanity", in Elizabeth Kowaleski Wallace (ed.), *Encyclopedia of Feminist Literary Theory*. London and New York: Routledge, pp. 212–214.

Radford, Andrew, 2009. *Victorian Sensation Fiction: A Reader's Guide to Essential Criticism*. Basingstoke: Palgrave Macmillan.

Rance, Nicholas, 1991. *Wilkie Collins and Other Sensation Novelists: Walking the Moral Hospital*. Basingstoke and London: Macmillan.

Roberts, David, 1978. "The Paterfamilias of the Victorian Governing Classes", in Anthony S. Wohl (ed.), *The Victorian Family*. London: Croom Helm, pp. 59–81.

Ruskin, John, 1849 [1903–1912]. "The Seven Lamps of Architecture", in E. T. Cook and Alexander Wedderburn (eds.), *The Works of John Ruskin*, 39 vols.; vol. 8. London: George Allen; New York: Longmans and Green.

Ruthven, K. K., 1984. *Feminist Literary Studies: An Introduction*. Cambridge and New York: Cambridge University Press.

Sanders, Valerie, 1996. *Eve's Renegades: Victorian Antifeminist Women Novelists*. Basingstoke and London: Macmillan.

Schaffer, Talia, 2016. "The Sensational Story of West Lynn: The Problem with Professionalism", *Women's Writing*, 23, 2, pp. 227–244.

Sergeant, Adeline, 1897. "Mrs. Crowe, Mrs. Archer Clive, Mrs. Henry Wood", in Mrs. Oliphant, Mrs. Lynn Linton, Mrs. Alexander, Mrs. Macquoid, Mrs. Parr, Mrs. Marshall, Charlotte M. Yonge, Adeline Sergeant, and Edna Lyall, *Women Novelists of Queen Victoria's Reign. A Book of Appreciations*. London: Hurst & Blackett, pp. 149–192.

Showalter, Elaine, 1977. *A Literature of Their Own: British Women Novelists from Brontë to Lessing*. Princeton: Princeton University Press.

-----, 1985. *The Female Malady: Women, Madness, and English Culture 1830–1980*. New York: Pantheon Books.

Shuttleworth, Sally, 1992. "Demonic Mothers: Ideologies of Bourgeois Motherhood in the Mid-Victorian Era", in Linda M. Shires (ed.), *Rewriting the Victorians: Theory, History, and the Politics of Gender*. New York and London: Routledge, pp. 31–51.

Simpson, Vicky, 2012. "Not-So-Happy Homemakers: Women, Property and Family in Ellen Wood's *East Lynne*", *Women's Writing*, 19, 4, pp. 584–601.

Smiles, Samuel, 1859 [2002]. *Self-Help: With Illustrations of Character, Conduct, and Perseverance*, edited by Peter W. Sinnema. Oxford and New York: Oxford University Press.

Steere, Elizabeth, 2013. *The Female Servant and Sensation Fiction: 'Kitchen Literature'*. Basingstoke and New York: Palgrave Macmillan.

Sussex, Lucy, 2010. *Women Writers and Detectives in Nineteenth-Century Crime Fiction: The Mothers of the Mystery Genre*. Basingstoke and New York: Palgrave Macmillan.

Tait, Lawson, 1877. *Diseases of Women*. London and Edinburgh: Williams and Norgate.

Talairach-Vielmas, Laurence, 2007. *Moulding the Female Body in Victorian Fairy Tales and Sensation Novels*. Aldershot and Burlington: Ashgate.

"Thackeray and Modern Fiction", 1864. *London Quarterly Review*, 44 (July), pp. 375–408.

Tosh, John, 1999. *A Man's Place: Masculinity and the Middle-Class Home in Victorian England*. New Haven and London: Yale University Press.

Trodd, Anthea, 1989. *Domestic Crime in the Victorian Novel*. London: Macmillan.

Tromp, Marlene, 2011. "Mrs. Henry Wood, *East Lynne*", in Pamela K. Gilbert (ed.), *A Companion to Sensation Fiction*. Malden, MA, and Oxford: Wiley-Blackwell, pp. 257–268.

Vrettos, Athena, 1995. *Somatic Fictions: Imagining Illness in Victorian Culture*. Stanford: Stanford University Press.

Wagner, Tamara S., 2008. "'Essentially a lady': Resistant Values of the Shabby-Genteel in Ellen Wood's Novels of High Life", *Women's Writing*, special issue: "Ellen (Mrs. Henry) Wood", edited by Emma Liggins and Andrew Maunder, 15, 2, pp. 199–218.

----- (ed.), 2009. *Antifeminism and the Victorian Novel: Rereading Nineteenth-Century Women Writers*. Amherst, NY: Cambria Press.

-----, 2018. "Mrs. Henry Wood's Model Men: How to Mismanage Your Marriage in *Court Netherleigh*", in Carolyn Lambert and Marion Shaw (eds.), *For Better, For Worse: Marriage in Victorian Novels by Women*. New York and London: Routledge, pp. 116–129.

Wallace, Elizabeth Kowaleski (ed.), 1996. *Encyclopedia of Feminist Literary Theory*. London and New York: Routledge.

Wohl, Anthony S. (ed.), 1978a. *The Victorian Family*. London: Croom Helm.

Wohl, Anthony S., 1978b. "Sex and the Single Room: Incest among the Victorian Working Classes", in Anthony S. Wohl (ed.), *The Victorian Family*. London: Croom Helm, pp. 197–216.

Wolff, Janet, 1988. "The Culture of Separate Spheres: The Role of Culture in Nineteenth-Century Public and Private Life", in Janet Wolff and John Seed (eds.), *The Culture of Capital: Art, Power and the Nineteenth-Century Middle Class*. Manchester: Manchester University Press, pp. 117–134.

Wood, Charles W., 1887. "Mrs. Henry Wood. In Memoriam", *The Argosy*, 43 (January-June), pp. 251–270, 334–353, 422–442.

-----, 1894. *Memorials of Mrs. Henry Wood*. London: Richard Bentley & Son.

Wood, [Ellen] Mrs. Henry, 1860 [n.d.]. *Danesbury House*. London and Fellingon-Tyne: The Walter Scott Publishing.

-----, 1861 [2000]. *East Lynne*, edited by Andrew Maunder. Peterborough: Broadview Press.

-----, 1862 [1897]. *Mrs. Halliburton's Troubles*. London: Richard Bentley & Son.

-----, 1863a [n.d.]. *The Shadow of Ashlydyat*. London: Milner and Company.

-----, 1863b [n.d.]. *Verner's Pride*. London and Glasgow: Collins' Clear Type Press.

-----, 1864a [1872]. *Lord Oakburn's Daughters*. London: Richard Bentley & Son.

-----, 1864b [1904]. *Oswald Cray*. London: Macmillan.

-----, 1866a [1903]. *Elster's Folly: A Novel*. London: Macmillan.

-----, 1866b [1893]. *St. Martin's Eve: A Novel*. London: Richard Bentley & Son.

-----, 1867. *Lady Adelaide's Oath*, 3 vols. London: Richard Bentley.

-----, 1868a [1896]. *Anne Hereford: A Novel*. London: Richard Bentley & Son.

-----, 1868b [1898]. *The Red Court Farm: A Novel*. London and New York: Macmillan.

-----, 1870 [1872]. *Bessy Rane: A Novel*. London: Richard Bentley & Son.

-----, 1871. *Dene Hollow*, 2 vols. Leipzig: Bernhard Tauchnitz.

-----, 1872 [1891]. *Within the Maze: A Novel*. London: Richard Bentley & Son.

-----, 1874a [1895]. "Coming Home to Him", in *Johnny Ludlow: First Series*. London: Richard Bentley & Son, pp. 64–79.

-----, 1874b [1895]. "Major Parrifer", in *Johnny Ludlow: First Series*. London: Richard Bentley & Son, pp. 48–63.

-----, 1876. *Parkwater*. London: Richard Bentley & Son.

-----, 1880a [1905]. "Abel Crew", in *Johnny Ludlow: Second Series*. London and New York: The Macmillan Company, pp. 56–74.

-----, 1880b [1905]. "Hester Reed's Pills", in *Johnny Ludlow: Second Series*. London and New York: The Macmillan Company, pp. 36–55.

-----, 1881 [1898]. *Court Netherleigh: A Novel*. London: Richard Bentley & Son.

-----, 1885a [1899]. "Dr. Knox", in *Johnny Ludlow: Third Series*. London and New York: The Macmillan Company, pp. 135–157.

-----, 1885b [1899]. "Janet Carey", in *Johnny Ludlow: Third Series*. London and New York: The Macmillan Company, pp. 112–134.

-----, 1890 [1896]. *The House of Halliwell: A Novel*. London: Richard Bentley & Son.

-----, 1899 [1901]. "The Mystery at Number Seven", in *Johnny Ludlow: Sixth Series*. London and New York: The Macmillan Company, pp. 1–53.

Woolf, Virginia, 1929 [2000]. *A Room of One's Own*. London: Penguin.

-----, 1931 [1981]. "Professions for Women", in Virginia Woolf, *The Death of the Moth and Other Essays*. London: The Hogarth Press, pp. 149–154.

Wynne, Deborah, 2001a. "'See what a big wide bed it is!': Mrs. Henry Wood and the Philistine Imagination", in Emma Liggins and D. Duffy (eds.), *Feminist Readings of Victorian Popular Texts: Divergent Femininities*. Aldershot and Burlington: Ashgate, pp. 89–107.

-----, 2001b. *The Sensation Novel and the Victorian Family Magazine*. Basingstoke and New York: Palgrave.

Zipes, Jack, 1983 [2006]. *Fairy Tales and the Art of Subversion: The Classical Genre for Children and the Process of Civilization*. New York and Abingdon: Routledge.

Index

"Abel Crew", 125–7
adolescence, 69–70, 112
adultery, 51–5, 60, 74, 79–81, 84, 105–6, 132
affect *see* emotion
agency, 95, 126–7, 130–1, 142–3, 166–8, 174–5, 179–82
aggression, 108, 119–20, 150, 152, 153
Ainsworth, William Harrison, 8
Alcoff, Linda, 24–5
alcohol/alcoholism, 94, 149, 172, 173–4, 176, 177–8
Allan, Janice M., 161
ambivalence, of characters, 68, 79–82, 94–5
anger, 100, 108, 119–20, 150, 152, 153
Anne Hereford, 39–40, 70, 91, 164–5
anorexia, 72, 74–5, 81, 85, 88–9, 199 n.6
anti-feminism, 13, 15–21, 35; versus proto-feminism, 17, 19–20, 28–9, 75, 133, 191–2
anti-heroines, 117–18, 120–2
appetite, 149–51, 176–7, 203 n.12; *see also* anorexia
Argosy (journal), 7–8, 161, 195 n.4; "Mrs. Henry Wood. In Memoriam", 4; *Johnny Ludlow* stories, 10, 123, 125; "Log-Book", 12; "Female Suffrage" (King), 15–16
aristocracy, 129–55, 183; transgressive, 129–38; stereotypical, 138–42; and femininity, 142–6; and performativity, 146–50

Bakhtin, Mikhail, 150–1, 154, 177–8
Beauvoir, Simone de, 143, 148; *The Second Sex*, 23–4
Beller, Anne-Marie, 82
Bentley, Richard, 4, 8, 161
Bentley's Miscellany (journal), 8
Bessy Rane, 49; and forbearance, 62, 69–70, 85, 92, 94; and class, 139, 181–3
bigamy, 59–60, 89–90, 91, 150, 152
bildungsroman, 13, 29, 162–3
Boccaccio, Giovanni, 29, 70
Bodichon, Barbara Leigh Smith, 18–19, 57, 143, 168
bodies, 5, 23–6, 107–8, 149–51; diseased, 6, 107, 175; gendered, 23–4; commodified, 25–6, 47, 63–4; ornamented, 110–11; wasted, 110–11; fat, 150–1, 176–8; *see also* corporeality
Bourdieu, Pierre, 177
Braddon, Mary Elizabeth, 2, 9, 195 n.5, 195 n.8; *Aurora Floyd*, 82–3; *Lady Audley's Secret*, 110, 114, 121, 201 n.6, 203 n.11
breastfeeding, 45, 172, 203 n.12
Bronfen, Elizabeth, 63–4

217

Brontë, Charlotte, *Jane Eyre*, 42–3, 91, 114, 162, 164, 175, 199 n.3
Brooks, Peter, 107
Broughton, Rhoda, 2–3
Burgauer, Rolf, 10, 159, 185
Butler, Judith, 24–5, 148

camouflage techniques, 9, 16, 30, 37, 66, 191; *Court Netherleigh*, 45, 48; *The Shadow of Ashlydyat*, 77, 81–2; *St Martin's Eve*, 122; *East Lynne*, 134
canonicization, 3, 191
Cixous, Hélène, 98–9, 200 n.2
class, 30–1, 62, 66, 114, 129–30; middle classes, 14, 129–31, 132–5, 144–5; gentility, 22–3, 55–8, 143–4, 161; and ladylike qualities, 55–7, 143–4, 146–7, 154, 161, 203 n.11; and immoderacy, 102, 149–51; and morality, 129–30, 132–3, 134, 178, 183; bourgeoisie, 129–31, 132–5; and masculinity, 130–1; and marriage, 130, 135, 137–8, 159–61; and emotion, 132–3; and irony, 132, 159, 167, 170–1, 182–3; and mothers/motherhood, 135–6; and sensation fiction, 172, 175; and inequality, 173–4, 179–80; *see also* aristocracy; lower classes; upper classes
class mobility, 135, 142–6, 158, 159–70, 187; downward, 130, 133–4, 137–8
clothing, 41, 42–3, 176–7
Collins, Wilkie, 2, 203 n.11, 203 n.13, 204 n.14; *Man and Wife*, 114; "The Diary of Anne Rodway", 182
comedy, 38, 59, 121–2, 153–4, 170–1, 176–7, 182–3, 203 n.7
"Coming Home to Him", 160
commodification: of bodies, 25–6, 63–4; of women, 25–6, 40, 41–4, 46–7, 54–5, 63–4, 69

conduct books, 13, 71, 78, 101–2, 192, 199 n.4, 203 n.12
consumerism, 40–6, 49, 110–11, 197 n.4
copyright, 8
corporeality, 74–5, 157; and feminism, 26; grotesque, 150–1, 154; and class, 175, 177–8, 185, 187, 189; *see also* bodies
Court Netherleigh, 36, 40–9, 61, 66, 69, 138, 195 n.3, 197 n.9
coverture, 9, 34, 58–9, 80, 93
Cox, Jessica, 133–4, 154
crime, 44, 53–5, 78, 94–5, 179–82; *see also* murder
crime fiction, 13, 31, 123–5, 182, 194
curiosity, 87–93; *see also* secrecy
Cvetkovich, Ann, 99, 134, 162

Danesbury House, 7, 60, 61, 94, 173–4, 185
daughters, 75–7, 86–8
deafness, 65
death, 10–11, 63–4, 78–9, 81–2, 103, 105–7; from 'broken hearts', 62; faked, 85, 181–2; of children, 117–18, 123, 125–6; suicide, 187; *see also* murder
debt, 41, 44, 78
Dene Hollow, 183
desire: consumerist, 40–1; sexual, 103–4, 105–6, 112–13, 123–5, 201 n.9, 204 n.4
detective fiction, 31, 123–5, 182
detectives, amateur, 54, 64, 121, 169, 179–82, 189
Dickens, Charles, *Great Expectations*, 112–13; *Martin Chuzzlewit*, 175
disability/impairment, 65
disease *see* illness
disobedience, 43–5, 74, 90, 92–3, 168–9
doctors, 81, 98, 108–9, 163; critique of,

INDEX

6, 92, 93, 166, 181–2, 202 n.14
domesticity, 8–9, 22–3, 33, 35–6, 37–8, 61
"Dr. Knox", 163
dress, 41, 42–3, 176–7, 204 n.3
drink/drunkenness, 94, 149, 172, 173–4, 176, 177–8
dysphagia, 81, 88–9

Earl's Heirs, The, 59–60
East Lynne, 7, 8, 13, 30, 193–4, 196 n.11; and marriage, 36, 39, 49, 59, 60; and forbearance, 71–5; and emotion, 99, 100; and transgression, 131–7; and class, 166–7
eating disorders, 72, 74–5, 81, 85, 88–9
Edgeworth, Maria, *The Modern Griselda*, 70
education: of women, 19–20, 56, 57, 117, 167–8; teachers/teaching, 56, 58, 64, 123, 159, 161–70
Elster's Folly, 49, 59, 88–91, 147–55
emotion, 23, 52–3; jealousy, 76–7, 84, 100, 114–16, 124, 132; repression of, 79–81, 100, 101–8; as feminine, 97–8; and gender, 97–8, 107–8; and victimization, 98–9, 106–8; immoderate, 99–107, 134; in sensation fiction, 99; excessive, 100–1; anger, 100, 108, 119–20, 150, 152, 153; and illness, 103, 105–7; and subjectivity, 104–5; and class, 132–3; regulation of, 164–5
Ensign Thomas Pepper letters, 9–10
Esquirol, Jean-Étienne Dominique, 113, 157
evolutionary theory, 81–2
excess *see* immoderacy

fairy tales, 13, 29, 37–8, 63–4, 67–70, 94–5, 164; "Beauty and the Beast", 46–7, 69, 197 n.6, 197 n.9;

"Cinderella", 69–70, 163; "Sleeping Beauty", 69; "Snow White", 69, 111; "Little Red Riding Hood", 70, 91; "Bluebeard", 90–3
fathers/fatherhood, 61–4, 75–7, 86–7, 115–16
femininity, 4, 11, 19–20, 81–2; and illness, 5, 71–2; and professionalism, 22–3, 57–8; respectable, 22–3; of working women, 57–8, 175–8; alternative models of, 82–4, 142–3, 162, 184, 188–9, 192–3; and emotion, 97–8; construction of, 136–7, 146–7, 157–8; critique of, 140–1; and class, 142–7; lack of, 149–50, 178–9
feminism, 3–4, 15–21, 191–2; suffrage, 15–16; Victorian, 15–21, 34–5, 57–8; ambiguous, 17, 20–1, 133; and space, 21–2; theorists, 21–6; phenomenological, 23–6; corporeal, 26; *see also* anti-feminism; proto-feminism
Fetterley, Judith, 28
fiction: gothic, 13, 37–8, 64, 84, 90, 101, 164, 194; supernatural, 13, 37, 85, 181, 203 n.10; crime, 13, 31, 123–5, 182; detective, 31, 123–5; *see also* narrative form; sensation fiction
food, 149–51, 176–7; *see also* anorexia
forbearance, 29, 67–95; and patriarchy, 29, 67–8, 75–7; and fairy tales, 67–70, 91–5; Griselda (Boccaccio character), 70–1; of wives, 71–5, 77–85, 88–95; and irony, 72, 73, 76–7, 80–2, 85; of daughters, 75–7, 86–8
foreigners, 169–71, 184
Freud, Sigmund, 63, 112

gambling, 42, 44, 197 n.6
gender: construction of, 10, 23–5, 136–7, 143, 147–8, 157–8;

219

performativity, 24–5, 146–51, 155; in fairy tales, 67–9; and emotion, 97–8, 107–8; and insanity, 111–14, 121–2, 124–5; and morality, 140–2; *see also* femininity; masculinity
gentility, 22–3, 55–8, 143–4, 161
ghosts, 37, 84, 85, 181, 203 n.10
Gilbert, Sandra, 3, 26, 29, 77, 99
Gilman, Charlotte Perkins, 35, 197 n.4
girls, 19–20, 69–70, 79, 112, 199 n.5
gluttony, 149–51, 176–7
gothic fiction, 13, 37–8, 64, 84, 90, 101, 164, 194
governesses, 123, 159, 161–70
Griselda (Boccaccio character), 29, 70–1, 73, 74–5, 77, 199 n.1
Grosz, Elizabeth, 26, 37
Gubar, Susan, 3, 26, 29, 77, 99

happy endings, 46, 68–9
hauntings, 37, 84, 85, 181, 203 n.10
Hawthorne, Nathaniel, *The Scarlet Letter*, 79–80
heredity, 113–14, 121–2, 124–5
"Hester Reed's Pills", 125–7
House of Halliwell, The, 92, 199 n.19; and marriage, 37, 60, 64–5; and immoderacy, 104, 121–2; and class, 142–3, 166
husbands, 14, 33–4, 60–1, 130–2; domineering, 27, 70, 72–3; abusive, 36, 49, 84; neglectful, 37, 39, 73–4, 116, 131–2; fond, 40–1, 44, 55; unfaithful, 51–5, 60, 79–81, 84, 105–6; murderous, 53–4, 84, 92–4, 168–9, 177–80; criminal, 78, 84–5, 92–4, 160
hysteria, 27, 74, 98–9, 101, 192; and immoderacy, 108–10, 112, 122–3, 125–6

illegitimacy, 154, 161, 204 n.14
illness, 15, 84, 110, 145; and femininity, 5, 71–2; psychosomatic, 5–6, 50, 62–3, 78, 99–100, 103, 105–7, 201 n.5; as rebellion, 50; of men, 72–3, 201 n.5; dysphagia, 81, 88–9; and repressed emotion, 103, 105–7; *see also* medicine; psychological disorders
immoderacy, 29–30, 97–127; and hysteria, 27, 74, 101, 108–10, 112, 122–3, 125–6, 192; consumerist, 41–6, 49, 110–11; emotional, 99–107, 134; and class, 102, 149–51; and irony, 103, 106–7, 125, 126; and insanity, 111–21, 124–5; and sexual desire, 112–13, 123–5; and motherhood, 113–14, 115–19, 122–3; gluttony, 149–51, 176–7
incest, 76–7, 186–7
infidelity, 51–5, 60, 74, 79–81, 84, 105–6, 132
inheritance, 66, 86, 116–17, 118; *see also* heredity
insanity, 26–7, 98–9, 111–25; gendering of, 108, 111–14, 121–2, 124–5; misdiagnosis, 109–10, 201 n.6; and desire, 112–13, 123–5; heritability of, 113–14, 121–3, 124; of men, 121–2; inducement of, 121, 122
intertextuality, 68, 90–1, 111, 163–4
invalidism, 4–6, 15, 71–2, 195 n.3; *see also* illness
Irigaray, Luce, 25, 26, 98–9, 136
irony: and marriage, 13–14, 19, 43–4, 46–7, 53–5, 59–60, 87; and motherhood, 37; and forbearance, 72, 73, 76–7, 80–2, 85; and immoderacy, 103, 106–7, 125, 126; and class, 132, 159, 167, 170–1, 182–3; and female transgression, 141, 146, 153; and performativity, 147–8

INDEX

"Janet Carey", 163
Jaquet, Alison, 183
jealousy, 76–7, 84, 100, 114–16, 124, 132
Johnny Ludlow stories, 10, 123, 125, 160, 163
Johnson, Joseph, 20, 58

Kaplan, E. Ann, 74
King, Alice, "Female Suffrage", 15–16
Kristeva, Julia, 37, 176
Kucich, John, 135

ladies, 55–7, 129–30, 161, 203 n.11; transgressive, 131–8; stereotypical, 138–44
Lady Adelaide's Oath, 84–5, 103–4, 121, 139–42, 170–1, 184
Langbauer, Laurie, 74
Lévi-Strauss, Claude, 25
Liggins, Emma, 82
Linton, Eliza Lynn, 19–20, 42, 79, 194, 199 n.5, 200 n.8
"Log-Book" (book reviews, *Argosy*), 12
Lord Oakburn's Daughters, 49; and marriage, 53–5; and forbearance, 75–7, 92–4; and class, 167–9, 170–1, 176–8, 179–80
love, 29, 38–40, 61–2, 72, 103–4, 105–6; *see also* desire
lower classes, 157–63, 170–2, 179–87, 193–4; *see also* servants, domestic

madness *see* hysteria; insanity; psychological disorders
maids, 123–5, 179–84, 205 n.10
"Major Parrifer", 160
Mangham, Andrew, 63–4, 84, 121, 140–1, 200 n.9
marriage, 6–7, 13–14, 18–19, 28–9, 33–66; coverture, 9, 34, 58–9, 80, 93; and irony, 13–14, 19, 43–4, 46–7, 53–5, 59–60, 87; companionate, 14, 34, 35, 39, 48, 196 n.1; mercenary, 20, 34–5, 39–40; and separate spheres ideology, 33–4, 36–7, 39; as transaction, 33–5; unhappy, 35, 49–55; for love, 39–40; separation, 44–5, 52; transactional, 44, 46–8, 54–5; risks of, 49–50; happy, 55; divorce, 59; bigamy, 59–60, 89–90, 91, 150, 152; polygamy, 59–60; second, 60, 75, 89, 115–17, 132–3, 135; and class, 130, 135, 137–8, 159–61; *see also* husbands; infidelity; wives
Married Women's Property Acts, 34, 49, 165
masculinity, 13, 27, 61, 91, 198 n.16; of women, 57–8, 82–3, 142–3, 147–9, 154, 189; dominating, 72–3, 75–6; and class, 130–1; lack of, 151–2, 153, 154
Matrimonial Causes Act (1857), 14, 34, 51
Maunder, Andrew, 1, 9, 136, 193
medicine: quackery, 5–6; nurses, 175–8; *see also* doctors
men: characterization, 13; weak, 27, 60–1; domestic, 38, 61; insane, 121–2; *see also* husbands; masculinity
menopause, 112–13
mental illness *see* psychological disorders
middle classes, 14, 129–31, 132–4, 144–5
Mill, John Stuart, *The Subjection of Women*, 18, 53
Mitchell, Sally, 58
money, 42, 197 n.6; and marriage, 34–5, 39–40; debt, 41, 44, 78; *see also* consumerism
"Montpellier-by-Sea", 123–5
morality: of women, 33–4, 55–7; and class, 129–30, 132–3, 134, 178, 183; gendering of, 140–2; and appearance, 178

221

Mormonism, 59
mothers/motherhood, 25, 36–7, 45,
    47–8, 149–50, 177–8; breastfeeding,
    45, 172, 203 n.12; stepmothers,
    60, 75, 94–5, 111, 114–20; and
    immoderacy, 113–14, 115–19,
    122–3; pregnancy, 113; and class,
    135–6; child care, 173–5
Mrs. Halliburton's Troubles, 14–15, 20,
    38, 123; and marriage, 55–9; and
    class, 169–70, 185–6, 187–8
murder, 139–40, 160, 166; accidental,
    40, 125–6; of wives, 53–4, 84, 92–4,
    168–9, 177–80; of women, 53–4, 84,
    92–4, 168–9, 177–80; of children,
    60, 94–5, 113–15, 117–23, 125–6,
    138, 161, 174–5; by women, 111,
    112–15, 117–25, 138, 161, 169–70,
    174–5
"Mystery at Number Seven, The",
    123–5

names, 25, 59, 132, 175; pseudonyms,
    9–10, 26
nannies, 174–5
narrative form, 2, 9–13, 28, 198
    n.18; bildungsroman, 13, 29,
    162–3; happy endings, 46, 68–9;
    intertextuality, 68, 90–1, 111, 163–4;
    see also camouflage techniques; fairy
    tales; fiction; sensation fiction
New Monthly Magazine, 8, 9–10, 122,
    161
non-disjunction, 68, 79–80, 93–4, 176
Norton, Caroline, 8, 195 n.5
nurses, 172–8; wet nurses, 172–4;
    medical, 175–8

obedience, 43–5, 70, 74, 102–3, 165,
    168–9
Oliphant, Margaret, 2–3, 18–19, 133,
    134, 167, 196 n.14, 197 n.8
Oswald Cray, 65, 86–8, 139

"Owen, the Milkman", 123–5

Parkwater, 161
passivity, 69, 71–4, 77, 79–80, 82, 85,
    111
patience *see* forbearance
patriarchy, 23, 61–3, 130–1; and
    commodification of women, 25–6,
    43–8; critique of, 27–8, 33–4, 74–5,
    107, 151–3, 165; and forbearance,
    29, 67–8, 75–7; and hysteria, 98–9;
    failures of, 130–1; and class, 149–56
performativity: gender, 24–5, 146–51,
    155; class, 146–9, 161
Phegley, Jennifer, 1, 12
plagiarism, 8, 195 n.5
poison, 92, 112, 125–6, 166, 173
poverty, 55–6, 173, 184–7
professionalism, 18–19, 73, 92,
    130–1, 144–5, 175–6, 182; of
    women writers, 4, 7–12, 15, 36; and
    femininity, 22–3, 57–8
prostitution, 185–6
proto-feminism, 15–21, 27, 40, 58;
    versus anti-feminism, 17, 19–20,
    28–9, 75, 133, 191–2; and work, 34,
    57, 143, 168
pseudonyms, 9–10, 26
psychological disorders: anorexia, 72,
    74–5, 81, 85, 88–9; self-harm, 74–5,
    119–20, 187; suicide, 187; *see also*
    hysteria; insanity
Pykett, Lyn, 1, 28, 157–8, 202 n.19

racialization, 114, 157–8, 169–71
rage *see* anger
readers, 12, 54; direct address to, 14,
    28, 38, 76–7, 137, 199 n.3
realism, 2, 12–13, 91–2, 137
Red Court Farm, The, 84, 105–7, 143–7
religion, 10–11, 19, 88, 149–51;
    Mormonism, 59; evangelical, 188,
    196 n.9

respectability, 9, 22–3, 38, 129, 143–4, 157, 192; maintenance of, 14–15, 55–8, 100; loss of, 104, 161–2
revenge, 54, 74, 93, 113, 169–70, 180
Riddell, Charlotte, 11
Ruskin, John, 42, 102; "Of Queen's Gardens", 18

sacrifice, 47–8, 62–3, 75–6, 81–2, 83, 85
Sanders, Valerie, 17, 35, 196 n.18
Schaffer, Talia, 73
secrecy, 79–80, 87–8, 89–90, 92–3, 139–40, 164–5
self-help, 38, 56–7, 77, 143, 145, 185, 187–8
self-restraint, 75, 79–80, 100, 101–8, 134
sensation fiction, 2–3, 9, 12–13, 114, 193–4, 196 n.12; and gender, 27, 46, 99; and fairy tales, 43, 68; and sexual inequality, 51; and domesticity, 137, 203 n.6; and performativity, 146; and class, 172, 175
separate spheres ideology, 14–16, 18–19, 33–4, 36–7, 39, 52, 129
Sergeant, Adeline, 1, 23
servants, domestic, 161–84; maids, 123–5, 179–84, 205 n.10; governesses, 123, 159, 161–70; wet nurses, 172–4; nannies, 174–5
sex, biological, 23–4, 147–8
sexual desire, 103–4, 105–6, 112–13, 123–5, 201 n.9, 204 n.4
sexual double standard, 49, 51–3
sexuality: of women, 52–3, 164–5; incest, 76–7, 186–7; and insanity, 112–13
Shadow of Ashlydyat, The: and marriage, 37, 49, 200 n.9; and forbearance, 75, 77–84, 94; and emotion, 100–1, 102–3, 105
shopping, 41–6, 49, 110–11

short stories, 8, 10, 123–7, 160, 163, 198 n.18
Showalter, Elaine, 3, 6, 17, 26, 98, 99
Simpson, Vicky, 36
Smiles, Samuel, *Self-Help*, 56, 77, 170–1, 185, 187
social determinism, 185, 187
space, 4, 15, 21–2, 33, 37–8, 197 n.2
spinsters, 38–9, 64–6, 112
St Martin's Eve, 36; and marriage, 60, 62–4, 110–11, 127; and forbearance, 69, 94–5; and immoderacy, 94–5, 114–21; and class, 138, 174–5
Steere, Elizabeth, 172
stepmothers, 60, 75, 94–5, 111, 114–20
subjectivity: and gender, 24–5; assertion of, 41, 43–4; and emotion, 104–5; renunciation of, 106–7; desiring, 110–11; of lower classes, 179–83
suffrage, 15–16
suicide, 187
supernatural fiction, 13, 37, 84, 85, 181, 203 n.10

Tait, Lawson, 112, 157
Talairach-Vielmas, Laurence, 43
teachers/teaching, 5, 56, 58, 64, 123, 159, 161–70
Temperance Movement, 71, 173
Trollope, Anthony, *Miss Mackenzie*, 70
Tromp, Marlene, 133

upper classes, 129–55, 183; transgressive, 129–38; stereotypical, 138–42; and femininity, 142–6; and performativity, 146–50

Verner's Pride, 49, 59, 61, 108–11, 121, 186–7
violence, 119–20, 123–4; domestic, 5, 36–7, 92; of women, 94, 101, 108,

113–15, 161; *see also* aggression; murder
voyeurism, 43, 62–4, 69, 111

Wagner, Tamara, 17, 45–6
wet nurses, 172–4
widows/widowhood, 38–9, 55–8, 116–17, 143, 145–6, 169
wills, 66, 86, 116–17, 118
Within the Maze, 49–53, 71, 100, 121, 176, 184
wives: rebellious, 43–5, 48–9, 74, 92–4, 138; murder of, 53–4, 84, 92–4, 168–9, 177–80; forbearance of, 70–5, 77–85, 88–95; liberation of, 72–3
women: redundant, 14–15, 56, 161–2, 167; single, 14–15, 38–9, 55–9, 64–6, 112; suffrage, 15–16; girls, 19–20, 69–70, 79, 112, 199 n.5; education of, 20, 56, 57, 117, 167–8; respectable, 22–3; commodified, 25–6, 40, 41–3, 46–7, 54–5, 63–4, 69; spinsters, 38–9, 64–6, 112; widows, 38–9, 55–8, 116–17, 143, 145–6, 169; power of, 39, 40, 79, 132, 142–3, 151–4, 181, 183, 201 n.7; masculine, 57–8, 79, 82–3, 142–3, 147–9, 154, 189; adolescent, 69–70, 112; daughters, 75–7, 86–8; violent, 94, 101, 108, 113–15, 161; anti-heroines, 117–18, 120–2; *see also* ladies; mothers/motherhood
women, work of, 18–19, 30–1, 34, 64, 159, 187–8, 191, 193; and respectability, 14–15, 55–8; and class, 142–6, 158, 175, 185; *see also* servants, domestic
women writers, 3, 4, 7–12, 15, 36, 195 n.6
Wood, Charles, 4, 8–9, 10–11, 16–17, 159
Wood, Ellen (Mrs Henry Wood):

professionalism, 1, 4, 7–12, 15, 36, 191, 195 n.6; reputation, 1, 2–4, 11, 13, 17, 21, 133, 193–4, 196 n.12; domesticity, 4, 8–9, 15, 22–3, 35–6, 129, 191; political views, 16–17, 158–9
Wood, Ellen, works: *Danesbury House*, 7, 60, 61, 94, 173–4, 185; *Ensign Thomas Pepper* lettes, 9–10; *Johnny Ludlow* stories, 10, 123, 125, 160, 163; "Log-Book" (book reviews, *Argosy*), 12; *Court Netherleigh*, 36, 40–9, 61, 66, 69, 138, 195 n.3, 197 n.9; *Anne Hereford*, 39–40, 70, 91, 164–5; *Within the Maze*, 49–53, 71, 100, 121, 176, 184; *Elster's Folly*, 49, 59, 88–91, 147–55; *Verner's Pride*, 49, 59, 61, 108–11, 121, 186–7; *The Earl's Heirs*, 59–60; *Oswald Cray*, 65, 86–8, 139; *Lady Adelaide's Oath*, 84–5, 103–4, 121, 139–42, 170–1, 184; *The Red Court Farm*, 84, 105–7, 143–7; "Montpellier-by-Sea", 123–5; "The Mystery at Number Seven", 123–5; "Owen, the Milkman", 123–5; "Abel Crew", 125–7; "Hester Reed's Pills", 125–7; "Coming Home to Him", 160; "Major Parrifer", 160; *Parkwater*, 161; "Dr. Knox", 163; "Janet Carey", 163; *Dene Hollow*, 183; *see also Bessy Rane*; *East Lynne*; *House of Halliwell, The*; *Lord Oakburn's Daughters*; *Mrs. Halliburton's Troubles*; *Shadow of Ashlydyat, The*; *St Martin's Eve*
Wood, Henry, 6–7, 36
Woolf, Virginia, 21–3; *A Room of One's Own*, 21–2; "Professions for Women", 22
work *see* professionalism; servants, domestic; women, work of

youth, 19–20, 69–70, 112

www.ingramcontent.com/pod-product-compliance
Lightning Source LLC
Chambersburg PA
CBHW060950230426
43665CB00015B/2135